The scholarship of Rich Furman is just plain lovely—original, inviting, and emotionally accessible. This powerful, thought-provoking collection beautifully weaves together the tools and sensibilities of autoethnography with poetic inquiry as few have done before. Reading his work makes me wish to read more, and more, and more. Brilliant. Expansive. Elegant. Radiant. Inspirational. Luminous."

Laurel Richardson, PhD Professor Emeritus of Sociology, The Ohio University. Qualitative sociologist, seminal practitioner of autoethnography, and author of many books, including *Writing Strategies, Reaching Diverse Audiences*

Rich Furman's *Poetry as Therapy, Research, and Education* is a treasure trove of the some of the best articles ever penned on the healing and transformative power of poetry. Furman writes in a lucid yet scholarly style. Like that of a fine artisan, his work is well crafted, attractive, and engaging. It is a one-of-a-kind text, unrivaled in its comprehensiveness and insightfulness. It is worth investing time and energy in because the knowledge it provides is timeless.

Samuel T. Gladding, PhD, Professor of Counseling, Wake Forest University, author of many books, including *Counseling: A Comprehensive Profession*

The potential of poetry to heal, explore, educate, and elevate the human mind is an inexhaustible resource. In his seminal work, Rich Furman shows that poetry really matters, opening new perspectives on self-reflection, and changing our conventional scripts of understanding. Guided by well-grounded professional values, ethics in therapy, and research, as well as social and educational work, Furman adds deep personal dimensions to the narrative and poetic ways of inquiry that encourage us to appreciate our own growth and well-being.

Juhani Hans, PhD, Senior Lecturer in Psychology, University of Helsinki, Finland, author of *Transformative Words: Writing Otherness and Identities*

In this evocative and readerly text, Furman advances the case for poetry beyond its literary questions, providing a rich terrain of knowledge for social science and humanities researchers. With thoughtful, qualitative reasoning, Furman shows us how poetry has the capacity to clarify and magnify existence: We learn how poetry inspires existential and phenomenological research questions; how poetry can be both the data and the analytical frame; and how the writing and reading of poetry can be a therapeutic and emancipatory process. In this text, Furman reveals ways to reconceptualize our lived experience, reorient our assumptions, search out new perspectives, and find new means for experimenting with our relationships with ourselves and others. Regardless of your background in poetry, this will be a text to welcome you into the ways of the poem.

Dr. Sean Wiebe, Associate Professor of Education at University of Prince Edward Island, Leading voice in A/R/Tography and poetic inquiry

Dr. Rich Furman's book provides an essential read for clinicians working with poetry therapy in a variety of settings, as well as within differing therapeutic models. He honors past theorists of poetry therapy, describes his social work practice, including writing exercises, and provides case studies that give us insight into the power of poetry therapy in action. One of the most effective threads woven throughout various chapters is how he demonstrates the power of metaphor as a "tool" to help clients move outside themselves to witness stance, and thus find meaning and value to enlarge their lives. In today's world, this is necessary "bread," as poet Mary Oliver describes poetry itself.

Perie Longo, Past president of the National Association of Poetry Therapy, Former Poet Laureate of Santa Barbara, Registered poetry therapist, Leading voice in poetry therapy

This collection of Dr. Rich Furman's articles, published over a twenty-year period, contributes in a significant way to the field of poetry therapy. Reflecting and integrating in-depth knowledge of the humanities, social sciences, and the social work profession, Dr. Furman's book provides a rich compendium of lucid and substantive articles that highlights the power of poetic expression to enhance clinical practice, increase the authenticity of qualitative research, and provide meaningful innovations in social work education.

> Geri Giebel Chavis, Author of *Poetry and Story Therapy: The Healing Power of Creative Expression*
> Professor of English and Gender Studies at St. Catherine University
> Licensed Psychologist and Certified Poetry Therapist

Rich Furman's vast research into poetry therapy is gathered in this vibrant collection of selected papers published across his career. Often combined or juxtaposed with other therapies and approaches, poetry therapy draws out the curative and healing nature of poetry long revered by artists and philosophers. Indeed, this remarkable book has countless poems that stretch our understanding of poetry-based research and therapeutic practices. What could be hard to disclose becomes possible when we tap into our creative processes and maximize our own emotional resources. Poetry becomes a very powerful method for practitioners interested in expanding their repertoire. This is a rich resource not to be missed and definitely a gift for all professionals!

> Rita L. Irwin, Distinguished University Scholar, Professor, Art Education, The University of British Columbia. Leader in arts-based research and A/R/Tography

As a research poet, Furman is bold yet vulnerable—willing to place his personal experiences alongside research participants through powerful poetry. This valuable volume brings together the breadth and depth of Furman's poetic scholarship in one place. By challenging research poets to draw on poetic forms from the arts, Furman's scholarship has transformed the landscape of research poetry. His vision stretches my personal writing and that of my students in ways that are rich and invigorating as we seek to represent participants' experiences.

Maria K. E. Lahman, PhD, Qualitative Methodologist, Professor of Applied Statistic and Research Methods, University of Northern Colorado

Poetry as Therapy, Research, and Education:
Selected Works of Rich Furman

Rich Furman, MFA, MSW, PhD

Colorado Springs, CO
www.universityprofessorspress.com

Copyright © 2022

Poetry as Therapy, Research, and Education: Selected Works of Rich Furman
by Rich Furman

All rights reserved. No portion of this book may be reproduced by any process or technique without the express written consent of the publisher.

First Published in 2022, University Professors Press. United States.

ISBN (Hardcover): 978-1-955737-02-9
ISBN (Paperback): 978-1-955737-03-6
ISBN (eBook):   978-1-955737-04-3

      UNIVERSITY PROFESSORS PRESS
      Colorado Springs, CO
      www.universityprofessorspress.com

Cover Art by Marguerite Laing
Cover Design by Laura Ross

Permissions listed at the end of the book

Table of Contents

Forward by Nicholas Mazza — i
Preface by Rich Furman — iii

Part I: Poetry, Healing and Practice — 1

Chapter 1   Poetry Therapy as a Tool for Strengths-Based Practice (2002) *with E. P. Downey, R. L. Jackson, & K. Bender* — 3

Chapter 2   Poetry Therapy as a Tool of Cognitively Based Practice (2006) *with C. L. Langer* — 19

Chapter 3   Poetry Therapy and Existential Practice (2003) — 34

Chapter 4. The Mundane, the Existential, and the Poetic (2007) — 46

Chapter 5: A Poetry Group for Cognitively Impaired Older Adults: A Brief Report (2012) — 66

Chapter 6: Poetry Therapy, Men and Masculinities (2012) *with L. Dill* — 74

Chapter 7: Poetry Matters: A Case for Poetry in Social Work Practice (2012) *with M. Enterline, R. Thompson, & A. Shukraft* — 88

Chapter 8: Exploring Friendship Loss Through Poetry (2004) — 99

Part II: Poetic Inquiry: Poetry and Research — 107

Chapter 9: Poetic Forms and Structures in Qualitative Health Research (2006) — 109

Chapter 10:	Autoethnographic Poems and Narrative Reflections: A Qualitative Study on the Death of a Companion Animal (2006)	118
Chapter 11:	Poetry and Narrative as Qualitative Data: Explorations into Existential Theory (2007)	134
Chapter 12:	Poetry as Qualitative Data for Exploring Social Development and Human Experience in Latin America (2004)	150
Chapter 13:	Autoethnographic Explorations of Researching Older Expatriate Men: Magnifying Emotion Using the Research Pantoum (2015)	171
Chapter 14:	The Tenderness and Vulnerability of Older Expatriate Men: A Poetic Inquiry of Research and Autoethnographic Poems (2019)	185
Chapter 15:	Extreme Data Reduction: The Case for the Research Tanka (2015) *with L. Dill*	192
Chapter 16:	Poetry and Photography: An Exploration into Expressive/Creative Qualitative Research (2005) *with P. Szto & C. Langer*	205

Part III: Poetry and Education/Teaching   229

| Chapter 17: | Using Poetry and Written Exercises to Teach Empathy (2005) | 231 |
| Chapter 18: | Beyond the Literary Uses of Poetry: A Class for University Freshmen (2014) | 241 |

| Chapter 19: | An International Experience for Social Work Students: Self-Reflection Through Poetry and Journal Writing Exercises (2018) *with A. Coyne & N. J. Negi* | 249 |
| Chapter 20: | The Poet/Practitioner: A Paradigm for the Profession (2006) *with C. L. Langer & D. K. Anderson* | 263 |

Permissions   283
Index   287
About the Author   291

Foreword

Rich Furman, one of the leading scholars in poetry therapy, is both a distinguished poet and social work educator. This collection of his "greatest hits" relating to poetry therapy captures the scope and depth of the field and is a "must read" not only for those actively involved in the creative arts therapies but all those in the helping professions interested in acquiring a deeper sense of the human element in teaching, practice, and research. Dr. Furman has effectively integrated poetry therapy with well-established theoretical frameworks (e.g., existential, cognitive, constructivist, and strengths-based). This includes the use of metaphors, story, creative writing, and journaling. Indeed, while not discarding the DSM-5 with its focus on formal assessment and diagnosis, he goes beyond identifying clearly visible symptoms and recognizes the importance of "story" in our lives.

Particularly compelling in this book is the explicit and implicit attention to how poetry speaks to the importance of our values. With reference to his own profession, Furman noted: "Without clear guidance from social work values, we are at risk of becoming a technocratic profession of social engineers, instead of the champions of the disadvantaged and oppressed." This is consistent with the potential of poetry to be incorporated in advocacy as it relates to both clinical practice and social policy/administration.

Furman's attention to poetry and research represents leading-edge studies in qualitative research, particularly as it relates to poetic inquiry, autoethnography, and narrative. He offers a critical and necessary complement to traditional quantitative research. Drawing from his international experience in Latin America, he is also able to link research to social development. He masterfully identifies and integrates various poetic devices as well as photography research methods. The personal use of the loss of his pet provides an even deeper look at autoethnographic poems and reflection. In another personal instance, reflecting on a poem relating to friendship, he wrote:

> I still think of him. Sometimes I look for my phonebook, or catch myself wondering why he does not call. Then I catch myself: He's dead… Reading the poem again, I continue to think about

my responsibility towards other friends. What does it mean?... Loss, sadness. What is it that keeps us from making friendships more central in our lives? In missing him, I miss others who I have lost connection with.

I suspect this resonates with so many of us at various life stages but certainly in later life. Poetry and narrative, with its attention to memory and aspirations, are especially valuable as we navigate those life stages.

Furman's attention to poetry and education/teaching is especially welcome because in addition to teaching a course on poetry therapy, I have used poetry in teaching crisis intervention, group therapy, family therapy, and a variety of foundation courses in social work. I can state without hesitation that Dr. Furman knows what he is writing about and masterfully uses poetry in the classroom. The examples and exercises relating to self-reflection and empathy presented by Furman relate to students on both personal and professional levels.

Rich Furman has addressed the three major domains of poetry therapy (Receptive/Prescriptive, Expressive/Creative/ Symbolic/ Ceremonial; Mazza, 1999, 2017) in an informative and engaging manner by including solid theoretical background, excellent techniques, and rich case examples. He has contributed to an ever-growing research base, in particular new dimensions in qualitative research. The content for social work educators and other helping professions, including numerous references and resources, should serve them and their students very well. The personal development and healing capacities of poetry therapy is affirmed and expanded, with a call for us to continue its unfinished exploration and application.

Nicholas Mazza, PhD, is Professor and Dean Emeritus at the Florida State University, College of Social Work, Tallahassee, FL. Dr. Mazza holds Florida licenses in psychology, clinical social work, and marriage and family therapy and has been involved in the practice, research, and teaching of poetry therapy for over 40 years. Dr. Mazza is the author of *Poetry Therapy: Theory and Practice*, 2nd edition, and editor of a four-volume series, *Expressive Therapies* (published by Routledge). He is also the founding (1987) and current editor of the *Journal of Poetry Therapy: The Interdisciplinary Journal of Practice, Theory, Research, and Education.* He is the current (2018–2020) president of the National Association for Poetry Therapy (NAPT). In 1997, Dr. Mazza received the *Pioneer Award*; and in 2017, the "Lifetime Achievement Award" from NAPT.

Preface

In 1992, I was sitting in the library at the University of Pennsylvania reading articles from the *Journal of Poetry Therapy*. Only a year before, as a first-year MSW student, had I discovered poetry therapy. I was shocked to find a discipline that brought together many of the great passions of my life: poetry, writing, a constellation of tools perfect for facilitating self-reflection, and a means of facilitating change that privileges creativity and a strengths-orientation. I had long believed that in the healing power of writing, and discovering that there was an actual journal devoted to its practice was personally and professional transformative.

I remember holding a copy of the journal in my hand and fantasizing that maybe one day I would be able to publish something in the journal. It seemed like an ambitious, even audacious goal, but maybe, just maybe, one day it might happen!!

Needless to say, many years have passed, and I have had the fortune of having my work appear in the journal on many occasions. I am grateful for the kind words that Nick Mazza wrote in the Foreword to this compilation of articles. Nick is one of the founders of the field of poetry therapy and the longtime editor of the *Journal of Poetry Therapy*. Not only am I humbled by Nick's kind and generous words, but his Foreword saves me the painful task of writing about my own work in a detached, dispassionate way.

In this volume you will find a collection of many of my articles on poetry as research, teaching, and therapy. They are broken down into separate sections, yet many of them overlap and explore aspects of each of these domains. What perhaps they most accomplish, if I have been at all successful, is to explore poetry as a vehicle for expressing core existential truths of the human condition. Whether through research, teaching, therapy, self-reflection, or actual engagement in poetry or creative writing as an art form, the act of writing can be a transformational act. Writing, indeed, has been my daily means of exploring the world, myself, and my connections to the world. I have written my way through my father's cancer, my (ex)wife's disability, our divorce, the death of friends and cherished companion animals, the challenges of parenting, and now, my quiet movement between midlife and older adulthood. I am grateful to writing; it has given me so much. I hope that this collection inspires you, the reader, to engage in the adventure of writing in new and novel ways.

Part I:

Poetry, Healing, and Practice

Chapter 1

Poetry Therapy as a Tool for Strengths-Based Practice[1]

Currently, the strengths perspective is rising to the fore as one of the most important and influential guides to practice for social workers (Chapin, 1995; Lewis, 1996; Logan, 1996; Saleebey, 2002; Van Wormer, 1999). While many of the values and principles of the strengths perspective are not new (Maluccio, 1981; Robinson, 1949 Smalley, 1967; Taft, 1939), its development and conceptualization as a separate perspective dates back only slightly more than a decade (Graybeal, 2001; Weick, et al., 1989). While the underlying assumptions, values, and precepts have been well articulated (Early, 2000; Saleebey, 2002), intervention techniques and practice methods related to the perspective need further development and articulation (De Jong & Miller, 1995). There do, however, exist techniques that readily lend themselves to possible inclusion under the rubric of the strengths perspective. One such approach is poetry therapy, the structured and therapeutic use of reading and writing poems that seeks to draw out the innate resources and healing power that lie within each individual. As such, it is highly congruent with the basic assumptions of a strengths-based approach to clinical practice. The purpose of this article is to demonstrate the ways in which poetry therapy is consistent with the strengths perspective and to discuss methods for its utilization in clinical settings.

Several issues will be explored in this article. First, a discussion of the healing and growth-inducing aspects of poetry and poetry therapy will be presented. Second, the nature of the strengths perspective as complementary to poetry therapy will be discussed. Third, the congruence between poetry therapy and the strengths perspective will be explored by discussing key elements of the strengths perspective and how these elements can be actualized through the use of poetry and

---

[1] Co-authored with E. P. Downey, R. L. Jackson, & K. Bender (2002).

poetry therapy. Fourth, case studies will be explored that demonstrate the integration of theory and practice vis-à-vis poetry therapy and the strengths perspective.

The Curative Nature of the Poem and Poetry Therapy

As tools, poetry and poetry therapy have been successful in drawing out the inner capacities of individuals from many different populations including the chronically mentally ill (Goldstein, 1987, the elderly (Edwards & Lyman, 1989), troubled children and adolescents (Alexander, 1990; Langosch, 1981; Mazza, 1987, 1996; Mazza, Magaz, & Scaturro, 1987), veterans (Geer, 1983), the terminally ill (McLoughlin, 2000), substance abusers (Bump, 1990 Leedy, 1987), and families (Gladding, 1995). Practitioners working in diverse settings including women's shelters (Hynes, 1987), nursing homes (Edwards, 1990; Kazemek & Rigg, 1987) and elementary schools (Gladding, 1987) have made use of poetry and poetry therapy. Additionally, poetry has even been incorporated into family work (Mazza, 1996), diversity work (Holman, 1996), community work consciousness raising (Kissman, 1989), and research (Poindexter, 1998).

Poets and philosophers have been aware of the curative and healing nature of poetry for millennia. Long before there were social workers or other helping professionals, poets and storytellers helped people deal with their deepest fears by echoing the struggles of humanity in their poems, myths, and stories. In hearing these works, people have learned that they are not alone with their pains, that they are part of a greater struggle. The Aristotelian concept of psychagogia (Lerner, 1991), "the leading out of the soul through the power of art" (p. 8), predates Freud's notion of sublimation by over a thousand years. Aristotle discovered that through the process of creating poetry people were able to transform their problems into power and their sadness into strength.

Many poets have discovered the liberational power of the poem in helping them maximize their own emotional and spiritual resources. For example, American counterculture poet Charles Bukowski (1991) saw poetry as the "ultimate psychiatrist." While poetry has been therapeutic for many "professional" poets, poetry can be therapeutic for and used therapeutically with many different groups of people.

As a discipline, poetry therapy falls into the broader classification of bibliotherapy, the intentional use of poetry and other forms of literature for healing and personal growth (Reiter, 1997). While many types of therapy are poetic in nature, poetry therapy is a separate entity (Rothenberg, 1987), with several professional organizations and journals devoted to its development (NAPT, 2001)[2]. Those who identify as poetry therapists include, psychiatrists, psychologists, counselors, substance abuse specialists, and social workers.

Lerner (1991) defines poetry therapy as the structured use of the reading and writing of poetry and similar literary genres to facilitate therapeutic goals. He draws a distinction between a poetry therapy group and a poetry workshop, in that the former uses poetry as a means to accomplish treatment goals. Poetry therapy uses poetry as a means to an end. Gladding and Heape (1987) note that popular music, such as rap, can be used to make the medium more accessible.

The Strengths Perspective and Implications for Therapy

To many, the construct of therapy represents an activity of practice that necessitates hierarchical patterns of practice that perpetuate or even accentuate social inequities. Many models of therapy are associated with the medical model of practice in which the professional therapist seeks to help the patient "fix" some deficit or problem that lies within them. In many ways, the strengths perspective has been developed as a reaction against such approaches that pathologize instead of empower. Unfortunately, therapy itself is now often identified with practice that disempowers and blames. This is unfortunate because therapy does not have to be conceptualized as a relationship between unequals that blames a client's problems on personal deficits. Finding new means of reframing the process of therapy is essential, as this is one of the most common tasks that social workers undertake in their practice (Gibelman, 2000). Fook (1993) has explored therapy and casework as means of overcoming oppression as well as altering social and personal inequities. Creative uses of therapy and therapeutic arrangements can assist clients in exploring the social causes of their struggles and finding ways of overcoming their structurally created bonds, thus freeing energy for personal and social growth and transformation (Fook, 1993; Lee & Pithers, 1980; Mullally, 1993.)

One principle of the strengths perspective is that the worker is encouraged to work in collaboration and dialogue with the client. Therapy need not be something that is done "to" people (Saleebey, 2000) but can be conducted as a collaborative experience guided and

---

[2] A list of resources is provided at the end of the article.

driven by the client as a means of helping them maximize their internal and external resources and achieve their dreams. Based upon the literature of resiliency, the strengths perspective challenges social workers to help people utilize their skills and competencies in overcoming life's problems. The strengths perspective does not deny the existence of problems but asserts that maximizing the strengths and resources of individuals and groups is the best means of helping them overcome life's challenges. Saleebey (2002) describes the strengths perspective in the following way:

> Practicing from a strengths orientation means that everything you do as a social worker (or therapist) will be predicated, in some way, on helping to discover and embellish, explore and exploit clients' strengths and resources in the service of assisting them to achieve their goals, realize their dreams, and shed the irons of their own inhibitions and misgivings (p.3).

Poetry Therapy as a Tool in Strengths-Based Practice

The strengths perspective rests upon a number of assumptions including empowerment, dialogue, and collaboration between worker and client, membership, resilience, healing and wholeness (Saleebey, 2002). These assumptions are also consistent with the use and application of poetry in therapy and poetry therapy.

The very engagement in the creative process can tap into inner strengths that are not always apparent, and can draw out well-hidden resiliencies (Makin, 1998). In his expansion of Maslow's hierarchy of needs, Gil (1990) postulates that creative expression is an essential human drive. It has been argued that when this drive is expressed, humans are freer to solve their problems, think creatively, and maximize their potential. If it is the case that creative expression can be difficult for clients with multi-stressors and overwhelming responsibilities, engaging clients in creative processes such as the creation of poetry can help liberate energy to be utilized for growth and healing (Wade, 1997).

Talerico (1986) notes that engagement in the creative process encourages the development of many skills that social workers attempt to instill in their clients, such as expression of feelings, confidence through risk-taking, development of new insights, problem solving, conflict resolution, and reduction of anxiety. Other skills and resources can be maximized to develop writing and verbal abilities that are essential to successful participation in most social institutions.

Johnson (1990) asserts that the process of creation unleashes the healing potential within each person. A key precept in strengths-based practice, this idea can find its roots in social work practice with the early functionalist scholars and practitioners. Poetry therapy is not something done "to" people; it is a means of engaging them in the process of maximizing their strengths and helping them achieve their hopes and desires.

The strengths-based approach is entwined with constructivist practice insights and ideas. In both theories, one can view the lives of people as stories that are constantly evolving and changing. As authors of the stories of their own lives, people can reposition themselves and other characters and can change the script to better reflect their visions and dreams. In therapy and other helping experiences, the worker thus helps the client develop new ways of envisioning their future.

The metaphors that lie at the heart of client stories, as well as narratives that guide how we see people, are extremely powerful in shaping our behavior (Mazza, 1999). Cowger and Snively (2002) discuss how the powers of certain metaphors of disease have greatly shaped social work practice.

> Deficit, disease and dysfunction metaphors have become deeply rooted in the helping professions, shaping contemporary social work practice through the emphasis on diagnosis and treatment of abnormal and pathological conditions within individuals. (p.106)

One effective way of helping clients re-author their lives is through helping them develop alternative metaphors for their lives. Metaphor and metaphoric language are key therapeutic elements in poetry and poetry therapy. The metaphor, the symbolic use of language where an object or event represents another object or event, is a core means of organizing the human experience. People hold core metaphors that represent their images of themselves, their lives, and their futures. When the metaphors that clients hold for their lives are characterized by disability or hopelessness, they see little hope in changing their lives.[3]

---

[3] It is important to note that the use of metaphor is not appropriate for all client populations. For example, people with chronic and persistent mental illnesses such as

Often, metaphors are how clients talk about their lives. By speaking in metaphoric language, clients are able to safely discuss issues that are often too painful to address directly. An example from the practice of the first author of this chapter illustrates this point clearly. One male client with a history of addiction and depression envisioned himself as a bird that was locked in an iron cage. As he pounded his head against the bars day after day, year after year, he imagined that somehow this desperate act would free him from the agony of his enslavement. Metaphorically, he was able to discuss how he used his teenage drug habit to escape his memories of molestation. By constructing such a metaphor, he was allowed to explore events that he was not ready to face directly. Poetic explorations such as these enable one to test their ability to deal with painful events and feelings slowly and safely. By helping a client discuss their prevailing metaphors and stories and affirming their creativity and courage in sharing, workers can help clients learn to see themselves as having strengths and the ability to conquer their pasts (Rothenberg, 1987; Zahner-Roloff, 1987).

Guidelines for the Use of Poetry Therapy in Practice

Discussed here are some guidelines for social work practitioners who want to integrate some of the techniques of poetry therapy into their strengths-based practice. In regard to structure, Lerner (1991) suggests that no table be placed between group members in order not to artificially distance them. Typically, the first author organizes the setting for poetry therapy groups using the same principles that guide more traditional groups, making sure that there is also a comfortable space for people to write when asked to do individual work. A few desks or tables should be provided since not everyone is comfortable writing in their chairs.

As previously discussed, the very idea of writing poetry can be anxiety producing for some clients. Houlding and Holland (1988) have designed several creative methods for reducing client anxiety. In the first session of groups, they pass out poems with certain phrases blocked out. Clients are asked to fill in the blanks with their own words. They found that this exercise eliminates the anxiety created by the forebodingness of a piece of blank paper. In early sessions, the authors utilize poems characterized by concreteness and neutrality, progressing to more metaphorical and emotionally laden work as

---

thought disorders might find metaphoric language confusing and frustrating. In such cases, poetry that is far more concrete is much more acceptable and useful.

members become more comfortable with one another and with the processes of poetry therapy.

Collaborative poems are useful in creating group cohesiveness (Mazza & Price, 1985), maximizing communication abilities and interpersonal skills, as well as in establishing a culture of productivity. One activity that is useful for groups is for the therapist to ask group members to identify feelings for which they would like to improve their ability to handle and resolve. Members are then broken off into pairs based on the feelings that they chose. Each subgroup is then given a poem that relates to the theme they have chosen, which they read and discuss together. The pairs are then instructed to write a poem together, exploring what the poem that was discussed meant to them. This process encourages empathy, as members wanting to gain acceptance from their peers usually try to include the ideas of others. Participants also learn that they are able to work with each other, and that their healing and recovery can be facilitated by other group members. This helps reinforce healthy patterns of mutual interdependence, an important concept in strengths-based practice.

In one group session with veterans attending group therapy in an inpatient substance abuse treatment center, a group of three men choose to work on the topic of fear. The triad who chose fear read a poem about the topic and then wrote the following poem, mimicking the style and format of the original work.

> Fear is getting old, not knowing who I am
> Fear is dying young, not knowing my children
> Fear is being wrong when I think I am right
> Fear is being right when I know I am wrong
> Fear is the pain of being hurt
> Fear is failure on life's own terms
> Fear is trying and then failing
> Fear is trusting and not belonging
> Fear is belonging and not trusting
> Fear is the future we don't know
> Fear is the past we know too well

After writing this poem, the triad shared its work with the larger group. They discussed the poem's content, as well as the process of working together. Group members were encouraged to explore and were helped to identify their own style of communication, areas of relating that were difficult for them, and behaviors of others that triggered difficult feelings or behaviors. The poem elicited a discussion on ways of coping with fears, a particularly difficult issue for veterans suffering from Posttraumatic Stress Disorder triggered by combat experiences. The first author, as the therapist in this group, helped the group focus on acceptance of this fear as a natural and normal consequence of having witnessed such horrors, and on the recognition of the enormous strength that it takes to live with such memories.

The creation of a collective poem is a collaborative exercise. Usually centering on a theme discussed previously in the group, each member writes a line for a poem in process (first lines can be created by the therapist or a group member or taken from an existing poem). An interesting extension of this exercise involves each group member writing a first line, and then passing the poems around so that each member adds a line. This often results in useful feedback for the creator of the first line.

Applications of Poetry Therapy and Case Examples

Geer (1983) helped a Vietnam veteran redefine his self-concept by using poetry therapy techniques to reconstruct his core life metaphor. During the intake, the client described himself as a "marine/machine," only able to experience his emotions violently as a marine or repress them as a machine. He saw himself as powerless over his feelings, and clearly saw how limiting these two options were. The more he tried to control his feelings, the more he was controlled by them. As a machine, he saw himself predetermined to act in a mechanistic, rote manner. The therapist encouraged him to search for a new metaphor for himself, one for the person he was capable of being and wanted to be. The therapist helped the client explore other possible ways of viewing himself, encouraging him to find a more flexible and expansive metaphor. In time, the veteran began to call himself the "poet of the rocks," referring to his newfound discovery of his creative, feeling self, and his growing love of nature. With this as his new guiding metaphor, he was able to explore behaviors that were more congruent with this new self-concept. He learned to maximize existing strengths and worked to create new ones.

Hynes (1987) utilized poetry therapy in her work with battered women. In strengths-based practice, it is important for the social worker to help normalize a client's feelings. While the ultimate aim of strengths-based practice is to help clients discover and develop strengths and resiliencies in the service of meeting their goals, it in no way implies the denial of current feelings. Therefore, before stories can be re-authored, they must be explored and constructed. Sometimes this is difficult for clients. Poems that approximate their experiences, or that can be used as jumping off points for dialogue about their personal stories, are valuable in helping clients begin the process of growth and healing. To this end, Hynes uses this poem to help battered women feel less isolated in their experiences.

> Understand
> I am beginning to understand
> the horror of my situation
> the bleakness of my life
> the emptiness of my future
> cuts me like a knife
>
> I am begging to understand
> the madness of who you are
> the hollowness of the day
> the sadness of the fighting
> what else can I say?
>
> I am begging to understand
> the joke life played on me
> how futile are my dreams
> the absence of my anger
> the silence of my screams.

After the poem was read out loud, each member was asked to identify what was significant about the poem to them or to identify an issue that needed to be talked about. The process allowed the women to express similar feelings in a safe manner.

In further expanding on Hynes' work from a strengths perspective, several other questions and experiences can be presented to such a group. Members can be asked to discuss how the person who wrote a poem might transform their experiences. What inner capacities and strengths have each group member learned from their oppressive and even abusive histories? How can they use the experiences to be more fully human and complete? Each member of the group can also be asked to write a follow-up poem of transcendence or reframing. For instance, how might the poem sound if one focused on positive, compensatory behaviors developed in the process of coping with abuse? How might a poem sound different if it were written a year later, after more healing had taken place?

The feelings of helplessness and powerlessness that are associated with oppression, such as racism and institutionalization, may lie at the heart of many emotional difficulties (Fanon, 1963; Gil, 1990; Van Wormer, 1997). Helping people become conscious of the roots of such oppression can lead to powerful emotional and behavioral changes (Freire, 1970). Again, poetry can be utilized to help people re-author their lives. Poems can be used to help explicate what people have learned about themselves from their history and then challenge these messages.

Poetry, often seen as being written for and by society's intelligentsia, can be used as a powerful tool in empowerment-oriented practices. The use of poetry in therapy has been used by feminist and minority writers for the purpose of community empowerment (Kissman, 1989). Using poetry techniques, clients can learn to understand their struggles in the context of institutionalized oppression, which can mark the first step away from self-rapprochement toward empowerment. When the mystique of poetry is deconstructed for clients, and they learn not only to understand it but also create it, an amazing sense of accomplishment and empowerment is achieved. They begin to realize that they can accomplish many of the things that that their internalized oppression has taught them they could not. Even the client who cannot read or write, who needs to recite their words for others to write down, can begin to acquire an increased sense of mastery and accomplishment.

The first author has used poetry therapy techniques with former patients of the state psychiatric hospital system who lived in community residences and attended a partial hospital program. Having suffered through years of institutionalization, most of these clients learned entrenched patters of helplessness and experienced feelings of worthlessness and expendability. These feelings clouded their perceptions and led them to attribute their social marginalization solely to their mental illnesses, not the effects of years of isolation and loneliness caused by institutional life. By helping them understand the etiology of these feelings, they started to blame themselves less and make real changes.

The group consisted of eight mental health consumers, ages twenty-five to sixty. Each was a member of a half-day partial hospitalization program, which they attended between three and five days a week. None had any previous experience writing poetry, and all reported a significant history of academic failures. The members also ranged in functional ability from one who planned on returning to college to another who could not remember how to read or write. They met for one and a half-hours, once a week, for three months.

Each session was composed of three phases. The first phase consisted of a simple didactic discussion on the elements of language and poetry. Topics such as the use of adjectives, nouns, metaphors, and sentence structure were explored to help each member improve the technical aspects of their writing and improve their sense of mastery.

During the second phase of each session, poetry was read aloud. Readings tended to be thematic, chosen by the therapist in consultation with the clients to reflect themes of therapeutic value to the clients, or were selected by the participants as they expressed the need. Themes included friendship and support versus isolation, love versus hate, prejudice versus acceptance, and apathy versus overcoming adversity. Trips to the local public and university libraries led to the selection of many poems by the group members. This in and of itself was empowering, as many of the group members did not know how to use a library. Learning to negotiate the library helped several group members feel a sense of efficacy. One member realized that if he could negotiate a library, he could perhaps one day return to work.

Group members were given much control over their group. The structure was only meant to provide order and a sense of safety. During a session one member asked the group to read a poem on helplessness. He had started to realize that during his 15 years of confinement at the state hospital, he learned to rely on staff to meet all of his needs. He started to realize that many of the decisions and choices that he continued to make emanated from the core belief that he was helpless. During a discussion of a poem by a paraplegic, several group members said they felt similarly, trapped and confined by their limitations. In time, they recognized that these limitations were not in fact truth, but were stories they learned about themselves that were open to analysis.

During this particular group, members began the process of writing about the themes of institutionalization and helplessness. Each member who was now comfortable and capable of working independently would work on a poem that reflected their response to the previous discussion or their reaction to the work. Members who were not capable of writing on their own dictated their thoughts to the therapist or worked with another member of the group. Both flexibility of structure and acceptance of where each member is at during each session are crucial for poetry groups to be safe and therapeutic environments.

After sufficient time had elapsed for all members to feel finished (with the previously established understanding that creative works often take many revisions, if the author so desires) members were encouraged to share their work with others. By the eighth session, group members had progressed to the point where all members either read their works or had others read them aloud. The following poem was written by the member who brought the topic to the group.

> I can't move my hands
> but they work O.K.
> I can't move my feet
> they taught me that way
> I sit by the TV
> I die in my room
> I die in the street
> there is nobody to meet
> I was not that bad
> before their rooms
> and their drugs
> and their thugs
> it will take some hard work
> it will cost quit a lot
> to get back all that I lost.

The author of this poem began to cry after reading this aloud. He said that it was one of the first times that he gotten in touch with the effects being medicated had on him. The members of the group shared in his pain and encouraged one another to explore how they could change some of these effects. The idea of changing many of their learned patterns of helplessness was both liberating and frightening, as many of these patterns had become simultaneously comfortable and depressing. Subsequent group sessions focused on group members finding or creating poems that focused on their transforming themselves.

Additional Considerations

Several additional implications and limitations of poetry therapy are important to address. First, claims of efficacy in this article are based upon unsystematic, clinical observations of individual cases and not upon systematic research. While many contributors to the field of poetry therapy have noted the effectiveness of the approach with various client populations, there exists little generalizable empirical research. Mazza (1999) has noted the importance for those who utilize poetry therapy to conduct evaluations of their practice. He calls for the use of various methodologies, including single-system design, ethnographic, and conventional experimental designs to improve upon the knowledge base. What research does exist tends to focus on process issues such as group cohesion and positive interactions, and not on client outcomes (Mazza, 1999; Rossiter & Brown, 1988). Similarly, little research exists on the efficacy of the strengths perspective in direct social work practice. Future research should also seek to validate the concepts and suppositions of the perspective.

Poetry and poetry therapy can also be valuable tools in social work education. Using poetry in classroom settings can lend variety to teaching methods. Teachers are encouraged to explore literature and poetry that has value to them and think of creative ways of using this material. When we utilize poetry that we have an emotional connection to, students are more likely to find value in it. The first author of this article has used poetry as a means of helping students understand various client situations. Poetry is especially helpful in teaching Human Behavior in the Social Environment, as poetry can help convey various psychosocial issues from the perspective of those experiencing them. The writing of poetry can also help students understand various issues on a personal level, thus improving their "professional use of self."

Conclusion

The use of poetry therapy allows clients, in conjunction with their social worker, to create a sense of freedom, accomplishment, insight, and connection with others. Clients dealing with issues that are difficult or painful to discuss in treatment can use poetry as a vehicle toward developing new capacities and resiliencies.

This article explores the connections and congruence between poetry therapy and strengths-based practice. The ability to use poetry therapy to help empower individuals master their emotions and experiences can aid the strength-based practitioner in assisting their clients toward growth and wellness. Similarly, the poetry therapist can work from a strength-based framework by guiding clients' creative expression toward future achievements and desired outcomes, and by maximizing their internal resources.

The social work field and other helping professions can benefit from integrating poetry therapy and the strength-based approach, two effective and complementary methods that can be linked together in creative ways to help social workers better meet the needs of clients.

References

Alexander, K. C. (1990). Communication with potential adolescent suicides through poetry. *The Arts in Psychotherapy, 17,* 125–130.

Bukowski, C. (1991). Writing. *Black Gun Silencer, 2.*

Bump, J. (1987). Innovative bibliotherapy approaches to substance abuse. *The Arts in Psychotherapy, 17,* 335–362.

Chapin, R. K. (1995). Social policy development: *The strengths perspective. Social Work, 40*(4), 506–514.

Cowger, C. D., & Snively, C. A. (2002). Assessing client strengths: Individual, family and community empowerment. In D. Saleebey (Ed.), The strengths perspective in social work practice (3rd ed.). Allyn and Bacon.

De Jong, P., & Miller, S. D. (1995). How to interview for client strengths. *Social Work, 40*(6), 729–736.

Early, T. J. (2000). Valuing families: Social work practice with families from a strengths perspective. *Social Work, 45*(2), 118–130.

Edwards, M. E. (1990). Poetry: Vehicle for retrospection and delight. *Generations, 14*(1), 61–62.

Edwards, M. E., & Lyman, A. J. (1989). Poetry: Life review for frail American Indian elderly. *Journal of Gerontological Social Work, 14,* 75-91.

Fanon, F. (1963). *The wretched of the earth.* Grove Weidenfeld.

Fook, J. (1993). *Radical casework: A theory of practice.* Allen & Unwin.

Freire, P. (1970). *Pedagogy of the oppressed.* Continuum.

Geer, F. C. (1983). Marine-machine to poet of the rocks, poetry therapy as a bridge to inner reality: Some exploratory observations. *The Arts in Psychotherapy, 10,* 9–14.

Gibelman, M. (2000). Say it ain't so, Norm! Reflections on who we are. *Social Work, 45*(5), 463–466.

Gil, D. (1990). *Unraveling social policy.* Rochester, VT: Schenkman.

Gladding, S. (1987). Poetic expressions: A counseling art in elementary schools. *Elementary School Guidance Counseling, 21*(4), 307–310.

Gladding, S., & Heape, S. (1987). Popular music as a poetic metaphor in family therapy. *Journal of Social Psychiatry, 7*(2), 109–111.

Gladding, S. (1995). Family poems: A way of modifying family dynamics. *The Arts in Psychotherapy, 12,* 239–243.

Goldstein, M. (1989). Poetry: A tool to induce reminiscing and creativity with geriatrics. *Journal of Social Psychiatry, 7*(2), 117–121.

Graybeal, C. (2001). Strengths based social work assessment: Transforming the dominant paradigm. *Family in Society, 82*(3), 233–242.

Holman, W. D. (1996). The power of poetry: Validating ethnic identity through a bibliotherapeutic intervention with a Puerto Rican adolescent. *Child and Adolescent Social Work Journal, 13*(5), 371–383.

Houlding, S., & Holland, P. (1988). Contributions of a poetry writing group to the treatment of severely disturbed psychiatric inpatients. *Clinical Social Work Journal, 16*(2), 194–200.

Hynes, A. (1987). Biblio/poetry therapy in women's shelters. *American Journal of Social Psychiatry, 7,* 112-116.

Johnson, L. (1990). Creative therapies in the treatment of addictions: The art of transforming shame. *The Arts in Psychotherapy, 17,* 299–308.

Kazemek, F., & Rigg, P. (1987). All that silver: A poetry workshop in a senior citizens' center. *Journal of Gerontological Social Work, 10*(2), 167–182.

Langosch, D. (1987). The use of poetry therapy with emotionally disturbed children. *The American Journal of Social Psychiatry, 7*(2), 97–100.

Lee, P., & Pithers, D. (1980). Radical residential care. In M. Brake and R. Bailey (Eds.), *Radical social work practice* (pp. 135–152). London: Edward Arnold.

Leedy, J. (1987). Poetry therapy for drug abusers. *The Journal of Social Psychiatry, 7*(2) 106–108.

Lerner, A. (1981). Poetry Therapy. In R. Corsini (Ed.), *Handbook of innovative psychotherapies* (pp. 131–152). John Wiley and Sons.

Lerner, A. (1981). Some semantic considerations in poetry therapy. *ECT: A Review of General Semantics, 48*(2), 213–219.a

Lewis, J. S. (1996). Sense of coherence and the strengths perspective with older persons. *Journal of Gerontological Social Work, 26*(3–4), 99–112.

Logan, S. L. (1996). Strengths perspective on Black families. In S. L. Logan (Ed.), *The Black family: Strengths, self-help, and positive change.* Westview.

Makin, S. R. (1998). *Poetic wisdom: Revealing and helping.* Charles C. Thomas.

Maluccio, A. N. (1981). *Promoting competence in clients.* The Free Press.

Mazza, N. (1987). Poetry and popular music in social work education: The liberal arts perspective. *The Arts in Psychotherapy, 14*(1), 293–299.

Mazza, N. (1996). Poetry therapy: A framework and synthesis of techniques for family social work. *Journal of Family Social Work, 1*(3), 3–18.

Mazza, M. (1999). *Poetry therapy: Interface of the arts and psychology.* CRC Press.

Mazza, N., Magaz, C., & Scaturro, J. (1987). Poetry therapy with abused children. *The Arts in Psychotherapy, 14*(1), 85–92.

Mazza, N., & Price, B. D. (1985). When time counts: Poetry and music in short-term group treatment. *Social Work with Groups, 8*(2), 53-66.

McLoughlin, D. (2000). Transition, transformation, and the art of losing: Some uses of poetry in hospice care for the terminally ill. *Psychodynamic Counselling, 6*(2), 215–234.

Mullally, R. P. (1993). *Structural social work: Ideology, theory and practice.* McClelland and Stewart.

NAPT—National Association for Poetry Therapy (2001). *Homepage.* http://www.poetrytherapy.org/main.htm

Perkins, K., & Tice, C. (1999). Suicide in elderly adults: The strengths perspective in practice. *Journal of Applied Gerontology, 13*(4), 438–454.

Poindexter, C. C. (1998). Poetry as data analysis: Honoring the words of research participants. *Reflections,* Summer, 22–23.

Reiter, S. (1997). Poetry therapy: testimony on Capitol Hill. *Journal of Poetry Therapy, 10*(3), 169-178.

Robinson, V. P. (1949) *The dynamics of supervision under functional controls.* Philadelphia: The University of Pennsylvania Press.

Rossiter, C., & Brown, R. (1988). An evaluation of interactive bibliotherapy in a clinical setting. *Journal of Poetry Therapy, 1*(2).

Rothenberg, A. (1987). Self-destruction, self-creation, and psychotherapy. *The American Journal of Social Psychiatry, 7*(2), 69–77.

Saleebey, D. (2002). The *strengths perspective in social work.* Boston: Allyn and Bacon

Smalley, R. E. (1967). *Theory for social work practice.* New York: Columbia University Press.

Taft, J. (1939). A conception of the growth process underlining social casework practice. *Social Casework,* (October), 72–80.

Talerico, C. J. (1986). The expressive arts and creativity as a form of therapeutic experience in the field of mental health. *Journal of Creative Behavior, 20*(4), 229–247.

Van Wormer, K. (1997). Social welfare: A world view. Chicago: Nelson-Hall

Van Wormer, K. (1999). The strengths perspective: A paradigm for correctional counseling. *Federal Probation, 63*(1), 51–58.

Wade, A. (1997). Small acts of living: Everyday resistance to violence and other forms of oppression. *Contemporary Family Therapy, 19(*1), 23–39.

Weick, A., Rapp, C. A., Sullivan, W. P., & Kishardt, W. E. (1989). A strengths perspective for social work practice. *Social Work, 89,* 350–454.

Chapter 2

Poetry Therapy as a Tool of Cognitively Based Practice[1]

Cognitive therapy and poetry therapy are therapeutic methods that have become increasingly important within social work and other clinical professions. Both are used to resolve multiple client problems within multiple treatment contexts. In many ways, the two methods are highly compatible and can be used creatively together. The purpose of this paper is to illustrate the potential uses of poetry and poetry therapy when working from a cognitively based model. Separate brief discussions of cognitive therapy and the uses of poetry and poetry therapy are presented. Next, the congruence between these two approaches is explored. Sample exercises are presented that illustrate this congruence as it occurs within actual practice situations. Limitations of this approach are also briefly discussed.

Cognitive Therapy

The scope of this section is to present the main precepts of cognitive therapy so that the reader can understand the connections made between cognitive interventions and poetry therapy. Kelly (1955) proposed a perspective of psychopathology that was based entirely on the cognitive processing of individuals. He pioneered the idea of "constructive alternativism," which asserts that individuals differ in their projections of cognitions about alternatives and options in their lives. Traditionally noted for contemporary contributions to the cognitive therapy model are Aaron Beck and his associates (Beck, 1976; Beck & Emery, 1985). Beck used Kelly's perspective on constructive alternativism in his work on client's feelings of worthlessness (Leahy, 1996). Beck's models of cognitive therapy have been empirically studied in over 325 clinical trials and have been found to be effective

---

[1] Co-authored with K. S. Collins & C. L. Langer (2006).

for disorders such as depression, anxiety, panic, substance abuse, and personality disorders (Beck Institute, 2000).

The umbrella of cognitive therapy also includes tenets from many theorists and disciplines (Werner, 1986; Mahrer, 1989; Payne, 1997). For example, cognitive theory includes Rational Emotive Behavior Therapy (REBT) (DiGiuseppe, 1981; Ellis, 1958, 1973 & 1976); Cognitive Behavioral Modification (Meichenbaum, 1977); cognitive restructuring (Mahoney, 1991); constructivist approaches to psychotherapy (Gergen, 1985) and reality therapy (Glasser, 1995). The differences among these approaches seem to be more superficial than some theorists postulate. For example, while Beck's cognitive therapy tends to focus more on the *processes* of cognition, and Ellis's REBT tends to be more concerned with the actual *content* of belief, both approaches focus considerable attention on both process and content. Often, the differences in focus stem from philosophical and personal preferences and fade at the level of actual practice.

The central notion in cognitive therapy is that the manners in which clients perceive their life situations and challenges is the most significant cause of emotion and behavior. Cognitive interventions tend to be time limited, focused on the present situations, and based on a problem-solving approach. It is the hope of cognitive therapists that their clients will be able to carry newly acquired skills and thinking patterns with them throughout the rest of their lives (Beck Institute, 2000). Stoic philosophers are often cited as the earliest thinkers who influenced the development of the cognitive approach. Epictetus, quoted in Walen, DiGuiseppe, and Wessler (1980) stated: "Men are not influenced by events, but by the views they hold of these events" (p. 23) That is, beliefs, attitudes, and patterns of thinking are largely responsible for the other realms of being. How one sees their world will impact their relationships to it, their feelings about it, and the manner in which they live. Individuals learn about their worlds through their families and through social institutions. These lessons are subsequently interpreted by the individual based upon their idiosyncratic differences in temperament and biology. The interaction of these differences is what subsequently leads to differences in cognition and belief (Leahy, 1996). Clearly, cognition is then not the only influence on human functioning, but is conceptualized as the most directly accessible in the therapeutic process (Beck, 1995; Ellis & Harper 1975, the change of which will lead to long-term symptom amelioration. Techniques that focus on behavioral and emotional systems are utilized to help change cognition. Modern cognitive theorists do not limit themselves to only cognitively based techniques, yet remain focused on the importance of cognitive change for the short- and long-term well-being of the client (Sharf, 2004).

In Beck's system of cognitive therapy, cognition is divided into three areas: 1) automatic thoughts, 2) intermediate beliefs, and 3) core beliefs. Automatic thoughts, the primary target of intervention, consist of thoughts that occur without any deliberation or reasoning. These are the actual images or thoughts that run through one's mind. As the name implies, they seem to automatically occur in the mind. Intermediate beliefs consist of the rules, attitudes, and assumptions that a person makes about their world and that of others. Core beliefs "are the most fundamental level of belief; they are global, rigid, and overgeneralized" (Beck, 1995, p. 16).

Ellis (1958) developed REBT, which is a therapeutic intervention that encourages emotional growth by teaching clients to replace their negative or self-defeating thoughts, feelings, and actions with new ones that are more effective for growth, healing, and personal development. The "ABCDE" practice method is used by REBT clinicians. The "A" in the system represents a client's activating event, or the situation or context in which the client is experiencing distress. In the system, "B" represents clients' beliefs, including images, values, and perceptions. Clients are taught a systematic method for evaluating the problems in their lives, which are represented as "C" (or consequences, either emotional or behavioral) in the paradigm. According to Ellis (1994), clinicians must disrupt (D) the irrational beliefs of the client in order for the client to enjoy (E) their newly discovered rational beliefs. Clients are helped to assess the connection between their beliefs and the difficult feelings and behavioral consequences that are transpiring in their lives (Ellis, 1958, 1973, 1994).

It is important to note that one of the most common misconceptions of REBT and other cognitive approaches is that the goal of treatment is to help clients not feel or to discount their emotions (Ellis, 1994). However, depicting REBT as anti-emotion is inaccurate. The goal of treatment is to help clients experience feelings in a deep and personal manner, and to modify intermediate and core beliefs which eliminate affective states that interfere with a client's realistic appraisal of the situation and their capacity to maximize their strengths and meet their goals. For example, sadness and grief are understood to be healthy human emotions that stem from upset and loss. According to Ellis (1994), depression occurs when patterns of thinking associated with sadness and loss become exaggerated, magnified, and globalized. In such cases it is essential that the therapist use their skills to "argue with the client" and challenge their belief system to help the client learn ways to alter these cognitive processes and content.

Narrative and constructivist approaches also may often draw from cognitive therapy. While certainly some key differences do exist, many interventions focus on a client's cognitive processes or content. As the authors explore later in this paper, the cognitive aspects of narrative therapy lend themselves particularly well to poetry therapy.

Poetry and Poetry Therapy

Poetry has been a means of exploring the human condition for perhaps as long as human language has existed (Silverman, 1993). In early societies, poets were relied upon to document and interpret the human experience and to share these insights with the community through public performance as well as through the written word. Before the scientific revolution, literature and the humanities were seen as the fundamental means of learning about the human condition (Postman, 1992). The curative power of the healer and shaman in many societies may not have been entirely due to the prescription but to the written word (Harrower, 1972). While the acceptance of poetic insights into the human condition may have diminished over the last several centuries due to the acceptance of logical positivism and the dominant epistemological position, even Freud (1963) states that the poets were the first to tap, and perhaps the best at tapping, into the mysteries of the human psyche. While the influence of poetry and the poem may have decreased, the power of the poem as a tool for healing and human growth continues to be recognized. Even in the medical profession, the power of poetry is recognized as a means of helping patients make sense of their medical conditions and the associated life changes with which they are forced to cope (Shelton, 1999).

While the discipline of poetry therapy can largely trace its history to the last thirty years, poetry has been utilized in therapy since the early and middle of the last century (Blanton, 1960; Leedy, 1969; Prescott, 1922; Shrodes, 1949). The therapeutic value of poetry has been recognized by parishioners from diverse disciplines, including nursing (Edwards, 1990), social work (Houlding & Holland, 1988; Mazza, 1996), psychology (McLoughlin, 2000), psychiatry (Langosch, 1987), as well as community organizers (Holman, 1996) and academics in the humanities. With the advent of the National Association of Poetry Therapy, and the establishment of credentials from this organization, poetry therapy has become an established member of the creative arts therapies. The discipline even has its own academic journal, the *Journal of Poetry Therapy*, dedicated to the practice, teaching, and research regarding the therapeutic potential of poetry.

In perhaps the clearest formulation of poetry therapy, Mazza (1999) discusses three basic domains of poetry therapy:

1. The receptive/prescriptive component, involving the introduction of literature into therapy.
2. The expressive/creative component, involving the use of client writing in therapy.
3. The symbolic/ceremonial component, involving the use of metaphors, rituals, and storytelling (p.17).

Reiter (1997), in testimony submitted to the National Coalition of Arts, posits many factors that are clearly congruent with cognitive theory. The goals that are most congruent with cognitive therapy are:

1. Encourage realistic thinking and problem solving.
2. Develop creativity, self-expression and greater self-esteem.
3. Strengthen communication, particularly listening and speaking skills.
4. Find new meaning through new ideas, insights, and/or information.

Poems are not the only tool of the poetry therapist. Journal writing, myths, fables, and personal metaphors can all be incorporated into treatment. Some authors do differ as to what constitutes a poem in poetry therapy. For instance, Wadeson (1981) draws the distinction between poetry and other forms of writing through asserting the literary qualities of the poem, including reliance on metaphor, imagery, sound, rhythm, and economy of expression. Other poetry therapists are less concerned with the technical aspects of poetry, but use any client expression for the purpose of helping a client make sense of their lives. Regardless of the philosophy to which one subscribes regarding the importance of technical or artistic issues, the focus in poetry therapy must be the person and not the poem. It is our contention that helping clients understand the power of metaphor, and the compressed nature of a good poem can help clients focus on what is "core" about their experiences. However, it is also essential that therapists demystify the process of writing for clients. Many clients who have had poor educational experiences can be intimidated by the very thought of writing poetry. Indeed, some clients are so deficient in basic writing skills that they will need the therapist to transcribe their poem from their conversations. This can be a powerful collaborative experience that can help facilitate the development of the helping relationships.

A Synthesis of Cognitive Therapy and Poetry

In order to best understand how these two therapies can be combined to effectively assist clients to better understand themselves and their relationships with others, as well as begin to effect change in their lives, it is necessary to identify some central assumptions of cognitive therapy and relate these assumptions to poetry.

First, cognitive therapy focuses on thoughts so powerful that they can control emotions, behaviors, and world views. Since these thoughts are largely outside the awareness of the client, it is the goal of therapy to bring them into awareness. Poetry has the capacity to do just this because while being the "poet," the client feels free to write about a thought or an idea as if it either is owned by another or has a life of its own. The therapist then has the opportunity to discuss with the client how this thought that appears in a poem actually impacts the client themself. Sometimes these thoughts can be perceived as taboo by the client, but once engaged in the web of words, the client feels safer to address them.

Once into the client's awareness, a second goal of cognitive therapy is to discover to what extent these faulty or irrational cognitions affect the world of the client. The use of the metaphor assists the client to describe their reality, which may be shaped by just such faulty or irrational cognitions. Using metaphor allows the client to distance the self and engage in a dialogue with the self that has the potential to demonstrate the irrational nature of the belief and the potential for change.

Finally, cognitive therapy helps the client to understand that they do not have to react to the whims of their irrational schemas that might have been with them since childhood. Clients can learn through poetry that they can create their lives. They have the capacity to sift away the disabling tapes that might have run through their heads for many, many years and replace them with powerful, compact phrases and words through poetry. These phrases and words provide a way for clients to think about things differently, to begin to see them differently, to feel them differently, and, therefore, to behave differently.

One of the central assumptions of cognitive therapy is that cognitions interplay with emotions and behaviors, but it is the cognitions that are the target of change. Thus, poetry therapy, which taps into thoughts and emotions, is a logical fit with cognitive restructuring, logical analysis, and other forms of interventions. Using few words to express the self, using metaphors to name the unnameable, and being fully engaged in this process are poetic techniques that lead to the opportunity for client and therapist to discuss the role of cognition in shaping the client's reality and to then make effective change through changing the cognitions.

Poetry Exercises in Cognitive Practice

In the following section, poetry therapy exercises are presented that are congruent with cognitive therapy goals. The uses and procedures for each exercise are discussed, and examples are provided.

Exercise 1: Identifying and Assessing Current Understanding of Irrational Beliefs

This exercise is useful for teaching clients a process for identifying and assessing the validity of their beliefs. It should be utilized only after the therapist has engaged in a fair amount of didactic and interpersonal work with the client, in helping him or her recognize the differences between rational and irrational beliefs. In this exercise, the client is asked to write a poem that specifically explores their irrational or unhelpful beliefs. The client is asked to write about their situation or personal story from the perspective of their irrational belief. That is, they take on the voice or persona of their irrational belief. After they complete this exercise, the client is asked to explore their beliefs in more detail. This allows the therapist and the client to dialogue about the client's current understanding of their problem from a cognitive perspective. Sometimes clinicians overestimate a client's understanding of the process of cognitive change and restructuring. Too often, clients will agree with the clinician's conceptualization of the problem as a means of gaining approval. Also, clients who have been historically disempowered must be helped to take ownership for their own therapy. This exercise allows the therapist to listen to the client responding to their own beliefs, and can help the therapist plan new cognitive restructuring experiences collaboratively with the client.

The following passage was written by a twenty-seven-year-old man suffering from depression. While medication had somewhat mitigated his symptoms and his self-downing cogitations, depression still remained a powerful part of his life. Traditional cognitive techniques were not able to dislodge his depressogenic beliefs. The technique described above helped the client begin to look at his beliefs in a more detached manner—"from this outside looking in." This helped him to be less defensive in therapy, and more open to exploring the relationship between his beliefs and his depression. He decided to write this in the form of a letter.

> Dear Bob,
> I hate you. You know that, right. The funny thing is, you think that it is you that I hate you. I have you tricked. When I speak, you listen, you confuse us. That is cool, huh? Well, here is the think. I really hate you. I don't really know why I hate you, but I do. And Bob, I am really good at getting you to believe what a loser you are. You see, I have good timing. I wait until you make mistakes, and I beat you up for them. And you listen sucker! You listen every time. For example, remember last week when you could not find your keys? I told you that only a worthless loser does that. I had you convinced to go to bed and call in sick. And then, for calling in sick, I had you convinced that that made you worthless. I want to thank you Bob for listening to me. I want to thank you for listening more to me than yourself.

Exercise 2: Exaggerated Irrational Beliefs Poem
In this exercise, clients are asked to write a poem that greatly exaggerates the force, intensity, and nature of their irrational beliefs. This exercise has much in common with paradoxical directives, which can be found in many family-oriented practices that utilize cognitive methods. Further, such use of paradox is also common within REBT practice. The procedures for this poem are as follows: First, the clinician asks the client to think about the event in their life that is causing them the most distress (usually the identifying problem, or a problem that the therapist and the clients are currently working on). Then, the clinician asks the client to consider the thoughts that are associated with this event (these events should have been previously explored in therapy). Next, the clinician has the client imagine that they actually *are* the belief. They have them imagine what it must be like, and what these beliefs would *say* if they were alive. Finally, clients write a poem from the perspective of the beliefs in the most forceful, exaggerated manner possible. After this is completed, the poem can serve as an effective

catalyst for dialogue about the content of the beliefs. Often, by writing from this exaggerated perspective, clients will start to question the veracity of their beliefs without prompting from their therapist. This exercise also helps the client externalize the problem (White & Epston, 1990). Adopted from narrative therapy, but congruent with cognitive practice, this intervention helps clients challenge their problems by looking at them in a more detached, objective manner (Epston, 1994).

The following poem, in the form of a haiku, was written by a middle-aged gentlemen struggling with the impact of schizophrenia. For years, he believed that he was worthless due to his illness. Externalizing his beliefs in an exaggerated, compressed form helped him to recognize them when they occurred. Note, it is important that therapists help their clients use poems such as this in service of their own growth and not to reinforce the negative cognitions.

> You, always nothing.
> A worm. Dung. Nothing. Worm. Dung.
> Your fault. You, nothing.

Exercise 3: The Knowing and Believing Poem
In cognitively oriented practice, it is important for clients to truly believe their newfound or developing rational beliefs. Belief is a matter of degrees. A client may believe something to be true theoretically or intellectually but may not believe it to be true on an emotional level. A client may have a sense that something is true but may not trust new, unfamiliar beliefs. For example, a client may realize in therapy that they have personal value and worth but may doggedly stick to more familiar notions or cognitive scripts of their own worthlessness. All too often, beginning clinicians do not spend enough time helping clients integrate new beliefs into their repertoire of cognitive processing. Lazarus (1981) explores how various emotionally evocative techniques can help clients integrate new beliefs into their schema—their core beliefs. Writing poems can be useful in this regard, as emotionally evocative language can help clients develop a deeper sense of belief.

In this exercise, clients are to write a poem in which they work hard at convincing themselves as to the veracity of their new belief. They are asked to write a poem with as much passion and emotion as possible. Their goal is to convince themselves of the genuineness, rationality, and importance of their newfound belief. This poem can also be written as a narrative or a speech. For example, they can visualize writing to an important group of people, such as Congress, further visualizing that the fate of the nation depends upon the degree to which they are convincing. The point is to help them work toward developing a sense of trust and true belief about newly adopted healthy cognitions.

After they write the poem, clinicians should ask the client to read the poem three times out loud, each time with increasing force and emotion. The clinician may also ask the client to read the poem several times daily as a means of helping integrate their new belief. The clinician may also read the poem to the client. The second author of this article has utilized this technique by performing the client's poem in a highly dramatic, performance-oriented manner.

The following poem was written by a young man attempting to remain drug free. Because he failed many times, he only partially believed that he had the capacity to live free of his drug of choice, heroin.

> Hey Keith!
> You can be a man!
> You can withstand!
> Ok, in the past you fell,
> you have seen the pits of hell,
> But man, you can do this!
> You can find other joys,
> New toys, and not a boy!
> I can do this!
> I know I can.
> My heart so wants to live
> And that needle drains it
> Like a sieve.
> You can be a man, Keith!
> You can do this!

Exercise 4: Goal Clarification Exercise

The cognitive therapies are concerned with the bottom line of therapy: helping people make positive, healthy changes in their lives. This emphasis has increased currency, given the realities of managed care. Therefore, cognitive therapists usually focus considerable attention on helping people reach concise and measurable goals (Beck Institute, 2000). In this poetry intervention, the client is asked to write about a goal that they have and what has gotten in the way of achieving this goal. The clinician should make certain that the client includes not only environmental or situational impediments but distortions in their thinking as well. After the client has written about barriers or situations that deter their well-being, they are asked to write a second poem in which they imagine ways they can overcome these obstacles. The clinician explores with the client different ways to view their obstacles. Further, carefully considering shifts in attitude, a discussion on what thoughts may help them get closer to meeting their goals may be beneficial.

This exercise is particularly useful for cognitively oriented practice with groups. The intervention starts with Robert Frost's 1920 poem "The Road Not Taken" read out loud to the group members. In exercises in which a poem is read audibly, it is useful to read the poem multiple times. Members should also be provided with a copy of the poem. Multiple readings seem to help clients experience a poem on multiple levels. Group members begin to immerse themselves and find self-meaning of the poem.

Frost's (1920) poem, which is widely used in poetry therapy, presents the metaphor of a traveler making decisions about which path to take on a road, just as our clients make important life choices in their own journey. After the reading, clients are asked to discuss their paths and how they would go about achieving their aims. The clinician may generate discussion about taking the more difficult path in life versus taking what appears to be an easier one. Clients are able to explore what they think may get in the way of choosing the path that would be most satisfying. Often, clients will recognize cognitions associated with fear, low frustration tolerance, or self-doubt. After these beliefs are exposed, group members may help one another develop goals to challenge negative thoughts.

The simple poem that follows was written by a teenage girl in a therapy group at a residential treatment facility. Through her poem she honestly explores her fear of an uncertain future and despairs about how she views her potential outcomes, based upon her troubled past. One can also see the impact of cognitive therapy as she recognizes the role that her own cognitions now play in perpetuating her fear. After writing this poem, she read it to the group, and gained valuable support from members who had similar experiences and feelings.

> I don't know about any roads less traveled.
> Every day I see drugs and thugs.
> They pretend to do good,
> but they all crooks.
> This is where I come from.

I don't know anything else?
How can I dream,
When I lived too many nightmares.
You think this 'ant real?
Its real, and this is what I have
ta get out of my mind.
Ok, so its only real in my mind.
It feels real to me, so how do I
see it as a lie?
Why can't I make it go away?

Limitations

One key aspect of both therapies and their synthesis is their reliance on higher order linguistic skills. Practitioners working with the severe and persistently mentally ill must watch for signs of frustration and disorganization when practicing these techniques. The cognitive introspection that is stimulated by these techniques can overwhelm clients prone to disorganized patterns of thinking and may at times be contraindicated. The same may be true with extremely anxious clients. Also, it is important to realize that the primary symptoms of thought disorders should not be the target of cognitively based interventions. Hallucinations and delusions are usually biologically based and are more effectively treated with psychopharmacological interventions. However, secondary symptoms often can be treated using these techniques. For example, a client my feel less about him/herself due to their diagnosis. Self-downing cognitions that lead to depression and self-loathing may certainly be targeted by these techniques.

Lastly, Furman (2003) warns that regardless of what theory or technique is used, practitioners must be sure that their practice is guided by clear adherence to their professional values and ethics and a concern for social issues such as discrimination and oppression. By continually paying attention to the role of values and ethics in treatment, therapists can avoid the tendency to blame clients for the problems they seek help with. A clear distinction must be maintained between blame and responsibility.

Conclusion

Cognitive therapies have been gaining influence in the psychological and helping professions. One of the main criticisms of working from this perspective is that therapy can feel mechanistic to clients and clinicians alike, or can lack depth. Integrating poetry and poetry therapy into cognitive practice can go a long way toward resolving this problem. Hirshfield (1997) stated that the goal of poetry is the "magnification and clarification of being" (p. 5). This is the goal not only of cognitive therapy but most types of psychotherapy concerned with human potential. The goal of therapy is to help clients develop the ability to live their lives more successfully. One of the most important things that a client can gain from treatment is the ability to resolve their own dilemmas without professional intervention. By helping clients use poetry and written exercises to explore and resolve their distorted and maladaptive thoughts, therapists empower clients with the tools to improve health and well-being. For some clients, poetry can become a source of fulfillment that stems beyond its use as a tool for growth. As a means of exploring what it means to be human, writing poetry can add depth to human lives.

References

Beck, A. T. (1976). *Cognitive therapy and the emotional disorders.* Grune & Stratton.
Beck, A. T., & Emery, G. (1985). *Anxiety disorders and phobias.* Basic Books.
Beck, J. S. (1995). *Cognitive therapy: Basics and beyond.* The Guilford Press.
Beck Institute (2000). The Beck Institute for cognitive therapy and research. http://www.beckinstitute.org/about.htm
Bernard. M. E., & Joyce, M. R. (1984). *Rational emotive therapy with children and adolescents.* John Wiley & Sons.
Blanton, S. (1960). *The healing power of poetry.* Thomas Crowell.
DiGiuseppe, R. (1981). *Using rational–emotive therapy effectively.* Plenum Publishing.
Edwards, M. E. (1990). Poetry: Vehicle for retrospection and delight. *Generations, 14*(1), 61–62.
Edwards, M. E., & Lyman, A. J. (1989). Poetry: Life review for frail American Indian elderly. *Journal of Gerontological Social Work, 14,* 75–91.
Ellis, A. (1958). Rational psychotherapy. *Journal of General Psychology, 59,* 37–47.
Ellis, A. (1973). My philosophy of psychotherapy. *Journal of Contemporary Psychotherapy, 6,* 13–18.
Ellis, A. (1976). *Conquering low frustration tolerance* (cassette recording). Institute for Rationale-Emotive Therapy.
Ellis, A. (1994). *The essence of rational-emotive therapy.* Institute for Rational-Emotive Therapy.
Ellis, A., & Harper, R. A. (1975). *A new guide to rational living.* Prentice-Hall.

Epston, D. (1994). Extending the conversation. *Family Therapy Networker, 18*(6), 31–37.

Freud, S. (1963). *General psychological theory: Papers on metapsychology.* With an Introduction by Philip Rieff (Ed.). Collier Books

Furman, R. (2003). Cognitive and existential theories in social work practice. *The Social Work Forum, 36,* 59–68.

Gergen, K. (1985). The social constructionist movement in modern psychology. *American Psychologist, 40,* 266–275.

Glasser, W. (1995). *Reality therapy: A new approach to psychiatry.* Harper & Row.

Harrower, M. (1972). *The therapy of poetry.* Charles C. Thomas.

Hirshfield, J. (1997). *Nine gates: Entering the mind of poetry.* HarperCollins.

Holman, W. D. (1996). The power of poetry: Validating ethnic identity through a bibliotherapeutic intervention with a Puerto Rican adolescent. *Child and Adolescent Social Work Journal, 13*(5), 371–383.

Houlding, S., & Holland, P. (1988). Contributions of a poetry writing group to the treatment of severely disturbed psychiatric inpatients. *Clinical Social Work Journal, 16*(2), 194–200.

Kelly, G. (1955). *Personal construct psychology.* Norton.

Langosch, D. (1987). The use of poetry therapy with emotionally disturbed children. *The American Journal of Social Psychiatry, 7*(2), 97–100.

Lazarus, A. A. (1981). *The practice of multimodal therapy.* McGraw-Hill.

Leahy, R.L. (1996). *Cognitive-behavioral therapy: Basic principles and applications.* Jason Aronson Publishers.

Leedy, J. J. (Ed.). (1969). *Poetry therapy: The use of poetry in the treatment of emotional disorders.* Lippincott.

Lerner, A. (1997). A look at poetry therapy. *The Arts in Psychotherapy, 24*(1), 81–89.

Mahoney, M. (1991). *Human change processes.* Basic Books.

Mazza, N. (1996). Poetry therapy: A framework and synthesis of techniques for family social work. *Journal of Family Social Work, 1*(3), 3–18.

Mazza, M. (1999). *Poetry therapy: Interface of the arts and psychology.* CRC Press.

Mahrer, A. R. (1989). *The integration of psychotherapies: A guide for practicing therapists.* Human Sciences Press.

McLoughlin, D. (2000). Transition, transformation, and the art of losing: Some uses of poetry in hospice care for the terminally ill. *Psychodynamic Counseling, 6*(2), 215–234.

Meichenbaum, D. (1977).*Cognitive-behavior modification: An integrative approach.* Plenum.

Payne, M. (1997). *Modern social work theory* (2nd ed.). Lyceum.

Postman, N. (1992). *Technopoly: The surrender of culture to technology.* Random House.

Prescott, F. (1922). *The poetic mind.* Macmillan.

Reiter, S. (1997). Poetry therapy: Testimony on Capitol Hill. *Journal of Poetry Therapy, 10*(3),169–178

Shelton, D. L. (1999). *Healing words*. Washington, DC: AMA Staff News. Retrieved April 25, 2003 from http://ama-assn.org/scipubs/amnews/pick_99/feat0517.htm.

Shrodes, C. (1949). *Bibliotherapy. A theoretical and clinical experimental study*. Unpublished doctoral dissertation, University of California, Berkeley.

Silverman, H. L. (1993). Poetry as a psychotherapeutic intervention. In R. Kapnick & A. A. Kelly (Eds.), *Thinking on the edge* (pp. 33–50). Agamemnon Press.

Wadeson, H. (1981). Self-exploration and integration through poetry writing. *The Arts in Psychotherapy, 8*(3), 1981.

Walen, W. R., DiGuiseppe, R., & Wessler, R. L. (1980). *A practitioner's guide to rational emotive therapy*. Oxford University Press.

Werner, H. D. (1986). Cognitive theory. In F. J. Turner, (Ed.), *Social work treatment* (pp. 91–129). The Free Press.

White, M., & Epston, D. (1990). *Narrative means to therapeutic ends*. Norton.

Chapter 3

Poetry Therapy and Existential Practice

The purpose of this paper is to demonstrate how poetry and poetry therapy are useful tools in existentially oriented psychotherapeutic practice. This paper will accomplish this aim in several ways. First, a brief introduction to poetry therapy will be presented. Second, the main principles of existential therapy will be explored. Third, the congruence between poetry therapy and existential theory will be addressed. Fourth, exercises will be presented that can be used in existentially oriented practice. Last, a case example demonstrates the use of poetry and poetry therapy in existential psychotherapy.

    This article represents a departure from most scholarship on poetry therapy, the majority of which is rooted in psychoanalytically oriented traditions. It appears that the preponderance of theorists in the expressive arts therapies in general have been those influenced by psychoanalysis and modern psychoanalytic theory (Mazza, 1999). This is lamentable, since therapists who practice from theoretical orientations not congruent with this approach may not explore the uses of poetry and poetry therapy in their work. I contend that poetry and poetry therapy are congruent with many additional theoretical orientations. For the field of poetry therapy to progress and expand its current boundaries, scholars must demonstrate its relevance to other theoretical and practice orientations. Previously, such work has been conducted with the strengths perspective of social work treatment (Furman et al., 2003).

Poetry Therapy

Poets and philosophers have been aware of the curative and healing nature of poetry for millennia. Long before there were helping professionals, poets and storytellers helped people deal with their deepest fears by echoing the struggles of humanity in their poems, myths, and stories (Harrower, 1972). In hearing these works, people have learned that they are not alone with their pains, that they are part of a greater struggle. The Aristotelian concept of psychagogia (Lerner, 1981), "the leading out of the soul through the power of art" (p. 8), predates Freud's notion of sublimation by more than a thousand years. Aristotle discovered that through the process of creating poetry, people were able to transform their problems into power and their sadness into strength.

Many poets have discovered the liberational power of the poem in helping them maximize their own emotional and spiritual resources. For example, American counterculture poet Charles Bukowski (1991) saw poetry as the "ultimate psychiatrist." While poetry has been therapeutic to many "professional" poets, poetry can be therapeutic and used therapeutically with many different groups of people.

Recently, Mazza (1999) has developed a model for poetry therapy practice that has helped delineate its therapeutic components. This model is presented, as it lays the groundwork for the types of exercises and interventions that are possible for the therapist utilizing poetry in practice. Its components are:

1. The receptive/prescriptive component, involving the introduction of literature into therapy.
2. The expressive/creative component, involving the use of client writing in therapy.
3. The symbolic/ceremonial component, involving the use of metaphors, rituals, and storytelling.

Existential Theory

Prior to a discussion of existential theory, it should be noted that, in a very real sense, any attempt at categorizing the central principles of the theory is bound to fail. At its core, existential thought applies a phenomenological approach, advocating for understanding human phenomena in the present moment, as an unfolding process (Spinelli, 1989). To the existentialist, life is a phenomenon that constantly unfolds in each moment. This description applies equally to the theory of existentialism itself; it is best understood not as a set of isolated, abstract principles, but through the unfolding drama of actual lives (Sartre, 1965). At its core, existential theory helps provide guidance into what makes for meaningful and fulfilling lives for people in general, and for individuals in particular (Mullan, 1992). Existential theory is predicated upon basic truths about human existence (Krill, 1978). Van Deurzen-Smith (1997) asserts that in existential psychotherapy "The objective is to enable people to stand courageously in the emotion of life in a way that ennobles and revitalizes them, whilst taking account of the context and horizons of the world in which they live" (p. 3).

For half a century, existential psychotherapy has had a profound impact on various helping professions (Frankl, 1963). In spite of its impact, misunderstandings about the theory may have inhibited its popularity and influence. With concepts such as dread, angst, and bad faith, existential theory is often thought of as presenting a pessimistic view of humankind. However, at its core existentialism professes a positive and optimistic view of humankind (Willis, 1994). People are seen as being able to accept the harsh realities of existence and come to live an authentic, full life (Heidegger, 1927). Existential principles that will be explored in this paper are meaning, death, anxiety, creation, and responsibility. This list is by no means exhaustive, yet can be found in much of the existential literature and has particular relevance to poetry therapy.

What is the meaning of life? What is the meaning of my life? These are questions that both philosophers and the common person have grappled with since human beings began to possess language. Meaning, and a person's ability to construct a meaningful life, lies at the heart of existential thought (Bugental, 1978). People are thought to process the capacity for creating meaning and fulfillment even within the direst social contexts. Frankl (1963) noted that even those living in Nazi concentration camps were often able to establish a sense of relevance and meaning in life. Indeed, existentialists believe that each person possesses the capacity to create a meaningful, worthwhile existence in spite of not only external circumstances but painful pasts as well.

Sartre (1956) posited that existence precedes essence. That is, existence and life spring forth naturally, and it is only after the conscious mind is *aware* of life that meaning is ascribed to it. To the existentialist, one of the great truths of life is that existence is inherently meaningless, which means that each person has both the freedom and responsibility to create their own meaning (Kierkegaard, 1954).

This proposition leads directly to the importance of personal responsibility in existential thought. Since life has no inherent meaning, each person is responsible for creating a life that brings them fulfillment (May, 1958). Since joy and meaning can be encountered in even the most oppressive situations, surely the majority of people who do not experience such trauma can lead a worthwhile life. The person who takes responsibility for their own meaning and joy is said to live an authentic existence (Krill, 1986). The person living an authentic life does not hide behind false ideologies or myths. They realize that while some of life's greatest joys occur with others, each person is ultimately responsible for their own happiness.

Anxiety is a normal consequence of living. The realization of our own idiosyncratic creation of meaning leads us to realize that in a very real sense we are alone. A representative image of this notion is that of an individual naked in front of the universe, stripped bare of all pretense. This realization is painful and causes anxiety, which leads many to escape through addictions, false ideologies, and other "bad faith" self-deceptions (van Deurzen-Smith, 1997). Such self-deceptions become costly, as those who do not work toward living authentic, meaningful lives are bound to become lost in dread and neurotic anxiety (Tillich, 1952). Neurotic anxiety is anxiety not faced, the roots of which remains unrevealed. To the existentialist, the anxiety over unpaid parking tickets and other small worries helps people avoid facing the true source of anxiety: the omnipresent specter of death (Heidegger, 1927).

The reality of death is a key notion in existential thought (Moustakas, 1954). Being aware of their own death, the person living *authentically* examines their choices and consciously chooses to live to the fullest. They take chances in order to be their own person and are conscious of the often subtle, sometimes not so subtle, forces that pull them toward conformity and mediocrity. To paraphrase from Somerset Maugham's (1942) classic *Of Human Bondage*, upon waking up in the morning, the protagonist asks death what it has in store for them today. The awareness of death leads to anxiety. According to existential thought, this existential anxiety can be experienced in two different ways. It can be debilitating and overwhelming, leading to what is referred to as dread (depression), and the choice of escape through various dysfunctional behaviors or mood states. Conversely, it can be an energizing source that propels one to live life as fully and totally as possible. Faced with the prospect of death, the authentic or transparent person lives with a sense of awe and urgency (Jourard, 1964). Faced with the notion of death, petty worries and concerns seem less important and real. Authenticity demands awareness of the ultimate realities of life.

Existential psychotherapy is not a "system" that relies on specific techniques or interventions. Instead, it supports a view of clients as capable of shedding the barriers that stop them from living meaningful lives. The client encountered in the helping relationship is treated as a whole person (Jourard, 1968; May, 1979). While the existential practitioner does not ignore the past, they utilize the methods of phenomenology or constructivism, realizing that people can best be understood by examining their lives unfolding in the present moment (Buber, 1955; Yalom, 1980). The existential psychotherapist does not focus on fixing or altering pathology but on being a catalyst and witness to a client's journey toward meaning and truth (Willis, 1994).

Congruence Between Existential Theory and Poetry Therapy

Despite the strong influence of psychodynamic theories on poetry therapy, Mazza (1999) posits that it is congruent with many theories of practice. In referring to his model of poetry therapy addressed earlier, he states: "All three components have the potential to address the cognitive, affective, and behavioral domains of human experience. As such, poetry therapy can be adapted to most psychological models" (p. 17).

Several key aspects of poetry therapy are highly congruent with existential practice. Poetry, if nothing else, is a tool for helping individuals explore their lives and create meaning from their experiences. Hirshfield (1997) declared that the purpose of poetry is the clarification and magnification of being. This statement could easily be adopted as a manifesto for existential therapists as well.

W. H. Auden (as cited in Morrison, 1987) hinted at the congruence between poetry and existential thought. To Auden, poetry helps writers make sense of their worlds, put their own pain and suffering into perspective, and find meaning in their lives. Indeed, finding meaning in the context of suffering is a key theme in existential thought (Frankl, 1967).

The creation of poetry is the giving of voice to the human experience. In this sense, the poet pays witness to the unfolding occurrence of life itself. To Nietzsche (1908) the goal of life is to not merely endure existence, but to cherish its struggle and all that one has, each and every day. Perhaps this is what poets and artists do in the creation of poetry and other expressive arts: bear witness to and relish the struggle to live a meaningful life.

Existential theory—with its focus on the creation of personal meaning, individual responsibility, self-awareness, authenticity, and commitment—helps therapists focus clients on growing. Developing the practice of writing poetry demands attention to the self; the poet must become aware of the relationship between themselves and their world. Through writing poetry, the poet must identify their emotions, and come to understand how these feelings relate to the natural and human worlds around them.

Poetry and Written Exercises for Existential Practice

In this section, I will describe useful exercises for existential practice. Many of these exercises can be used when practicing from various theoretical perspectives but have special application to existential practice. As such, some additional concepts from existential theory are interspersed throughout this section in order to help the reader make connections between theory and practice. For those who have not utilized poetry therapy previously, Mazza (1999) provides an excellent guide.

Automatic Writing
Since existential practice eschews the notion of the therapist as an expert in what the client needs, exercises that help clients get in touch with their own internal guides are congruent with the existential way of practicing. In automatic writing, clients are asked to write for five minutes (or more after they have done the exercise several times) without putting down their pen. This exercise can be utilized with any topic in which the client would benefit from an increase in insight. Automatic writing exercises have been useful with young adults as well as children (McKinney, 1976). The therapist should make certain that the client has permission to write whatever comes into their mind. The goal is to help the client explore, not edit. I have found it valuable to tell the client that even if they write the word "the" repeatedly for five minutes, they are to keep writing.

Visioning Meaning Exercises: "With My Grand Future I Will"
In this exercise clients are asked to use writing to get them in touch with what is important to them. When we project ourselves into the future in this manner, we tend to think in terms of our dreams and passions. When we think of ourselves in the present, we are more likely to look through the filter of self-doubt or social expectation. The wording of the stem, *with my grand future I will,* seems to encourage the deep sense of visioning that is necessary in existentially oriented practice. As with the exercise above, clients are encouraged to write for five minutes (longer if they are accustomed to writing) and are asked to not censor their words. Clients will often be surprised at the degree of depth and the power of their writing. This presents the therapist with a good

opportunity to validate the client's own internal strengths and resources. In many ways, the goal for existential therapy, and perhaps all therapies, is to make the therapist ultimately expendable.

Mission Statement Exercise

In this exercise, clients are asked to write a poem about what their life stands for, or what it means. They are asked to imagine themselves as an organization and dream up organizational goals and actions. Depending upon the client, this exercise can be written as a prose statement or in poetic form. I have found it useful to have clients conduct this exercise with some degree of formality and to include feedback from people in their lives. Some clients have sought input from important "members of the board" and have had their mission statements printed on fine paper and mounted on a plaque.

Strength and Motivation from Death

In discussing the work of Martin Heidegger, van Deurzen-Smith (1997) states: "In spite of the ineluctable anxiety that is triggered by the potential loss of all we care for, we nevertheless tend to take the essentials of life for granted" (p. 36).

As previously explored, death as reality in our daily lives can be a powerful motivator in helping us come to terms with our passions. When we possess an acute and emotionally immediate sense of ourselves as finite, we are less likely to live blindly. Time and life can come to be seen as precious gifts that must not be wasted. In the following exercise, death is used as a motivator to help clients explore the manner in which they live.

For this exercise, the client is asked to clearly and carefully imagine their own funeral. Utilizing as many senses as they can, they are asked to imagine themselves as a witness to the ceremony. In this ceremony, many people speak about them and how they lived their life. Afterward, they are encouraged to write about the event, focusing upon what was said about them, and their own feelings. The writings that emerge from this exercise can be powerful motivators for exploration and change.

Case Example

Jeff was an African American man in his mid-forties who lived in a large city in the northeastern United States. He was a participant in a social rehabilitation day program for people suffering from persistent mental illness. Jeff, who had been diagnosed with schizophrenia, had been participating in the program for nearly ten years.

Jeff had his first psychotic episode while he was a graduate student in African American studies at a local urban university. He began hearing voices and became increasingly paranoid. He soon was hospitalized and had to drop out of school. Medication never stopped Jeff's auditory hallucinations, and he remained episodically paranoid. He started to receive disability payments and moved out of his parents' house. For several years, he became homeless and addicted to cocaine. He managed to quit using illegal drugs and moved into a boarding house for persons with mental illness.

By the time that Jeff started seeing me for therapy, he had become nearly completely marginalized from most people and experienced little meaning and purpose in his life. He participated in the activities of the program but seemed to derive little joy from them. In therapy, Jeff and I began to explore what his life had come to mean to him. Still capable of considerable insight, he began to discover that he had lost a great deal of what he valued. He explored how he had come to hide from having to truly live. He recognized that he had succumbed to the power of his painful and often debilitating mental illness. Hidden from himself under the depressing cloak of his current existence, one that provided little joy but much predictability, Jeff took little responsibility for his happiness. Upon realizing how he had wasted many years, he soon began to experience existential anxiety, the intense feeling that comes from realizing that one is wasting the only life they are guaranteed.

Jeff felt stuck. He came to realize that he needed to break free from his learned, internalized helplessness but did not know how. I asked him how he felt about exploring his life and its purpose through writing and poetry, which had been important to him while he was in college. Jeff agreed and started to keep a written journal of his feelings and thoughts. He began to write poetry on his own and in therapy. We had several goals for his writing. First, we hoped it would serve a means of helping him develop insight into his learned helplessness and be a vehicle for re-envisioning his future. Second, we also posited that the writing of poetry would, in and of itself, give his life renewed meaning. Third, we hoped that writing would be a good tool for helping him manage his anxiety. When working with people with persistent mental illness, it is essential that such affective states are kept within tolerable limits in order not to exacerbate psychotic symptoms.

One of the first poems that Jeff wrote explored his sense of loss and sadness over having lost many years to mental illness and inertia. It is untitled.

> When I broke
> I just broke
> I fell asleep like
> Rip Van—I don't even remember
> his whole name.
> And *that*, is the shame.
> The years have past me by
> while I have waited here
> wanting to do what, why?
> With the medication
> my mind and soul
> and one proud spirit
> starting to fry?
> I feel sick
> being able to see myself
> from the outside
> as if now
> I am both in my body
> and on Mars
> high above the stars
> staring down at me.
> It may be time to start living.

After several months of writing, Jeff began to feel increasingly hopeful about his life for the first time in many years. He started to experience a sense of motivation and got in touch with feelings he had not experienced since before he became ill. He also saw how his own behavior had led people to treat him as a *patient* and not as a whole person. He began to develop awareness of his own behavior, and would ask those around him to have higher expectations for him. The following poem was written as a mission poem, as described in the preceding section.

> **My Mission Statement**
> Ok, will the real me please stand?
> Can the *I* within open his hand
> to reach out to life?

> Perhaps it is too late to be
> a professor of African American Studies
> or a great
> anything.
> But I can write these words
> I can speak my voice
> and my voice and my words
> can help educate and free
> if not anyone else
> at the very least me.
> I may be alone some days
> in my room
> but now I don't stare at the blank walls
> I fill these blank pages.
> I fill me.
> Maybe some magazines will reject them
> but I will never reject me.
> I have come too far
> and have some more
> distant mountains to climb.

By the end of treatment, which lasted over one year and consisted of approximately fifty sessions, Jeff had made significant progress toward his three goals. Poetry helped him understand how he had limited himself through the socially constructed label of "mental patient." Through his writing, he began to create new metaphors for himself that challenged his self-imposed understanding of his limitations. Further, writing became a source of meaning for him. He began to see himself as a writer, and enjoyed the time he spent writing in his journal. He even read his poetry at a few community poetry readings. He began to feel useful, and reported experiencing hope for the first time in many years. He also learned that writing could be a useful coping mechanism to help him deal with anxiety, depression, and other difficult mood states. He understood that poetry would not cure his mental illness, but that it greatly enriched his life and increased his overall sense of well-being.

Conclusion

The preceding case example illustrates how poetry can be useful in helping people create meaning and value in their lives. Poetry therapy is an important expressive arts therapy, congruent with many different theories and practice models. Through the demonstration of its use in existentially oriented practice, it is hoped that therapists who have not experimented with its varied aspects will become interested in the use of poetry. For the existentially oriented practitioner, the use of poetry is an ideal tool for helping people come to terms with the realities of existence. It is my hope that practitioners working from various perspectives will explore the uses of poetry in practice and will publish their results as a means of adding to the developing body of literature.

References

Buber, M. (1955). *Between man and man*. Beacon.
Bugental, J. F. (1978). *Psychotherapy and process: The fundamentals of an existential-humanistic approach*. Random House.
Bukowski, C. (1991). Writing. *Black Gun Silencer, 2*.
Frankl, V. (1963). *Man's search for meaning: An introduction to logotherapy*. Pocket Books.
Frankl, V. (1967). *Psychotherapy and existentialism: Selected papers on logotherapy*. Simon & Schuster.
Furman, R., Langer, C. L., & Anderson, D. K. (2006). The poet/practitioner: A paradigm for the profession. *J. Soc. & Soc. Welfare, 33*, 29.
Harrower, M. (1972). *The therapy of poetry*. Charles C. Thomas.
Hirshfield, J. (1997). *Nine gates: Entering the mind of poetry*. HarperCollins.
Heidegger. M. (1927/1981). *Being and time* (A. Hofstadter, Trans.). University Press
Jourard, S. M. (1964). *The transparent self: Toward a psychology of being*. Norstrand.
Jourard, S. (1968). *Disclosing man to himself*. Van Nostrand Reinhold.
Kierkegaard, S. (1954). *Fear and trembling and the sickness unto death*. Doubleday.
Krill, D. (1978). *Existential social work*. Free Press.
Krill, D. (1986). Existential social work. In F. J. Turner, (Ed.), *Social work treatment* (pp. 181–218). The Free Press.
Lerner, A. (1981). Poetry Therapy. In R. Corsini (Ed.), *Handbook of innovative psychotherapies* (pp. 131–152). John Wiley and Sons.
Maugham, W. S. (1942). *Of human bondage*. The Modern Library.
May, R., Angel, E., & Ellenberger, H. F. (1958). *Existence*. Simon and Schuster.
May, R. (1979). *Psychology and the human dilemma*. W. W. Norton.
Mazza, N. (1999). *Poetry therapy: Interface of the arts and psychology*. CRC Press.
McKinney, F. (1976). Free writing as therapy. *Psychotherapy: Theory Research and Practice, 3*(2), 183–187.
Morrison, M. R. (1987). Poetry and therapy. In M. R. Morrison (Ed.), *Poetry as therapy* (pp. 21–26). Human Sciences Press.

Moustakas, C. (1954). *The self: Explorations in personal growth.* Harper & Row.
Mullan, H. (1992). Existential therapists and their group therapy practices. *International Journal of Group Psychotherapy, 42*(4), 453–458.
Sartre, J. P. (1956). *Being and nothingness.* Philosophical Library.
Sartre, J. P. (1965). *Essays in existentialism.* Carol Publishing Group.
Spinelli, E. (1989). *The interpreted world: An introduction to phenomenological psychology.* Sage.
Tillich, P. (1952). *The courage to be.* Yale University Press.
van Deurzen-Smith, E. (1997). *Everyday mysteries: Existential dimensions of psychology.* Routledge.
Yalom, I. D. (1980). *Existential psychotherapy.* Harper/Collins Publishers.
Willis, R. J. (1994). *Transcendence in relationship: Existentialism and psychotherapy.* Ablex.

Chapter 4

The Mundane, the Existential, and the Poetic

Poetry is an existential act. At its best, poetry is an attempt to explore, and create, meaning in existence. At its core, successful poetry reduces life to its essential elements. In a very real sense, poetry is a highly subjective, highly personal exploration into the realm of sub-atomic physics. Or, to paraphrase what a poet friend Jim Smith once said, poetry is the distillation of the essence of being. Yet, what is this essence? From an existential perspective, the essence of human existence is nothingness (Furman, 2003a). The world exists; we are born into it, and at some point become aware of the void that is both terrifying and wonderful (Yalom, 1980). The essence of the world is characterized by this dialectical experience of nothingness (Krill, 1969). The void is our essence, our salvation, and the source of our deepest fears, all at once. The void is nothingness; it is empty. The void is the essence of all that is mundane and profound. Notice the careful juxtapositioning of these two concepts.

Sartre (1965) asserted that there is no inherent meaning to life. The significance and value ascribed to objects, events, and relationships are our own conscious and unconscious projected meanings we place upon the world. In this sense, all that separates the mundane from the profound is the vehicle of perception. It is not my intention to advocate for moral relativism at this point, only to set a context for understanding the role of human perception in a conceptualization of the mundane.

Now, the reader might wonder how this dark, existential tangent is connected to poetry. First, let's consider poetry as data. Better, let's think of poetry as a highly subjective form of qualitative data capable of capturing affect. One of the strengths of poetry lies in its ability to convey complex and powerful emotions. The power of juxtaposing images can help convey conflicting and co-existing emotions that characterize complex experiences and relationships. Poetry is the affective microchip (Furman, 2003b). At its best, it captures the deep emotion of lived experience in a highly compressed form (Richardson, 1994).

Many people write poetry, or at least poetic language written as a vehicle for self-expression and revelation. Adolescents spontaneously write poetry as a means of coming to grips with the biopsychosocial developmental changes that characterized their world. The adolescent uses poetry as a means of bringing order to their chaotic, highly labile world. During my early years of college, I began to write poetry as a means of understanding my growing sense of self and my relationship to the world. This is personal poetry; personal narratives, and lyrics written mostly for the self.

At some point, some young writers of poetry decide to move beyond this self-revelatory/therapeutic function and attempt to communicate to the outside world. At first, the new poet writes about that which is most troubling or shocking. This is what they are accustomed to writing about. They also believe that these exceptional experiences are the essence of what they *must* communicate through their writing. Narcissistically, although developmentally appropriate to young adulthood, we assume that our experiences are perhaps more profound than those of others. Also, while there is a sense of emotional risk involved in sharing such personal experiences, at the same time it is safe—safe in the sense that we know they will make an impact on our audience just by the nature of the content of the poems.

It is easy to write powerfully about monumental events, about life trauma and pain. Plucking the heart strings is not difficult. Write about war, romance, incest, oppression, with even a modicum of poetic skill and leave the average audience moved. This is not to denigrate or minimize these horrific human phenomena. They are real, they exist, and those suffering through them deserve deep empathy, support, and healing. Yet, in this mode of writing, the poem is still a means to an end. The poem is a vehicle, an object, a fetish even. The *experience* is what evokes the reader's response, not the poem itself. The poem exists to communicate in the same way that advertising is designed to elicit a buying response. The dynamic is one of manipulation, a desired cause and effect. There is little room for the personal experiences and constructions of the reader. The poem is a vehicle through which to present and explore the marked.

Yet, at some point, the maturing poet may wish for something else from poetry, from life perhaps. They may seek to move beyond self-absorption and into the world of others. Perhaps this inclination represents a movement into the world of the aesthetic, perhaps a desire to chronicle human events outside the self. Still, their work and processes are characterized by a focus on the external, on the need to find *something* to write about, perhaps an important event to share. Again, they remain committed, without consciously being aware of it, to a poetics of the marked.

Yet, I believe that the poet who wants to make a go of poetry as a lifetime experience begins to chronicle objects and events around them that seem fairly mundane. Perhaps they realize that they have already written about all the most painful and important events in their lives. Perhaps this evolution is about honesty. Brekhus (2001) notes that the scholarship of the marked is a scholarship of bias. By studying the extraordinary, the true nature of social phenomena is distorted, and often wholly ignored. This applies equally to poetry. A poetics of the mundane is far more honest than a poetics of the extraordinary. We live in a world of objects, events, and relationships that are seemingly ordinary. The poet that seeks to document and bring life to the ordinary seeks to reach out and experience the world around them in an authentic way. They seek to bring their real selves into a dynamic, honest relationship with their day-to-day world as it really is. Buber (1955) describes this authentic relating to others and the world as an I–thou experience. The world and others are not treated as a series of objects to capture or use. In the I–thou relationship, the goal is to experience the true nature of the other and, in a very real sense, transcend the separation between the self and the world. Yet, why would one want to have such a relationship to everyday objects? Aren't these everyday objects boring, banal, mundane?

The poet who becomes aware of the sublime nature of the ordinary becomes transformed in the same way that the student of Zen finds enlightenment: The simple becomes the profound; a blade of grass becomes the universal. For William Carlos Williams (1923), it was a red wheelbarrow that glistened in the sun. In this classic poem the image that is conjured in the mind is of objects that might be passed by a hundred times a day without being noticed. Yet, the attention, caring, and linguistic dedication that he brings to these seemingly forgettable objects renders them unforgettable. The product is a poem that is simultaneously ordinary and extraordinary. In this sense, the poem perfectly captures the nature of existence, perhaps the purpose of an art and science of the mundane.

Compare this to the first line of a poem by Ginsberg (1972), the first line also being the title, "Done, finished with the biggest cock I ever had" (p. 54) Nothing ordinary here. The poet tells us that the extraordinary just happened; the immediacy of the event frames it as something that must be immediately documented. Clearly, the author of the poem was impacted. The event is sex with size, the conquest of the biggest or best. As the first line, it leaves the reader no doubt that this will be an extraordinary poem about an extraordinary event. We are given little choice but to recognize that something magnificent has occurred. Yet, is most sex really about the biggest and the best? Most sex probably occurs late at night when a couple is tired, after work, after the drudgery of chores, before the alarm clock ushers in more work and mundane, everyday existence.

I contend that the task of the poet is to make the mundane powerful, to add meaning to the meaningless. The poet experiences their world of objects and experiences, most of which are mundane. Their task is to experience these objects and make them meaningful. The poet—through comparison, metaphor, image, revelry, and juxtapositioning—transforms the world of the mundane into the world of the sacred. In fact, the poet merely demonstrates that the differences between what we typically call the mundane and the sacred are found not in the objects themselves, but within ourselves. Why is a small bush we ignore each day on our way to work less magnificent than the redwoods we see on vacation? The fault lies in imagination, and attention. This is where the poet enters, pointing out the magnificence of the small shrub.

Life for the most part is series of mundane tasks that each individual engages in before their ultimate death, with episodic experiences that appear to have currency and intensity—appear in the sense that the event just *is*; it has no inherent meaning other than that which we derive from our own personal and cultural experience. Again, life is meaningless. One person may become depressed when losing a job while another becomes ecstatic. The meaning that the individual ascribes to the event predicates how it will be defined.

While many will read this and wonder if the author has one leg tied to a large stone that he is ready to hurl into deep water, this realization is intensely liberating. Since life has no inherent meaning, we each have the capacity to create a sense of meaning within each moment. Since the most prevalent aspect of life is the mundane, the goal is to learn to cherish that which is mundane. Since the mundane is everywhere, there is much to cherish! Frankl (1963) observed the capacity to create meaning within the context of the Nazi death camps. Small acts, mundane acts, became powerful, became important.

The poet, constantly seeking to attach meaning to the mundane, possesses the capacity for revering even the most ordinary aspects of existence. This paper will explore poems the author has written that are concerned largely with the mundane. By exploring the mundane, the mundane become sacred and the sacred becomes mundane. It is perhaps this very dialectic that fuels the study of the mundane.

Three sections of poems and reflective comments about each poem will be presented: mundane objects, mundane events, and mundane relationships. These categories are somewhat arbitrary; there is considerable crossover between the three.

Mundane Objects

We live in a world of things. In American society, we learn to covet objects. We learn that having enough expensive, extraordinary things will somehow lead to personal satisfaction, even salvation. If you have an extraordinary car, you are a success. If you have an ordinary car, you are a failure. Yet, material fetishism can fix our lives. Ultimately, all objects fail to save us from death.

The first two poems are concerned with two objects that are perhaps so mundane and ordinary as to be invisible: dental floss and lint, two objects unworthy of poetry. Notice how observations regarding the mundane turn into explorations of time, creation, and death.

Dental Floss

Red strings of dental floss
spent in the waste basket
or floating in the toilet
knowing nothing of the madness
of our days working without reason
or our crying with no true pain
or loving well past the time to end.
But there they lie
as I shine old brown shoes
into renewal like an old whore
and her paint of sadness and economics
or the stripped and varnished desk
with its nails pulling to escape.
I cannot yet accept
the finality of gapping socks
shattered glasses or dreams

or the rim of gray that greets me
with wide open arms
facing the planes of time.

To The Lint from The Dryer

Why do we loathe you so?
Former flesh of our hands, fur of our dogs.
My step-daughter, frightened of your form-
she can barely be consoled.
What a burden to be so feared,
deemed so useless,
caste into corners, forgotten.
Some say, at the cellular level,
even sprouts scream when eaten.
Why vegetarianism is a form of murder,
yet no one considers you?

The next poem is about my wife's freckles. What is more ordinary than the small red marks that are the bane of so many children's existence. Freckles, as ordinary and American as a two-car garage.

Spot

The spots on your face
multiply in June.

It is the sun you say and
melanin spreading from exposure.

The great lie of science counsels the sacred.
Each one of the millions

earned by each loving act.
Rescuing a dying homeless dog,

driving home the disabled man
who pisses on the car seat,

soothing crying children,
calming muse to grouchy poet.

This next poem is about a pair of shoes that I wore as a teenager. Often, mundane objects become metaphorical for important, developmental issues.

Creepers

Misnamed   indelicate   plodding,
but with the right pair of jeans,

my feet grin fungal-smiles,
they remember for me.

The knobby rubber sole
that squealed even on carpet,

that I fumbled with when fleeing
faces on the brink   can barely recall

the clumsy metal buckle
the edge of dorm-room beds,

an eighteen-year-old boy
pretending he was a man,

wrestling crusted dishes   ramen dignified with shallots,
and the Infinity avoided like statistics,

and lips like whispering hammers on girls ready for love.
And now   I forget most of the details,

jeans faded from dancing thighs and sun,
clunky crimson *zapatos*   courage.

Early in my career as a social worker, I worked with developmentally disabled adults. The program was designed for men who were capable of living in the community, usually held jobs, but needed some help getting their daily needs met. This poem is about one of these men, who was able to find the ordinary extraordinary.

Glen

buys a ticket
to ride the carousel
at the pier

Glen is thirty
giggling
conferring with Glen

I watch him from a bench
as blood drains into distant sands

Glen is retarded
autistic
schizophrenic

Glen laughs
wonderfully oblivious
his world commencing and ceasing
with the raising and falling, the corkscrewing
antique painted pony.

After each whirling revolution
Glen salutes me with a thrusting fist
like the Black power sign
mumbling
hysterical
pure glee.

Mundane Events

Look around the room where you are reading this. What is it filled with? Perhaps a work of art or two, something truly powerful. Yet, look further. Perhaps a cheap ballpoint pen without a top or even the cap on the back? A coffee cup with a half inch of day-old coffee and a stain around the rim? Discarded paper? In all likelihood, the objects you see are not those designed to help you engage in epic adventures. We encounter mundane objects while engaging in mundane events. We brush our teeth. We clean the carpet. We watch moths return.

The Return

The Miller moths flutter overhead
as we die at varying rates.

The lament of a hardened heart
unknowing the passing of weeds

or black car coughing dirge.
Before she sleeps

her legs flail towards the ceiling,
lips bustle and swerve

like the mind anticipating an accident.
Somehow, always imagining myself

a dignitary, this Nile green coarseness,
this fist that pummels time,

or an extortionist with amnesia
or the clutching embrace of lies

spoken with crossed fingers
resting on separate hips.

Mundane events often do not seem mundane. Sometimes they weigh us down with anxiety and dread. Sometimes we recognize the folly of being controlled, angered, or depressed by events that we will forget about in time. Oftentimes they seem to take on near existential proportion. The degree to which one is able to separate themselves from such events, or at least place them in perspective, is the degree to which they can live authentically.

Speaking with Death on A Wednesday

Nothing
that should not

peer at its center
laugh

even
when cancer devours

the IRS levies
the mind whispers

brutal acts
the hands

contemplate obeying
I examine my hands

tan ridged scars
crossing blue green veins

and look at death
with challenging glance

across my aging face
spit in the eye of time

bark at beckoning winds.
I will wait for you

in this rooted space.

I wrote the following poem on the first truly warm day of spring while I was still living in Colorado. Sipping a beer, enjoying the sun, feeling the rays warm my face, I wrote this poem, inspired by the fleeting glance of a young woman.

On Watching A Stranger Walk By

You will miss her death bed.
Kisses.

Stripping the *number seven*
printed on her shirt,

watching it fall to the floor,
that it will appear to be a *number one*

crumbled in a lonely pile,
or whispering that she looks lovely

as she tries to hide
ashamed.

This poem delves into a strange, extraordinary event contextualized within day-to-day life. It explores how the ordinary becomes extraordinary through dialogue and relationship. This poem easily fits into this or the next section.

Forty Cats

He tells me about the woman
found with forty cats in her freezer
as he grills chicken in the rain
while his wife pan-fries frozen vegetables

in virgin olive oil and seasoning salt.
I finish the packaged Spanish rice
as we wax about the poem and the past.
Trying to hear with my heart

distracted ears fail me,
I creep towards the freezer
and marvel at how organized one would have to be
to pack forty cats inside.

We roam and shoot a few a games
I sink an unmakeable bank
and chock on the gifts.
Stumbling home he whispers

about his father
who criticizes received criticism
about being overly critical
about his friend the tie die junky

greasy stands of hair and Rorschach shirts
who fails at music and love
owes everyone a grand or so
and now caresses little baggies

small flames and prays
the linings in his nose will last.
Ambling down Pearl Street
in Boulder Colorado in two thousand and three

the moment prefect like mountain oysters and a beer
after draining starvation hike over two miles high
or marvelous like rows of felines
in plastic bags, mouths carefully turned

to delicate smiles,
and this moment mysterious
like the reason they were saved
in the first place.

This poem chronicles a night of documenting the activities of patrons in bars in a trendy area of Denver.

Late Night Lodo

1
She, a hobby horse
in a diagram of sadness.

Painting her flesh
with Van Gogh desperation

on the beer balcony
behind the stadium

on the swirling end
of shock and awe existence

on stink well of norotia
and unbalance

overdoing this game
of chronic seeking

an overexertion of lacking
the boys all say

she is a nice
play thing.

2
Yellow breasts
and hands facing east

her loss
and poison grass venom

a fallow wasted field.
Tonight, she might fight

a new champion
of forgetting.

After, they will watch
television.

It will seem nothing
like love.

3

His muscle shirt screaming
I take steroids

and have a small penis
he will not make

the anxious blond from the suburbs.
The waitress stuffs her check holder

into the back of her pants
a middle-age brunette

discards pretense
a paltriness of longing

we pretend
 to forget.

4
As the homeliest girl
of the group

you *must*
try harder.

A bodymaker crafting
herringbone suits

for men twenty years
your senior.

It is this
or finding what?

Meaning alone?
Facing that void without vodka?

Pitching a tent around
the grasslands of reason-

answer your cell phone.
Quickly.

5
Mistake one.
Ask her to make anything.

She spins together Jim Beam
and something.

It tastes like emptiness
and she calls you hon'

and she is maybe near forty
and looks maybe fifty

black shirt and gold lamé
and small slits on each side

with some flesh pushing between
it tells me *I'm Sexy*

and I ask for something
to make the drink sweet

adds a bit of Seven-up
I don't want to kill you

just yet hon.
and there is an old white guy

his face skimming the bar top
his chained wallet in back pocket

but he'd give it up for
some head or a knife

or maybe not,
nothing ventured nothing lost,

and the gay men
in Spanish ball caps

check all eyes for signs
and the middle-age women

wishing for things of these men
they will not deliver

but might anyhow
for rent, or even a few drinks.

Mundane Relationships

Relationships are the essence of life. In social work, a quality helping relationship is recognized as perhaps the most important factor in ensuring successful client outcomes for a variety of psychosocial problems (Goldstein, 1990). Television and film often portray relationships during their most intense, usually problematic or euphoric moments. Yet, relationships are often day-to-day grinds. Friends listen to each other's problems, talk about trivial things. In marriages and significant-other relationships, partners worry about bills and who is going to scrub the toilet. You eat, make love, work; day-to-day relationships shape the meanings of our lives.

The first poem is another poem about my wife's freckles. It focuses more on the importance of daily occurrences within our relationship.

Freckles

The first thing I see each morning
are her freckles.
This cannot be helped.
I have to describe them to her,
tell her how amazing they are
that she might have more freckles
than there mini-malls in
all of suburbia.
She rolls her eyes.
She never cared for them much.
And you can see how she must
have suffered as a child.
Yet, they are a wonder.
Drawing out her eyes
they match her tenderness,
her innocent belief in others
her childlike resolve to love.
I watch them throughout the day:
they shift and change their form
depending upon the light,
upon her womanly moods.
I pick up the paper:
wars,
inflation,

the crash of markets.
I look at her freckles
as she loves the dogs
raises our kids.
There is order in those things
that truly matter.

Friendships are often devalued in the United States. Kinship ties are seen as more significant and important to the developmental process (Hutter, 2001). Yet, friendships are essential for healthy growth and development. Often, little transpires between friendship, other than *being* together. It is this being that is essential, as mundane as it appears from the outside. Relationships also are full of mundane and petty misunderstandings.

Between Us

The beer not between us,
the swaying willow of our shame.

Your uneasiness sober?
A chest-thumping ape.

In a bookstore
a young woman half our age,

torn jeans and pale belly shirt
underwear exposed

flips through *The Cat Encyclopedia*
and *Puppies of the World,*

her breasts are ivory amulets,
and you would understand

if I told you her softness
is bleeding like time,

is airbrushed contentment.
What is the cost of beer ol' buddy?

This poem again explores a friendship, this time one that has been lost.

For A Lost Fried

A limping Villanelle

What do I seek in those sleeves?
Potted time, crimson longing, a vector,
the pinning of sweat on my chest a reprieve?

I have loved the dead, they return and leave
aches and welts under skin as leather.
What do I seek in those sleeves?

You failed to ever please,
women and girls, in your sadness, better
to surrender? They left you dusty on your knees.

And for juxtaposed failures, you wheeze,
and I die to you, underneath the feaster.
What do I seek in those sleeves?

Ol' buddy, I have tried to appease,
my years and heart only redder,
to surrender? I'm, left on dusty knees.

And after all these years? More reprieve,
you fade, as a seventeen-year-old specter
finally now, in Omaha heat, I'm ready to leave,
but what do I seek in those sleeves?

For the final poem, a vulnerable poem with a surreal tone. Somehow, no additional elaboration seems appropriate.

Final

Toilet paper rolls and Mesopotamian tombs
have nothing in common, or anything
to do with why your bank balance crawls
to zero   a black earth slug   hambone.

Caught in the chill   no sex for three days
after a run of twelve. She eyes you over her
book as you return   talk is tense
descend to your wood-paneled basement

slide into the stiff oak captain's chair,
this elbow grease scouring the abrasion of Alone,
this nappy, shaggy waiting, this recollection

witnessed like petty theft, like an organ donor,
so solace in a box, when writing on eternity
with the caulk of self.

How long til' you ascend
those fragile, indebted stairs? Casting a spell
upon the final design?

Conclusion

I am tempted to let the poems stand for themselves and serve as their own conclusion. Yet, finishing this paper in a café, I am struck by a conversation that I am overhearing (eavesdropping on?). Two young women are discussing whom to confide in among their circle of friends; whom to be increasingly vulnerable with. I am sitting very close to these two young women, both dressed in sweatpants, both a bit disheveled. From afar, they are ordinary, both plain. I listen to their gentle explorations of their relationships, their desire for connection and community, their desire to be known. I glance over again, somehow they both are suddenly beautiful, quietly extraordinary. They are both profoundly, yet mundanely, poetic.

References

Brekhus, W. (2001). A mundane manifesto. *Journal of Mundane Behavior 1.*
    http://www.mundanebehavior.org/index.htm
Buber, M. (1955). *Between man and man.* Beacon.
Frankl, V. (1963). *Man's search for meaning: An introduction to logotherapy.*
    Pocket Books.
Furman, R. (2003a). Cognitive and existential theories in social work practice
    The Social Work Forum 36, 59–68.
Furman, R. (2003b). Exploring step-fatherhood through poetry. *Journal of*
    Poetry Therapy 16, 91–96.

Ginsberg, A. (1972). *The fall of America: Poems of these states 1965–1971*. City Lights.
Goldstein, H. (1990). The knowledge base of social work practice: Wisdom, analogue, or art. *Families in Society, 71*, 32–43.
Hutter, H. (2001). On friendship. *Contemporary Sociology 30*, 579–581.
Krill, D. (1969). Existential physiotherapy and the problem of anomie. *Social Work, 26*, 165–182.
Richardson, L. (1994). Nine poems: Marriage and the family. *Journal of Contemporary Ethnography, 23*, 3–13.
Sartre, J. P. (1965). *Essays in existentialism*. Carol Publishing Group.
Williams, W. C. (1923). *Spring and all*. Contact.
Yalom, I. (1980). *Existential psychotherapy*. Harper/Collins Publishers.

Chapter 5

A Poetry Group for Cognitively Impaired Older Adults

Poetry has frequently been used as a tool of practice with older adults (Edwards, 1990; Kazemek & Rigg, 1987; Reiter, 1994; Silverman, 1988). Some research has noted that various types of cognitive stimulation, including poetry therapy and related expressive arts approaches, may help improve quality of life and overall functioning for this population (Hagens, Beaman & Bouchard-Ryan, 2003; Papadopoulos, Wright, & Harding, 1999; Stuckey & Nobel, 2010). Poetry therapy and poetry groups have been used to help achieve many goals, such as to increase happiness through reminiscing, improve quality of life, and facilitate improved communication (Flood & Phillips, 2007).

In poetry group work with all populations, the first and second group sessions hold special importance as they set the tone for later work. This may be especially true when working with older adults, and certainly for adults with cognitive impairments, whose cognitive deficits and associated emotional difficulties may make engaging in new activities at times anxiety producing and stressful.

The purpose of this brief note is to present a discussion of the first two sessions of a poetry group conducted with moderately to more severely cognitively impaired adults in a nursing home in the eastern part of the United States.

The nursing home where the sessions took place provided residential care for people suffering from Alzheimer's disease and other types of dementia and cognitive impairments. It was a medium-sized facility and utilized many creative modalities to help improve the quality of life for people suffering from these disorders. I became involved in the center while supervising a social work intern doing her field practicum there. After several months of working together, the director of the center learned about my interest in using poetry in therapeutic settings and asked me to conduct a group. We decided that the group would not be therapeutic in the sense of seeking formal, systematic change but one in which poetry would be used to help improve the quality of life and enjoyment of the members. In this sense, the group was congruent with a strengths-based approach to utilizing poetry as a practice tool (Furman, Jackson, Downey, & Bender, 2002). I conducted ten sessions over a fourteen-week period. Knowing the importance of beginnings, I took particularly good notes of the activities and actual sessions for the first two meetings. Below, I present these notes.

Session 1

The assistant director of activities, Lisa, went to each room to gather the participants. While she previously had spoken to each resident about the group, people with cognitive impairment often are not able to remember information such as this from day to day. She let them know that a poetry group was starting and that she believed they would enjoy it. One by one, six residents appeared and sat with me at a small wooden table in the common area in front of the residents' rooms. Loretta was the first to sit next to me, and from the initial session was the most actively involved in the group. Loretta was an elementary teacher, and had been living in the nursing home for two years. Her dementia was just beginning to progress to the point of causing significant impairment. As each member sat down, I introduced myself, and thanked them for coming. I focused on being warm and engaging while adopting a calming tone.

Once all members arrived, I re-introduced myself to the group, and had each member introduce themselves, if they were able. I informed them that our group would be like a club meeting or a class without grades that focused on enjoying poetry and learning how poetry could enrich their lives. I said that during our poetry group, I would read poetry to them and help them write poetry if they wished. I let them know that they could participate as much or as little as they wanted, and that I was glad they were there. Given that each of the adults was cognitively impaired, I stressed that it was not always important to understand each poem, but that it was sometimes enough to just enjoy how a poem sounded, what it felt like, or to appreciate what it reminded them of. I asked members if they had any questions. I then asked them if they would like to hear a few poems that I brought with me. I did this to encourage participation, and to help set the tone of participation and choice.

After a positive response, I read Edgar Allan Poe's (1984) "Eldorado." I chose to start with Eldorado for its rhyme, sound and emotional tone. It is a dramatic poem, and I wanted the residents to focus on the performance as a way of helping to engage them. I wanted them to feel comfortable and not feel pressured to participate. I read the poem two times very slowly; from my experience, it is nearly never enough to only read a poem once, regardless of the population. After I read the poem twice, I asked if anyone had anything to share about the poem, or about how it made them feel. Loretta commented that what she liked about poetry was that "it is like a voice that comes over you." I validated her for her participation, and jotted down her words on a piece of paper. I told her and the group that I thought her response was very poetic, and that if we arranged it a bit, it could be the start of a poem or a complete poem. I chose simple line breaks and rewrote her words.

> Poetry
> Is like a voice
> That comes over you.

I repeated this several times and reaffirmed the poetic quality of her words. I wanted to stress how poetry can happen spontaneously that it did not have to be something that was overly intellectual, and that those of them that could speak could create poetry. I asked Loretta and the group if they could think of a next line or two for the poem. For a movement no one responded. I sensed that a couple members felt a bit pressured by this request, so I tried to lower the expectations by reframing the questions for Loretta: "Loretta, why don't you tell me something else about what you wrote, anything at all." I read her words again, with some added dramatic emphasis. She responded: "it is you and the voice." I wrote this down.

She digressed into a few unrelated thoughts. I asked her if she wanted me to write those down as part of the poem; she declined. I read her words together and again stressed how much I appreciated what she had created. I wanted her and the other members to feel that I valued them, their stories, and their words. Two of the other group members smiled at this point. Suzette, an 80-year-old African American woman, said that Loretta was already a good poet. I smiled, told her that I agreed, and thanked her for her support of Loretta and her good taste in poetry. After a moment, I asked if they would like to hear another poem. Nods and positive responses filled the air.

I wanted the second poem to be one with simple language, and chose Gerald Locklin's (1976) "Weightlifting." I chose this poem for its wonderful extended metaphor about friendship. Irene, a thin woman with attentive eyes, followed the words carefully on the copies I handed out. She said nearly nothing during the session, but was fully engaged in listening and following. This could also be said of Helen, another participant. It is important that facilitators of poetry groups with this population keep their expectations in line with the group members' capacities and preferences.

We briefly discussed the poem, and Helen and Luisa said they preferred this poem to Poe's, as it was easier to understand. I affirmed that the language was more modern, and that I appreciated their sharing their feelings. At this point, I asked the group if they liked or used to like any exercise or any specific physical activities. Lisa said that Jack liked to bowl. I asked Jack if this was true, and he spoke a few sounds that I could not understand. Jack's Alzheimer's is fairly advanced. I mentioned to Jack that next week I would bring in a poem about bowling. His face lit up with joy, which Lisa later told me was a relatively rare occurrence.

After our discussion, Loretta began to tell me and the group a bit more about her life, and about how she always lived poetry. I wrote down her words, and quickly condensed them and her previous words into the following poem.

> Poetry
> Is a voice
> That comes over you
> It is you
> And the voice.
>
> Always was interested
> In poetry
> All my life.
>
> Never afraid
> To speak
> Or talk.
>
> It's just me
> And the voice.

I read her poem out loud, dramatically. I asked her if it felt like "hers," if I "got it right." She smiled and said that I did. Several members smiled and nodded when I asked them what they thought of Loretta's poem. I commented how wonderful it was that she could create such a powerful poem so quickly, and I looked forward to helping each of them, if they wished, to do the same. I again stressed that this would be their choice, and that they were free to listen if they chose or to participate in any way they wished. After some closing remarks, I asked the group about other potential topics to help me in selecting poems for the following week. No one spoke up, so I said I would find some poems about bowling, and perhaps another special poem or two for the following week.

Session Two

During the week before the meeting, I searched for poetry about bowling. I also decided that I would bring more poems with me to read, as the listening seemed to be the most joyous part of the experience for the residents. This realization makes this group, at least at this stage of development, a bit different than other poetry groups I have conducted. Typically, the presentation of poems serve as a vehicle through which discussion and individual and collective exploration occurs. This group was different, and it was clear I had a great deal to learn about working with older adults with cognitive disorders. Cognitive limitations must be carefully assessed and accounted for so a poetry group is seen as pleasurable, and not something that highlights the limitations of group members. A goal certainly can be to help stimulate cognitive processes, yet this must be balanced with an awareness of the impact of such activities on individual members' identity and sense of self.

I opened the second session by reintroducing myself, and let them know how much I enjoyed my time with them the previous week, and how I thought about each of them during the week. The first poem that we read was the one created by Loretta from the previous week. I clearly introduced this as her poem, about which she expressed a great deal of joy and satisfaction. I read the poem slowly and clearly, with a great deal of tension and drama. The members listened attentively. Afterwards, I commented how wonderful it was that Loretta was able to create such a wonderful poem!

After, I asked Jack if he was ready to hear the poems about bowling that I found. He quickly moved from inattentive to extremely attentive; his eyes met mine for the first time. Unable to find what I considered high-quality poems about bowling, I read a rhyming poem I found online that did describe someone's love for the sport. Unable to talk, Jack listened intently to this poem, and to two others about the joy of bowling. He seemed to especially appreciate the sensory images of the sounds of bowling balls striking the pins. Lisa, the assistant activities director, informed me later that this was the most engaged that Jack had been in some time.

For a closing activity, I read Raymond Carver's (2000) poem "Happiness." It is a wonderful poem full of simple, concrete images and explores how happiness transcends being able to talk about happiness, that it is just something that one feels. I asked each of the group members to consider one thing that made them happy. Two members were able to provide responses without prompting. One of the women said that quilting was what made her happy, and asked if I had any poems about her favorite hobby. I told her I did not have any with me, but promised to bring some the following week.

Conclusion

The subsequent eight sessions followed a similar format and loose structure. The composition of the group changed somewhat from week to week as the moods and health of some of the members shifted and changed. Three members attended all group sessions, including Loretta and Jack. While no formal evaluation was conducted, and no therapeutic goals were established, staff believed that Jack, who was not able to speak other than the occasional guttural utterance, appeared to be more engaged with others at the center and less agitated than he previously had been.

Poetry therapy often focuses on helping clients change life conditions they wish to improve or personal attributes in need of alteration. While poetry therapy may hold the potential for therapeutic benefit for older adults suffering from cognitive impairments, it is certainly not a cure. A more humble goal of poetry groups such as this may be to provide joy to those who suffer, a chance to re-experience memories, to connect to others, and create moments of increased value and meaning. Increasing the frequency of moments such as these is a valuable therapeutic aim in and of itself.

References

Carver, R. (2000). *All of us: The collected poems*. Vintage.

Edwards, M. E. (1990). Poetry: Vehicle for retrospection and delight. *Generations, 14*(1), 61–62.

Flood, M., & Phillips, K. D. (2007). Creativity in older adults: A plethora of possibilities. *Issues in Mental Health Nursing, 28*(4), 389–411.

Furman, R., Jackson, R. L., Downey, E. P., & Bender, K. (2002). Poetry therapy as a tool for strengths-based practice. *Advances in Social Work, 3*(2), 146–157.

Hagens, C., Beaman, A., & Bouchard-Ryan, E. (2003). Reminiscing, poetry writing and remember boxes: Personhood-centered communication with cognitively impaired older adults. *Activities, Adaptation & Aging, 27*(3/4), 97–112.

Kazemek, F., & Rigg, P. (1987). All that silver: A poetry workshop in a senior citizens' center. *Journal of Gerontological Social Work, 10*(2), 167–182.

Locklin, G. (1976). *The Criminal mentality*. San Francisco: Red Hill Press.

Papadopoulos, A., Wright, S., & Harding, S. (1999). Evaluating a therapeutic poetry group for older adults. *Journal of Poetry Therapy, 13*(1), 27–37.

Poe, E. A. (1984). The *complete poems and stories of Edgar Allan Poe*. Doubleday.

Reiter, S. (1994). Enhancing the quality of life for the frail elderly: RX, the poetic prescription. *Journal of Long Term Home Healthcare, 13*(2), 12–29.

Silverman, S. (1988). Poetry therapy with frail elderly in a nursing home. *Journal of Poetry Therapy, 2*(2), 72–83.

Stuckey, H. L., & Nobel, J. (2010). The connection between art, healing and public health: A review of current literature. *American Journal of Public Health, 100*(2), 254–263.

Chapter 6

Poetry Therapy, Men, and Masculinities[1]

Therapists and clinicians have long utilized poetry and poetry therapy with various at-risk male populations. For example, poetry has frequently been used in clinical settings with male veterans (Geer, 1983), inner city male youth (Tyson, 2002), and prisoners (Berger & Giovan, 1990). Yet, in spite of its use, poetry therapists have long been aware of the dilemmas in using poetry with a population whose behavior and identity may at times run counter to the core tenants of poetry therapy. For instance, poetry therapy stresses the importance of expressing softer emotions such as vulnerability and doubt, the centrality of human creativity, self-awareness and introspection, and the willingness to engage in a process that at times does not have clear outcomes (Mazza, 2003). Each of these conflict with aspects of traditional masculinity.

Scholars have noted that men and boys may often be resistant to poetry due to their own conceptions of masculinities. Gardner (1993), in discussing her work with runaway youth, noted that "A number of the boys resisted the idea of poetry altogether, finding it too threatening for their masculinity or protected themselves from exposure by refusing to cooperate" (p. 218). Poetry is often viewed as a feminine art form. Indeed, this compounds the tendency that art in general may be viewed as anti-masculine by traditional, working-class men.

While the frequent use of poetry with men and boys is evident, what has not been fully explored are the specific mechanisms of masculinities that may hinder and/or facilitate the uses of poetry in therapy with men. This is lamentable, as understanding masculinities and how they may influence practice, is essential to the success of our interventions with men (Addis & Mahalik, 2003). This recognition is congruent with culturally competent and sensitive approaches to practice which contend that different cultural factors, in this case

---

[1] Co-authored with L. Dill (2012).

gender socialization, will have profound impacts on treatment outcomes (Kosberg, 2002, 2005). This article will help prepare poetry therapists, creative arts therapists, and other clinicians to become more sensitive to gender issues and utilize this understanding in their practice. It explores some of the key concepts from gender and masculinities studies and provides examples of how these concepts can be used in practice as well.

Poetry Therapy and Masculinities

A review of the literature reveals little in terms of the relationship between poetry therapy and gender. Hodas (1991) utilized music lyrics to help adolescents explore their gender identity and sexuality. Travis and Deepak (2011) utilized hip-hop music lyrics to explore the connections between positive youth development and empowerment, and between person and environment. While poetry therapy has been practiced extensively with men, little has been written about engaging men as men. In other words, what knowledge, skills, and values do we need to possess in order to more successfully engage men in poetry therapy as men? In this section, key issues from masculinities and gender studies that can be used in poetry therapy are explored.

A central concept from gender studies is that gender itself is largely socially constructed (Kimmel, 1996; Oliffe, 2005). We are born male or female, but we become men and women through the socialization of our families, schools, and other important social institutions. Society teaches men the rules by which masculinity must be performed, what is expected of them, and what they are expected not to do. It is also important to recognize that masculinities, as are many other factors related to human identity and culturally sensitive practice, are diverse. Men from different societies and at different times in history understand and "perform" masculinities differently (Connell, 2003; Correia & Bannon, 2006). However, within each society a dominate form of masculinity is evident, one by which men are judged by themselves and others: hegemonic masculinity (Connell & Messerschmidt, 2005).

While masculinities often vary, within North American society there is normally one accepted form of masculinity which becomes the model that shapes and contours men's feelings, thinking and behavior; this is referred to as hegemonic masculinity. Most of us can identify various traits of this "ideal," and clearly recognize when a man is breaking the rules of hegemonic masculinity. This ideal includes traits such as bravery, sexual prowess, stoicism, control, autonomy and independence, competitiveness, and aggressiveness. Men are also supposed to be well employed in a good profession, powerful, heterosexual, muscular, and homophobic. A real man must not share his feelings, admit to vulnerability, or admit weakness.

These roles and traits are often exceedingly restrictive, and often lead to poor health outcomes (Courtenay, 2000, 2003) and poor longevity (Shye et al.,1995). In addition, few, if any, men can actually achieve these overly restrictive roles, try as they may, because of powerful socializing forces that tell men what "real men" must do and be. Mahalik, Lagan, and Morrison (2006) explain that:

> one potential explanation of why men have less healthy lifestyles is that males are socialized to adopt masculine ideals that may put their health at risk. A gender role socialization framework posits that males are reinforced for adopting behaviors and attitudes consistent with traditional masculine norms (e.g., risk taking, self-reliance, and emotional control) and punished or shamed when they do not conform to traditional masculine norms. (p.192)

The consequence of not being able to achieve these roles is referred to as gender role strain (Pleck, 1981), the constant pressure and awareness that a man is always, to some degree or another, failing in his most important task—to be a man. This pressure, and men's perceived failure of falling short of achieving this ideal and being "real men" can engender many emotional and psychological problems that lead to and present strategic dilemmas in therapy.

> The more disengaged and disconnected men become from their traditional sources of meaning, from social institutions, and from their capacity to conform to social expectations about what it means to be a man, the more likely they are to act out their emptiness, pain, and angst. (Furman, 2010, p. 39)

Many men come from communities where conceptions of masculinities are at odds with some aspects of the hegemonic ideal. This leads to a further exacerbation of a variation of gender role strain. Minority men and men from oppressed communities often face intense conflicts when attempting to honor their "local" masculine identity and the hegemonic ideal.

There are several implications of the notion of hegemonic masculinities for therapists utilizing poetry with men. Most significant, the very act of poetry therapy runs counter to the hegemonic ideal. Creating poetry demands an attention to the subtleties of one's feelings, in particular what are often referred to as "softer" feelings such as sadness, doubt, tenderness, and fear. Hegemonic masculinities teach men that the only acceptable feelings are anger and lust. While identifying softer feelings is difficult for many men, even some men who are able to identify a broad range of feelings are reluctant to share them with a stranger, thereby admitting weakness. This at times requires a great deal of patience on the part of therapists, as they slowly work with their male clients on becoming more acclimated to expressing a wide range of emotions. Men who do not express "softer" emotions are not being resistant, but instead are performing what is expected of them in many social situations.

Given this lack of fit between therapists' views of emotions and those of many men, Glicken (2005) contends that therapists must pay careful attention to what their male clients want from the helping process in general, as well as from each individual session. This builds from a collaborative relationship based on respect for a man's belief system. As such, therapists should work with men on selecting the types of poetry to be read and experiences to be engaged in for each session, carefully working with clients to establish weekly links between the client's stated desires and overall treatment goals.

There are several techniques therapists can use to counter some of the dilemmas caused by hegemonic traits and help their clients engage with poetry. First, since poetry is often viewed as feminine, it is important to find ways to counter and challenge this perspective. One of the ways to do this is to begin by reading, with clients, song lyrics—particularly those written and performed by men with whom clients may identify. The reading of poetry can be a helpful first step in helping men begin to engage in the affective aspects of the therapeutic process. Reading poems can be used to help men who have a hard time identifying their feelings. The reading of poems with clear emotional content can help a man learn to increasingly identify his feelings and find resonance between the work that is being read and his feelings. This can serve as a springboard to writing exercises and the creation of his own poetry. For instance, the lyrics to Bruce Springsteen's song, "The River" is a wonderful portrayal of many of the emotions of working-class men, sung by a man who is usually viewed as masculine. Another way to challenge the notion of the femininity of poetry is to focus on poetry by men who conform to more traditional forms, such as the counterculture poet Charles Bukowski. Throughout his work, Bukowski admits to his struggles with depression and uses writing as a means of overcoming it. Therapists can encourage their male clients to reflect upon how these artists were able to express feelings of vulnerability without having their sense of masculinity diminished. Therapists can also help men discuss what it would mean for them to express their feelings in such a manner, and what it would mean to their own sense of masculinity.

This is not to say that these are the only poetic sources that should be presented to men, but they may be valuable during the initial phase of therapy, to borrow a term from social work, to "start where the client is" (Cameron & King, 2010). Of course, it is essential that the therapist carefully select poems that do not inadvertently reinforce aspects of hegemonic masculinity that are implicated in the client's challenges. For men whose alcohol abuse is at least partially an expression of their own sense of masculinity, poetry that presents a glamorization of drinking or glamorizes the impact of alcohol use on masculinity should be avoided, or at least used carefully and be balanced by poetry that presents the deleterious impact of alcohol on the lives of men.

Another important concept from masculinities studies is the notion of masculine scripts. Mahalik, Good and Englar-Carlson (2003) developed an approach to understanding male behavior that describes the various scripts by which men live their lives. These scripts offer easy ways to understand the internalization of many rules and roles by which hegemonic masculinity operates. In different contexts and for different reasons, men will often blindly follow each role with as much faithfulness as an actor would his lines.

- The strong-silent-type script propels men toward emotional restriction and stoicism. Mahalik and his colleagues reported powerful consequences of adhering to this script, including depression, anxiety, and social isolation.
- The tough-guy script is learned from an early age, as boys must act bravely and suppress any vulnerability. Boys learn that real men should never be soft. Boys fight and do not back down from fights, thereby placing themselves at a high risk of violence or harm. By adopting this script, not only do men and boys increase their risk of perpetrating and being the victims of violence, but they learn to act out their feelings instead of discussing them.

- The give-em-hell script, a close relative to the tough-guy script, suggests the ideal that men do not back down from conflicts but instead demonstrate their power and willingness to use violence as a means of exerting their will (Gomez Alcaraz & Garcia Suarez, 2006). Men who conform to this script are at high risk of engaging in violence in intimate relationships and may have legal problems as well.
- When men live their lives by the playboy script, they seek sexual relationships not connected to emotional intimacy. Having suppressed the capacity to feel and express their own emotions, they use sex as a primary means of achieving connections. Men who live out this script equate their ability to gain sexual conquests with their own personal worth. Sexual conquests become a means of achieving personal acceptance. Adhering to this norm predisposes men to problems maintaining long term, loving partnerships and places them at risk for sexually transmitted diseases.
- The homophobic script has powerful consequences for men and their capacity to form intimate relationships with each other. Men adhering to this script seek to prove their own manhood by shunning connections with other men, for fear of being viewed as homosexual. According to the hegemonic ideal, homosexuality is anti-masculine; men adhering to the homophobic script will go to great lengths to prove they are not gay, often eschewing any type of relationship that could be construed as homosexual. The homophobic script leads to isolation and often to denial of aspects of oneself.
- The authors note the importance of the winner script to American culture, in which men are expected to be competitive and successful. While competition has its place, and their material and career success is of value, rigidly holding this script as the only way to achieve value and meaning leads to difficult consequences. Extreme adherence to this script can be associated with heart disease and other health concerns. It may also make it difficult for men to connect to others in non-competitive contexts.
- The independence script refers to men's adherence to a hyper-independent relationship style that leads to isolation and disconnection. This script also has strong health-seeking consequences, as men who adhere to this script believe that

they can solve their problems on their own. Seeking and receiving help are viewed as weaknesses.

Clearly the concepts included in the notion of masculine scripts overlap other concepts we have addressed and will explore. The power of the notion of masculine scripts is that it provides an easy-to-understand metaphor that can help therapists and their clients explore the nature of their scripts and the impact on their lives. Each of these scripts lend themselves to personal reflection and discussion, and can become the fodder for the creation of poetry in therapy. In this sense, the use of masculine scripts can be both an assessment guide that can help therapists select other interventions or can be used directly with clients as a starting point to show how these scripts impact their lives.

The goal of therapy is not to compel men to eliminate their adherence to masculine scripts but to increase their self-awareness about when they are acting according to scripts so they can have more behavioral choices. For instance, a man who frequently employs the winner script should not be told this script is "bad" or "wrong" for him; given that his enacting this script may have often led to a great deal of success, a therapist would not have credibility if they implied it did not have value. One exercise that can help a man examine the script on which his behavior is based is for him to write two poems—one about when the script is working and one about potential negative situations. Writing two poems about the same phenomenon will help him explore the subtleties and complexities regarding how the script is applied. The therapist's role is to serve as facilitator of an open exploration of how masculine scripts impact their clients lives.

One of the areas in which each of these scripts manifests is in men's relationships with one another. Adhering to these scripts contributes to men treating one another as competitors and rivals. In so doing, men often devalue the place that friendships with other men can have in their lives; research has demonstrated the importance of friendships to psychosocial health and well-being (Greif, 2008). A poem that I have found useful in helping men dialogue about their friendships is Gerald Locklin's (1976) poem "Weightlifting." The simple narrative poem presents the bench-pressing ritual of the poet and his friend. It focuses on the simplicity of the task, yet throughout alludes to something more meaningful transpiring between them. The last paragraph pushes this theme to the center:

> we do not rush our workouts.
> there's time to speak of nixon, king lear, women.
> it is the best part of the week. we've something there,
> In our ramshackle gym, that many do not have

The first author of this article has frequently used this poem while working with men. Therapists should start with a slow and careful reading of the poem, remembering not to rush through it, in spite of its simplicity. After the poem is read, the therapist using this poem may ask the men to reflect on the poem and discuss what is occurring. At times, a more direct approach is needed, as men are often not accustomed to exploring the dynamics of their relationships. A good prompt to stimulate discussion is to ask clients to elaboration on the last sentence by asking, "What is it that they have that others do not."

In addition to treating one another as competitors or rivals, men also negotiate the complex processes of holding themselves and their peers accountable. One poem that speaks to this is Haki Madhubuti's (née Don Lee, 1970) poem "Change-Up."

> change-up,
> let's go for ourselves
> both cheeks are broken now.
> change-up,
> move past the corner bar,
> let yr/split lift u above that quick high.
> change-up,
> that toothpick you're sucking on was
> once a log.
> change-up,
> and yr/children will look at u differently
> than we looked at our parents

The second author of this article used this poem in working with a group of young African American and Latino men in middle- and high school. Written in Chicago during the Black Arts Movement, this poem still spoke to the group in present-day California. The young people felt that the straightforward word choice was effective in conveying the urgency to "keep it real" and "change your ways."

Men's Views of the Helping Process

As previously mentioned, men learn that they must be autonomous and independent. They learn that they must solve their own problems, pick themselves up by the bootstraps, and be there for others. When they need help, they perceive it as a failure. Not only did they fail, but they failed at being a man, in other words, they failed as a person.

As we have explored, there exist incongruities between the emotional repertoire of many man and therapy. Brooks (1998, as presented in Kosberg, 2011) explores the feelings that are typically required in the therapeutic process, and presents the corresponding emotion that hegemonic masculinity demands. Therapists must become familiar with this discrepancy, as it helps them work on their own expectations and reactions and contextualizes the behaviors of men engaged in the therapeutic process. Observe the list, and note how frequently emotions demanded by traditional masculinities conflict with therapy.

Typical Psychotherapy Demands	Masculinity Demands
Disclosing private experience	Hiding ignorance
Relinquishing control	Maintaining control
Nonsexual intimacy	Sexualizing intimacy
Showing weakness	Showing strengths
Experiencing shame	Expressing pride
Acting vulnerable	Acting invincible
Seeking help	Being self-reliant
Expressing feelings	Being stoic
Being introspective	Taking action
Addressing relationship conflict	Avoiding conflict
Confronting pain	Denying pain
Acknowledging failure	Feigning omniscience

Without becoming aware of this discrepancy, therapists risk shaming men for their current emotional capacities and skills and making them feel like failures in therapy. Such expectations decrease the likelihood that men will continue in treatment and make it less likely that they will seek help in the future. It is important to remember that the process of change is often slow, especially for changing decades-long patterns or learning to expand our emotional range and reactions.

Clinicians and therapists have several tools at their disposal to help a man feel less like a failure and become increasingly open to receiving, and ultimately seeking help. First, it is important to adopt a strengths perspective (Saleebey, 2002). A strengths perspective—where the primary focus of the work is on strengths, capacities, hopes and dreams, aspirations and successes—is highly congruent with poetry therapy and other arts-based approaches to change (Furman et al., 2002).

> talked about the feel of the cut stick, the way the ball sounds when it strikes another or drops its shot successfully into the pocket, the whirr of the dropping ball down the wooden chute beneath the table. I explored that pool wouldn't be the same without the sensations, and life would not be the same, and that poetry was simply a way of noticing and appreciating those aspects of experience that please and transform us (Gardner, 1993, p. 219)

The previous discussion most likely has led to the impression that the author and the literature contend that all men are the same, have the same responses and reactions to helping, and view poetry and poetry therapy in the same manner. This is untrue. Men are not a monolithic group, and hegemonic masculinity and the roles and rules that it forces upon men does not constitute the totality of who men are. In fact, when speaking about masculinity, it is often best to speak about masculinities, both in terms of the alternative forms of masculinities that exist within groups and the alternative masculinities within men. For instance, a man, by virtue of being brought up in American society, may adhere to some aspects of the hegemonic ideal yet may also have been influenced by a father who developed a more inclusive, feminist masculinity that includes an appreciation and acceptance of feelings and a strong valuation of male friendships. Many men do enjoy poetry. Men are able to explore a full array of feelings, and are able to engage eloquently in therapy. Indeed, many men have worked tirelessly at examining and exploring the deleterious effects of constraining men to develop their own conceptions of what it means to be a man. Yet, all men are powerfully shaped and pulled by the coercing, constrictive norms of hegemonic masculinity, and therapists would be well served to understand the powerful ways in which it influences consciousness, behavior, and feelings. As Sabo (2011) observes regarding his own sense of masculinity while teaching in a prison.

> It sounds crazy, but the twinges of paranoia almost feel good. Indeed, there are parts of me, call them "threads" or "echoes" of masculine identity, that embrace the distrust and welcome the presumed danger and potential for violence. (p.84)

Indeed, transcending the vestiges of our socialization, no matter how confining, is a complex process that never is fully complete.

Additionally, it is also true that not all aspects of traditional or hegemonic masculinities are always problematic. For instance, bravery may have potential health consequences when "applied" to all situations, but firefighters and police officers behaving bravely in crisis situations can ensure the survival of innocent people. Men know, intuitively, that some of these attributes of hegemonic masculinities have led to their success. Aggressiveness, competitiveness, an unwillingness not to "win" may be powerful attributes that lead to career success. Therapists should never challenge the powerful benefits that these traits have had; to do so would lead them to lose credibility with their clients. Instead, men should be helped to see the contextual nature of these attributes. For instance, aggressiveness may have a functional quality in some work contexts but may be extremely detrimental to personal relationships. Therapists can help men see these attributes as "tools," and help them learn how to develop new tools for new contexts.

One helpful exercise may be to help men create poems that explore the contextual usefulness of some of these attributes. For instance, asking them to write from the stem "My anger works for me" and then "my anger does not work for me" helps them view their anger from multiple perspectives. Exercises such as this encourage men to explore for themselves the complexities of their feelings and masculine identities and helps create awareness, along with cognitive and behavioral flexibility.

Therapists must always adopt a strengths-based approach when working with men, helping to maximize their resources and increase their capacities. Therapists who focus too much energy on what is "wrong" with men may find themselves seeing very few male clients for second or third sessions. Therapists must be aware of the impact of hegemonic masculinity without "forcing" men into this small and confining box. All human beings are a complex constellation of strengths, capacities, and concerns.

Once men are comfortable with exploring the emotional content within poetry and, hopefully, the emotional content of their own creative writing, more challenging material can be provided about the nature of masculinities. For example, the performance poem "Manly Man" by Bradley Hathaway (2010) presents a complex and nuanced perspective on what it means to be a man. The author explores the aspects of his personality that are congruent with the hegemonic ideal, yet also explores how his more traditionally "feminine" characteristics are equally representative of his masculinity. Playing the video of the performance, along with a study of the words, can help stimulate a powerful discussion regarding conceptions of identity. When therapists take such risks, they may find men responding with sexist or homophobic language. Much care must be taken in exploring the implications of these language choices. Failure to comment may be perceived as condoning sexism and homophobia, yet being confrontive may be shaming and thwart open dialogue. It is best that the therapist ask open-ended questions about the meaning of such language and help men explore the meaning of language that often comes up in such dialogue.

Conclusion

In this article, we explore some of the key concepts from masculinities studies and demonstrate their importance to understanding the therapeutic process and working with men. Practical suggestions for how to integrate this knowledge were presented. While this article discusses some key issues relevant to engaging men in poetry therapy, it by no means is a comprehensive exploration of masculinities studies and its implications for poetry and art therapy, which would be far beyond the scope of any single article. It is imperative that when therapists work with any culturally different population that the therapist becomes increasingly knowledgeable about culturally sensitive and competent practices. It is the contention of the authors of this article that men are indeed a culturally distinct population with their own preferences, capacities, and needs. Therapist and others who use poetry with men would be well served to continue to explore lessons from masculinities studies, gender studies, and theorists and practitioners who have integrated lessons from these fields into their work. Last, it is important for therapists to familiarize themselves not only with techniques and interventions useful for working with men but also with the poetry of and about men that can be a valuable means of understanding the experiences of men, for instance the classic anthology by Bly, Hillman, and Meade (1993).

References

Addis, M.E. & Mahalik, J.R. (2003). Men, masculinity, and the contexts of help seeking. *American Psychologist, 58*(1), 5–14.

Berger, A., & Giovan, M. (1990). Poetic interventions with forensic patients. *Journal of Poetry Therapy, 4*(2), 83–92.

Bly, R., Hillman, J., & Meade, M. (Eds.). (1993). *The rag and bone shop of the heart: Poems for men.* Harper Perennial

Brooks, G.R. (1998). *A new psychotherapy for traditional men* (P. 44). Jossey-Bass Publishers.

Cameron, M., & King, E. (2010). The common factors model: Implications for transtheoretical clinical practice. *Social Work, 55*(1), 67–73,

Connell, R. W. (2003). *Masculinities and masculinity politics in world society.* Paper of the November 25, 2003 lecture at Rutgers University Institute for Research on Women, Distinguished Lecture Series. Retrieved April 3, 2007 from http://irw.rutgers.edu/lectures/connelllecture.pdf

Connell, R. W., & Messerschmidt, J. W. (2005). Hegemonic masculinity: Rethinking the concept. *Gender & Society, 19*(6), 829–859.

Correia, M. C., & Bannon, I. (2006). Gender and its discontents: Moving to men—streaming development. In I. Bannon & M. C. Correia (Eds.), *The other half of gender* (pp. 245–260). The World Bank.

Courtenay, W. H. (2000). Engendering health: A social constructionist examination of men's health beliefs and behaviors. *Psychology of Men and Masculinity, 1*(1), 4–15.

Courtenay, W. H. (2003). Key determinants of the health and well-being of men & boys. *International Journal of Men's Health, 2*(1), 1–30.

Furman, R. (2010). *Social work practice with men at-risk.* Columbia University Press.

Furman, R., Jackson, R. L., Downey, E. P., & Bender, K. (2002). Poetry therapy as a tool for strengths based practice. *Advances in Social Work, 3*(2), 146–157.

Gardner, J. (1993). Runaway with words: Teaching poetry to at-risk teens. *Journal of Poetry Therapy, 6*(4), 213–227.

Geer, F. C. (1983). Marine-machine to poet of the rocks, poetry therapy as a bridge to inner reality: Some exploratory observations. *The Arts in Psychotherapy, 10,* 9–14.

Greif, G. L. (2008). *The buddy system: Understanding male friendships.* Oxford University Press.

Glicken, M.D. (2005). *Working with troubled men: A contemporary practitioner's guide.* Lawrence Erlbaum Associates.

Gomez Alcaraz, F. H., & Garcia Suarez, C. I. (2006). Masculinity and violence in Colombia: Deconstructing the conventional way of becoming a man. In I. Bannon & M. C. Correia (Eds.),*The other half of gender* (pp.93–110). The World Bank.

Hathaway, B. (2010). *Manly man* (performance poem video. From Badley Hathaway fan site: http://thebradley.net/uncategorized/manly-man-by-bradley-hathaway-4/

Hodas, G. (1991). Using original music to explore gender and sexuality with adolescents. *Journal of Poetry Therapy, 4*(4), 205–220.

Kimmel, M. S. (1996). *Manhood in America: A cultural history.* Free Press.

Kosberg, J. I. (2002). Heterosexual males: A group forgotten by the profession of social work. *Journal of Sociology and Social Welfare, 29*(3), 50–70.

Kosberg, J. I. (2005). Meeting the needs of older men: Challenges for those in the helping professions. *Journal of Sociology and Social Welfare, 32*(1), 9–31.

Kosberg, J. I. (2011, February). *Social work outreach and practice with men.* Presented at the National Association of Social Workers–New Mexico conference, Albuquerque.

Lee, D. (1970). *We walk the way of the new world.* Broadside Press.

Locklin, G. (1976). *The criminal mentality.* Red Hill Press.

Mazza, N. (2003). *Poetry therapy: Theory and practice.* Routledge

Mahalik, J. R., Good, G. E., & Englar-Carlson, M. (2003). Masculinity scripts, presenting concerns, and help seeking: Implications for practice and training. *Professional Psychology: Research and Practice, 34*(2), 123–131.

Mahalik, J. R., Lagan, H. D., & Morrison, J. A. (2006). Health behaviors and masculinity in Kenyan and U.S. male college students. *Psychology of Men and Masculinity, 7*(4), 191–202.

Oliffe, J. (2005). Constructions of masculinity following prostatectomy-induced impotence. *Social Science & Medicine, 60,* 2249–2259.

Pleck, J. H. (1981). *The myth of masculinity.* MIT Press.

Sabo, D. (2011). Doing time, doing masculinity: Sports and prison (pp. 82–86). In M. B. Zinn, P. Hondagneu-Sotelo, & M. A. Messner (Eds.), *Gender through the prism of difference* (4th ed.). Oxford University Press.

Saleebey, D. (2002). *The strengths perspective in social work.* Allyn and Bacon.

Shye, D., Mullooly, J. P., Freeborn, D. K., & Pope, C. R. (1995). Gender differences in the relationship between social network support and mortality: A longitudinal study of an elderly cohort. *Social Science & Medicine, 41*(7), 935–947.

Travis, R. & Deepak, A. (2011). Empowerment in context: Lessons from hip-hop culture social work practice. *Journal of Ethnic & Cultural Diversity in Social Work, 20,* (2),1–20.

Tyson, E. H. (2002). Hip hop therapy: An exploratory study of a rap music intervention with at-risk and delinquent youth. *Journal of Poetry Therapy, 15*(3), 131–144.

Chapter 7

Poetry Matters: A Case for Poetry in Social Work Practice[1]

Over the last twenty years, social work has become more aligned with the biobehavioral approach to human behavior and has largely adopted science as its dominant metaphor (Goldstein, 1987: Kreuger, 1997). While science certainly can be a valuable tool in creating and testing social work knowledge, there are many other metaphors for knowledge generation that may be more able to depict the life experiences of the vulnerable populations that social work traditionally serves (Heineman, 1981; Langer & Furman, 2004). Additionally, the over-reliance on science as a metaphor for practice has largely shifted the focus of social work from a relatively equal balance between values and knowledge to a valuation of knowledge as the central driver of social work practice. Gordon (1965) expressed concern about the diminution of values in social work as early as forty years ago. She asserted that when social workers base decisions upon knowledge when reliance upon values is indicated, interventions will be misguided, and perhaps even oppressive.

Scholars and practitioners have argued that social work has neglected the moral compass of its liberal arts- and humanities-inspired history (Goldstein, 1990; Kreuger, 1997). This is lamentable, since the social justice orientation of the profession in large part stems from, and is grounded in this tradition. The arts and humanities have been an integral part of social work since its inception (Furman, Langer, & Anderson, 2006). For instance, the work of the early functionalists, from which a great deal of social work practice wisdom and core values was derived, was based upon the teachings of artist-turned-psychoanalyst Otto Rank (Stein, 2010).

As explored in a previous article (Furman, Langer, & Anderson, 2006), the use of poetry and the work of the poet serve as a valuable

---

[1] Co-authored with M. Enterline, R. Thompson, & A. Shukraf (2012).

metaphor for social workers. This article seeks to contribute to an unfortunately declining literature that explores the importance of the arts and humanities to social work practice, education, and research through an exploration of poetry in social work practice and research. This article will achieve its aims in the following ways. First, the authors will explore the metaphor of the poet/practitioner, identifying what the practitioner can learn from the poet. Second, the authors will explore the use of poetry in therapeutic settings, identifying the strengths of using this tool in clinical practice. Third, the authors will discuss the use of poetry within the context of research, exploring how the research poem can be used as a tool of post-modern qualitative research to help social workers understand the lived experiences of their clients. Finally, we shall explore current and future consequences of the profession ignoring the arts and humanities.

Poetry as a Metaphor of the Poet/Practitioner

The importance of the helping relationship has been central to social work practice since the profession's inception. Not only has this centrality been supported by a century of practice wisdom, but also numerous studies have shown the relationship between helping relationships and positive outcomes. Traditionally, the helping relationship in social work has been characterized by a focus on empowerment, mutuality, and the self-determination of the client. However, the advent of managed care and the increasing medicalization of the profession have impacted the social work relationship. In the medical model, the practitioner is seen more as an expert or technician who provides evidenced-based solutions to their client. The focus is on the short-term amelioration of the problem. However, while this model may be effective for helping to alleviate the short-term suffering of clients, it may not be effective for empowering a client to commit to lasting personal and systemic change.

This section will demonstrate how the metaphor of the poet is perhaps more aligned with the values and practice realities of social work than is the metaphor of the scientist. While the poet and the scientist both value discovery, there are several key differences. Taking a poetic approach to social work practice, the practitioner recognizes the importance of the subjective, lived experience of the client. To the poet, there is no one single truth; rather, there is that which is constructed based upon a lifetime of experiences, values, and meanings. The poet/practitioner understands that the social work relationship is one in which clients construct their own narratives, and the social worker supports the client in reconstructing their story, and their lives.

The poet/practitioner understands that the act of creation, whether that creation is a poem or the construction of one's individual life space, is a highly personal act, demanding more witness than expert. Using the poet mindset to enrich analysis allows the practitioner a more tangible examination of the human experience through their own reflections on life and experience. In this way, poetry can act not only as a means of social work research, but also as the beginnings of an intervention, both for the client and the practitioner himself (Furman, 2004). The practitioner seeks to understand the human experience from a holistic perspective, while also striving to understand himself from this perspective. Both of these abilities will allow better insight into a client's perception and experiences. Since this interpretive approach assumes that people create their own social reality, it is essential that the practitioner attempt to see the client's social reality, to integrate the client's words, thoughts, feelings, and ideas into observations, as well as the helping process. In this way, he can see each client as an individual and strive to create the most effective treatments for them while learning new views and truths from them.

One way to understand the client's reality is to create connections. The poet/practitioner seeks to connect the client to the outside world and her inside feelings and beliefs simultaneously. He promotes a connection with others through personal expression of shared feelings, as well as promoting a connection to feelings through direct access of experiences and personal fallout from these experiences. He recognizes what people share universally—what is "normal," as well as what they carry alone, what is unique—as part of the human condition. Even though two people may experience the same event, the impact typically differs for each. Because of this, it is important to know how the individual experienced an event, as well as to normalize their feelings so they still feel connected to others.

In addition to connecting people inside and out, the poet/practitioner simultaneously seeks to separate the client from the inside and outside worlds. When people are faced with challenging experiences in their lives, they tend to want to disengage from their feelings so that those feelings are easier to examine from a more objective perspective. When looking at these feelings as metaphor, something that the poet/practitioner would commonly incorporate into practice, they are easier to extricate oneself from. Speaking of the client's life as a story or poem, it is as though the experiences and emotions within that life belong to the characters involved, not to the client.

On a larger scale, these metaphors serve to give ownership of experiences to the client, allowing them to create or utilize symbols that are meaningful to them alone. Metaphors have an internal consistency and coherence personal and unique to the client, and provide an avenue to inexplicit or consciously held ideas (Leavy, McSorley, & Bote, 2006). The evocative element of metaphor allows the teasing of connections that may not be accessible by direct questioning. In this way, through metaphor, implicit feelings become explicit by way of reflection on and representation of the client's narrative and provide a vehicle for further dialog. (Leavy et al., 2006). The poet/practitioner encourages clients to find or create metaphors that are personal, unique expressions of feelings that serve to separate their views from those of others. Although some of these may tap into archetypal or cultural symbology, such as the use of the Hero's Journey metaphor seen in Star Wars, or the orphan archetype symbolizing attachment and abandonment, among other things, to name a few examples. Carl Jung summarized what he called "archetypes of transformation" as places, situations, ways, and means that symbolize the transformation in question. Existing primarily as energy, these archetypes may be useful in interpreting and helping the client find meaning when used in such a way that they belong to the client alone (Jung, 1990).

When looking at the client's use of metaphor, it is essential that the poet/practitioner be able to observe and utilize patterns of behavior, language, and thought both on a personal and universal level. He recognizes the client's own ability to be an individual and a part of the collective, as well as recognizing the client's ability to take part in her own treatment. In this way, poetry empowers clients to take control of life and shape their own mold. The poet/practitioner approaches each individual as an individual, as a "partner in the co-construction of the helping experience" (Furman, Langer, & Anderson, 2006).

The final requirement of the poet/practitioner is flexibility. Although he should be well trained, as should any social worker, he should also be open to new learning experiences, be they formal, classroom experiences or lessons from the mouths of his clients. He should allow himself to retain knowledge of his training and experiences, but he does not hold onto this foundation so rigidly as to let it overshadow the client's individual needs. The poet/practitioner, like a poem, can grow and change with time, building on his strengths, editing his weaknesses, constantly striving to bring new insights into deeper focus.

Poetry in Practice

The therapeutic use of poetry has become an important tool of social work practice. In fact, poetry therapy has become its own discipline, complete with its own professional association and its own journal. Poetry therapy has been used with many client populations, including the chronically mentally ill (Goldstein, 1987), the elderly (Edwards & Lyman, 1989), troubled children and adolescents (Alexander, 1990; Langosch, 1987 Mazza, 1996, 1987; Mazza, Magaz & Scaturro, 1987), veterans (Geer, 1983), the terminally ill (McLoughlin, 2000), substance abusers (Bump, 1990 Leedy, 1987), and families (Gladding, 1987. Practitioners working in diverse settings including women's shelters (Hynes, 1987), nursing homes (Edwards, 1990; Kazemek & Rigg, 1987) and elementary schools (Gladding, 1987) have made use of poetry and poetry therapy. Additionally, poetry has even been incorporated into family work (Mazza, 1996), diversity work (Holman, 1996), and community consciousness raising work (Kissman, 1989). Goldstein (1987) contends that poetry is a way to enhance consciousness in lived experience.

Within a therapeutic context, writing poetry can provide tremendous insight into a client's experiences. Much of this insight comes through the use of metaphor, which can be a powerful tool (Collins, Furman, & Langer, 2006; Dalton & Krout, 2005; Rousseau, et al., 2005; Finn, 2003). One of the great strengths of metaphor in the therapeutic setting is how it lends itself to universality. So many symbols that clients use in their writing are archetypal, allowing for ease of interpretation, as mentioned in the previous section. Still others, though, are more personal in nature, and provide a window into how they perceive their experiences. In this way, metaphor serves to strengthen the ability to own and identify with emotions and behaviors, as if the poet has created her own reactions to a powerful event. Poetry uses the client's own words, allowing her to give voice to difficult feelings on her own terms. Though some consumers may be intimidated by the writing process, it can also be freeing, allowing them to let others in without a direct assault on their emotions. Rather, poetry pushes them to open up under the veiled guise of metaphor. This also allows the writer to impact the reader greatly because the imagery often taps into the emotions of the reader as well as the poet, giving practitioners a glimpse through client's eyes.

Besides allowing the client to open up through language, metaphor allows the practitioner to access the true voice of the client. Through metaphor and symbol, the poet/client can often access their core beliefs without the restrictions that they typically place on these beliefs (Collins, Furman, & Langer, 2006). Evocation of meaning is contained in the client's story, bringing to the forefront "presence, images, and sensibilities that are so crisp and real that they evoke reflective responses such as wondering, questioning, or understanding" (van Manen, 1997).

Meaning is relative to our experiences. Each person views an event differently, so writing can not only help to give perspective to others but also to normalize experiences, showing that some of the feelings that the poet/client is experiencing are shared with those around her who are facing the same challenges in life. Poetry can give an indirect pathway to access difficult feelings, or feelings surrounding difficult emotions. (Furman, 2004)

Poems lend themselves to repeated "visits." While they may have one meaning or impact for a client during the writing process, they may take on whole new meanings in later viewings, whether during the editing process or in sharing with others, such as the practitioner, Poetry allows us to face the portions of life we don't necessarily want to. French poet and philosopher Paul Valery once said of writing poetry that "a poem is never finished, only abandoned." Because of this ever-changing nature, poems lend themselves to re-examination over time. Add to this their brief nature and the ease with which the author can separate him or herself from the events and emotions within the poem, and it is easy to see why this genre can be therapeutic. The poet/client can revisit the feelings without owning them, should they choose. Rather, the emotions belong to a character, one the poet/client understands intimately but nonetheless can separate himself from, should he choose (Furman, 2004). The expressive and creative arts have become valuable tools for the social work practitioner (Szto, Furman, & Langer, 2005).

Poetry in Social Work Research

Social workers need knowledge to guide their practices. While quantitative methods can be extremely valuable for testing the efficacy of certain methods, qualitative methods are far more useful in helping social workers develop an in-depth understanding of clients. Through reading in-depth qualitative accounts, social workers can learn how clients perceive their social and emotional life spaces, their social relationships, and provide insights into how they experience social work services (Furman & Cavers, 2005). Ethnographic and other types of qualitative data help social workers understand the lived experiences of their clients. However, a great deal of quantitative data are dense and often difficult to penetrate with regard to the application to human emotion (Finley & Knowles, 1995). What social workers need is data that can provide the in-depth liveness of ethnographic studies yet be more condensed. Fortunately, a new method of expressive qualitative research, the research poem, or what has been referred to in the literature as poetic transcription (Faulkner, 2009), is just such a tool (Langer & Furman, 2003).

The research poem is, simply put, a condensed version of qualitative data about a client's life experiences (Langer & Furman, 2003). They discussed one methodology for creating the research poem. Using traditional methods, the researchers first conduct an interview to obtain qualitative data about the lived experiences of the client in her words. The interview data are then compressed into a draft of a poem using only the client's language and allowing the data to determine the structure of the poem. The idea is to utilize the visual components of poetry, such as line and stanza breaks, to give the data form and substance, as well as to access the fundamental nature of what the client is saying about herself (Langer & Furman, 2005). Although no words are added to the data, many are removed in order to help boil the data down into the essence of the client's words. In this way, the poem focuses ideas into key words and phrases of the client's making, which in turn focuses the writing and reading of the poem on what the client is truly feeling at the core of her experiences. This method utilizes the researcher's artistic sense, as well as interrater reliability between at least two researchers, in order to ensure that the poem is true to the client's original statements and expressed emotions (Langer & Furman, 2005). See Furman's previous work, poetic forms and structures in Qualitative Health Research (2006) for a more detailed description of methodology.

Poetry can be a powerful form of qualitative data collection (Poindexter, 2002; Richardson, 1994). Because it allows us such an intimate look at the client's emotions, it gives us a true picture of how they perceive the world and their problems in it. When studying human behavior and feelings, data are inherently social in nature, and this social data must be taken in a fitting manner. Because of the complex, personal nature of the human experience, a simple survey where choices are defined for clients would hardly suffice to give practitioners an accurate picture of the client's experiences and feelings associated with substantial events in her life (Furman, 2005; Finley & Knowles, 1995).

Poetry allows the social worker to gauge experiences, to hear the voices of clients and not simply to diagnose and treat their physical symptoms based on qualitative data. Through this medium, the practitioner is allowed to see the world through the poet's lens, filling in some of the more personal, more meaningful aspects of the client's experiences, which will allow the practitioner to better understand and more compassionately and competently treat her (Furman & Cavers, 2005; Richardson, 1994). This can give us an insight into the client that is both unique and personal, something that many practitioners strive for years to achieve.

Because of this unique perspective, poetry can be used to create a language around which true discussions of feelings and experiences can begin. Though the words of the poet are not statistically generalizable, readers can share the thoughts and the emotions held by the poet. Because of the accuracy of the picture that a poem can present about, say, Alzheimer's disease, or the experiences of someone dealing with bipolar disorder, or loss and grief, this type of data can give researchers new insight into the actual feelings that are being experienced, not just data sets and statistics. The poems can be generalized in the sense that they can give insight into what the writer is feeling about the experience, and those feelings, though often worded differently depending on the writer, can be shared by others experiencing the same events.

Conclusion

Much of what this implicates is a greater need for education within the field of social work in regard to the methods, effectiveness, and uses of creative and expressive arts in the contexts of general practice, therapy, and research. There are organizations that hold individual trainings, but, by and large, poetry is probably not high on the curriculum priorities of most BSW and MSW programs, whereas it could be spread liberally throughout the curriculum. Although poetry therapy has come a long way, there is still a need for effective techniques to be brought into the mainstream of the practice so that poetry can be seen as less intimidating as well as more effective than most people would think.

Additionally, in the area of research, more investigation into widespread application of findings will be useful for the field of social work.

Within the social work field, there are many ways to approach clients. The use of poetry is one method that needs to be more readily brought to the table. Although it can be intimidating to practitioners and clients alike, it does lend itself to self-determination in that a poem can be anything a poet or a reader wants it to be. There is no magic formula for a poem, especially not one written for personal use. The poem does not need to be "good"'; literary criticism is not the essential goal of social work in any arena of the field. Rather, the essential goal is to illuminate some truth from the client's perspective. This truth is universal in the sense that there are more than likely others experiencing the same feelings, but more so personal, subjective truth, the truth of experiences. In this way, social workers can see through the client's lens. The hope is that this lens will help them to better understand their clients so that they can continue to grow in their practice knowledge.

References

Alexander, K. C. (1990). Communication with potential adolescent suicides through poetry. *The Arts in Psychotherapy, 17,* 125–130.

Bump, J. (1990). Innovative bibliotherapy approaches to substance abuse. *The Arts in Psychotherapy, 17,* 335–362.

Collins, K., Furman, R., & Langer, C. (2006). Poetry therapy as a tool of cognitively based practice. *The Arts in Psychotherapy, 33,* 180–187.

Dalton, T., & Krout, R. (2005). Development of the Grief Process Scale through music therapy songwriting with bereaved adolescents. *The Arts in Psychotherapy, 32,* 131–143.

Edwards, M. E. (1990). Poetry: Vehicle for retrospection and delight. *Generations, 14*(1), 61–62.

Edwards, M. E., & Lyman, A. J. (1989). Poetry: Life review for frail American Indian elderly. *Journal of Gerontological Social Work, 14,* 75–91.

Faulkner, S. L. (2009). *Poetry as method: Reporting research through verse.* Left Coast Press

Finley, S., & Knowles, J. G. (1995). Researcher as an artist/artist as a researcher. *Qualitative Inquiry, 1*(1), 110–142.

Finn, C. (2003). Helping students cope with loss: Incorporating art into group counseling. *Journal for Specialists in Group Work, 28*(2), 155–165.

Furman, R., Langer, C. L., & Anderson, D. K. (2006). The poet/practitioner: A paradigm for the profession. *J. Soc. & Soc. Welfare, 33,* 29.

Geer, F. C. (1983). Marine-machine to poet of the rocks, poetry therapy as a bridge to inner reality: Some exploratory observations. *The Arts in Psychotherapy, 10,* 9–14.

Gladding, S. (1987). Poetic expressions: A counseling art in elementary schools. *Elementary School Guidance Counseling, 21*(4), 307–310.

Goldstein, M. (1987). Poetry: A tool to induce reminiscing and creativity with geriatrics. *Journal of Social Psychiatry, 7*(2), 117–121.

Goldstein, H. (1990). The limits and art of understanding in social work practice. *Families in Society, 80*(4), 385–395.

Gordon, W. E. (1965). Knowledge and value: Their distinction and relationship in clarifying social work practice. *Social Work, 10*(3), 32–39.

Heineman, M. B. (1981). The obsolete scientific imperative in social work research. *Social Service Review, 55,* 371–339.

Holman, W. D. (1996). The power of poetry: Validating ethnic identity through a bibliotherapeutic intervention with a Puerto Rican adolescent. *Child and Adolescent Social Work Journal, 13*(5), 371-383.

Hynes, A. (1987). Biblio/poetry therapy in women's shelters. *American Journal of Social Psychiatry.*

Jung, C. G. (1990). *The archetypes and the collective unconscious* (R.C.F. Hull, Trans.). Princeton University Press. (Original work published in 1959)

Kazemek, F., & Rigg, P. (1987). All that silver: A poetry workshop in a senior citizens' center. *Journal of Gerontological Social Work, 10*(2), 167–182.

Kissman, K. (1989). Poetry and feminist social work. *Journal of Poetry Therapy, 2*(4), 221–230.

Kreuger, L. W. (1997). The end of social work. *Journal of Social Work Education, 33*(1), 19–27.

Langosch, D. (1987). The use of poetry therapy with emotionally disturbed children. *The American Journal of Social Psychiatry, 7*(2), 97–100.

Leedy, J. (1987). Poetry therapy for drug abusers. *The Journal of Social Psychiatry, 7*(2) 106–108.

Mazza, N. (1987). Poetry and popular music in social work education: The liberal arts perspective. *The Arts in Psychotherapy, 14*(1), 293–299.

Mazza, N. (1996). Poetry therapy: A framework and synthesis of techniques for family social work. *Journal of Family Social Work, 1*(3), 3–18.

Mazza, N., Magaz, C., & Scaturro, J. (1987). Poetry therapy with abused children. *The Arts in Psychotherapy, 14*(1), 85–92.

McLoughlin, D. (2000). Transition, transformation, and the art of losing: Some uses of poetry in hospice care for the terminally ill. *Psychodynamic Counseling, 6*(2), 215–234.

Poindexter, C. C. (2002). Meaning from methods: Re-presenting narratives of an HIV-affected caregiver. *Qualitative Social Work, 1*(1), 59–78.

Richardson, L. (1994). Nine poems: Marriage and the family. *Journal of Contemporary Ethnography, 23*(1), 3–13.

Rousseau, C., Gauthier, M.F., Lacroix, L., Alain, N. Benoit, M., Moran, A. et al. (2005). Playing with identities and transforming shared realities: Drama therapy workshops for adolescent immigrants and refugees. *The Arts in Psychotherapy, 32,* 13–27.

Stein, E. (2010). Otto Rank: Pioneering ideas for social work theory and practice. *Psychoanalytic Social Work, 17*(2), 116–131.

Szto, P., Furman, R., & Langer, C. (2005). *Qualitative Social Work, 4*(2), 135–156.

van Manen, M. (1997). From meaning to method. *Qualitative Health Research, 7,* 345–396.

Chapter 8

Exploring Friendship Loss through Poetry

> We are, at the root of things, social beings existing with one another in a state of symbiosis, interdependence, and community. (Goldstein, 1990, p. 33)

Friendships are essential for healthy development throughout the lifespan (Baumeister & Leary, 1995; Hutter, 2001). In spite of its importance, friendship has been neglected when compared to research and scholarship regarding the necessity of the family and community to psychosocial health. Even less prevalent is scholarship dealing with the loss of friendship. In fact, a review of over one hundred articles on friendship found none dealing significantly with the concept of friendship loss. The purpose of this article is to begin to address this gap. This qualitative study will explore this phenomenon through the use of expressive arts research methods (Finley & Knowles, 1995). More specifically, it will do so through the use of autobiographical poetry and reflexive commentary. Poetry has become an increasingly important tool in the research literature, spanning disciplines as diverse as management and organizational development (Brearley, 2000), education (Percer, 1992), anthropology (Gee, 1991), sociology (Richardson, 1994), and social work (Poindexter, 2002).

Methodology

Poems are powerful sources of data for several reasons. First, one of the strengths of poetry lies in its ability to convey complex and powerful emotions. The power of juxtaposing images can help convey conflicting and dialectical emotions that often characterize complex experiences and relationships.

When dealing with autobiographical data in research, the researcher must continually be reflexive (Padgett, 1998; Patton, 2001). It is self-evident that researchers are biased. The reflexive and honest researcher explores their biases and presents them openly (Creswell,

1998; Constas, 1992). It is also key that researchers resist the temptation of trying to look good. Autobiographical data often contain information about the researcher's fears, difficult emotions, and vulnerabilities. It is a valuable lesson for researchers to push themselves toward self-revelation. Indeed, how can we expect our research subjects to be open to us if we are unwilling to be open ourselves?

The poems presented are taken from a series of nearly sixty prose poems about my friendships. They were written over a period of three months, spanning June through August of 2003. Since the area of friendship has been a substantive area of my research, for the last two years I have written considerable journal notes about my own friendships. In June of 2003, I attended a poetry workshop at the Greyrock Writing Institute at Colorado State University, where I was an assistant professor. During this time, I took a workshop on the vignette conducted by Angela Hodap, a recent CSU MFA graduate. During the workshop, we were asked to write a vignette about a person no longer in our lives. I started to think about a certain friend and almost immediately wrote an entire prose poem. During the rest of the workshop, I wrote several other prose poems that seemed to just pour from me. Over the next several days, I realized that the prose poem would be the perfect vehicle through which to explore friendships. In another article, I explore in depth the value of the prose poem as a tool of inquiry (Furman, 2003. In short, the prose poem, a synthesis of poetry and prose, allows for the compression, images, and metaphor of traditional poetry, yet utilizes the narrative structure of prose. The prose poem allowed me to tell the stories of my friendships using evocative and emotionally charged language.

The poems presented here are those that specifically deal with experiences of loss in friendships. Poems dealing with friendship in general can be found in Furman (2003). Along with each poem are my reactions after reading the poems. Each day for a week, I read each poem and reflected upon the reading. I subsequently made journal notes documenting my reflections. Some of these reflections are shared here. The journal notes that were used were left unedited so may contain grammatically incorrect phases.

The Death of a Friend

Five A. M. Reading Poems
Five a.m. reading poems as he ties up to shoot straight horse sadness into his veins. As the world turns useless, like a spoon to a ditch digger. As the working ones wake to wasted rituals. As he nods deep, bowing to the floor like a psychotic yogi, remaining silent, leaving forgotten secrets to guess. As life breathes, we tick, tock and junk or school, rule or game in yesterday's playgrounds. It's all about equal. Yet it isn't and we all rage some strange mystical rhythm.

Which We Will Never Know
The wasted hope of the leaves change colors amongst the dead, amongst the armies, villains, accountants, the forgotten gaze of what some suckers call god. Today I found out that he died a year ago to this day. Needle in his arms. They said things had changed, no worries, his biggest problem deciding between two women who loved him. Now they must visit his stone, the one with his drawing etched on its face, like the smile of an ugly idiot, and lay flowers that will turn to pulverized bits. As gravity pulls, and time expands, expelling us out of the gate, dazed and lost, eating the dust, of that which we shall never know.

*

I still think of him. Sometimes I look for my phonebook, or catch myself wondering why he does not call. Then I catch myself: He's dead. It does not seem real. I think about friends whom I have not spoken to in some time. Do I have the luxury of waiting? What stops me from reaching out to people?

*

Reading the poem again, I continue to think about my responsibility toward others friends. What does it mean? I think about the times I could have seen him more, other friends more, how will I feel if they die, and I have not been there for them, if I let the months slide by without contact? Loss, sadness. What is it that keeps us from making friendships more central in our lives? In missing him, I miss others who I have lost connection with.

Blood Is Thicker Than Water

No Longer
You saw company boogiemen behind every colonial arch, lurking through *La Prensa* pages, pale hawks gawking over small rodent revueltos. You insisted brown hippy leather sandals were government issued as obvious as square boxed blue sedans, that they tried to blend with pot smoking druggies by the lake. Watch, you whispered, we will wind up with CIA rap sheets, be interrogated, maybe drugged when we return home. A slightly less scraggly Jewish Latino Irish Ginsberg, knew every conspiracy theory as intricate webs ensnarling villages of machine gunned spiders. We hitched on truck backs cushioned with red platanos, bounced through dirt miles on school buses protected by sad faced Marys, across Honduras, almost until Nicaragua. Separated for a few days of cheap rooms, rats and rum, found you in an Esteli hotel sweating revolutionary songs through laughing frantic eyeballs. Marched through the streets drunk on Cuban rum and hope. Years later, I almost married your sister, but as things ended badly between us, so did you and I. Yesterday marked the twenty-third anniversary of the revolution. Long since expired, I remember it as a lost comapanero I may no longer love.

*

Again, cheated. Friendships second to family bonds. Is this right? I don't know, but it is the way things are, or at least the way they usually seem to play out. I admired him so. He made me think politically, deeply about international issues. The connections between our communities and the world. Just his presence, the way he lived his life. Perhaps this is why for the last several years, I have been less politically involved, more inclined toward other pursuits. Clearly, friendships impact greatly on our behavior, upon who we are. Through friendship, we access parts of ourselves that we may not be in touch with. Losing a significant friendship such as this, it seems I have lost, at least for now, a certain part of myself.

*

What would he think if I tried to reconnect with him? I think it has been maybe four years since we spoke. I tried to send him an e-mail a couple of years ago, but I don't even know if that was an active account. What would I want to say? That I am glad he was my friend, that he meant something to me. How often have I thanked people for being my friend, for what they have given me? I don't think we ever learn the vocabulary for dialoging with friends in this manner. Certainly not men. I look back at times I have thanked other men for their friendship, for their love. I remember telling another friend this, and he clearly was shocked. Touched, but shocked. I remember him crying, and then saying that he never heard those words before. What holds us back? Fear? Of what?

The End of A Friendship: Growing Apart?

The Fence
Why did Mrs. Finch, our first grade teacher assemble us at her home? To mobilize young outcasts? Was I a loser like you? I shudder now recalling years I would cry for no solid reason. Now, I know enough to at least rationalize. Thinking back, we formed and fried triangle shaped burgers, threw uncoordinated Frisbees, teaching our hands to obey our brains. Those struggles connecting us, linked us together for twenty years, our friendship a fence which I opened to show you what, life? You, locked for years behind your own Beverly Hills Berlin wall, a cell lined with velvet Elvises, rows of pristine records, virginity and masturbating into a terrycloth towel on your water bed. I recall your Nicaraguan maid begging you: *just grab life and take it Matt*. But you were weak. Like when you strained for that one pull up with all of us coaxing your chin upward. We stared into each other's eyes for that second before you surrendered. Perhaps nothing I gave you was useful either. I am sorry that we are no longer friends, but mostly that you may never open that fence for anyone else.

Of You
A white paint chip wedges deep under my nail. Pain shoots upward as blood trickles down my finger. Stains white gold of wedding ring. A polluted river spoiling the sea. I am reminded of you. Pry out most of it, a small biting edge breaks off. Festers and more blood. I am reminded of you. A court jester offering asparagus sprigs to the queen for her sadness. I pry a pin under the nail. Finally dig it out. My jagged skin frayed. A red clot remains swollen underneath. My old friend no longer, I am reminder of you.

*

It's one thing to lose a friend to death. That feels at least nature. When friendships end though, I feel cheated. It seems unnatural, as if some unwritten taboo has been broken. Sadness and shame. Again, deep loss. Even a friendship as with the one I had with Matt, where I felt as if I received so little. He had so little to give, perhaps, but the ending rattles me. Abandonment.

*

Again, feeling like I miss a ghost. Or perhaps not a ghost, but an image, a fantasy of what friendship could and should mean. Life long, enduring. Always. There is sadness; while I will make many new friendships in my life, I never again will have one that played with me in kindergarten. History is a powerful connector, provides a meaningful context for sharing.

A Most Recent Loss

Each time I write about friendships, I am forced to reconsider what each relationships means, and how I relate to friends. The other night, I decided to call several old friends I have not heard from in a while. Some friendships are that way, the connections transcend time or space. With others, sometimes time and distance leads to a diminished contact. Such is the case with Larry, a former student of mine while I taught at a community college on the East Coast. Larry was an older student, in his late forties. Having received a liver transplant five years before, Larry wanted to be a transplant coordinator. After a year and a half of school, shortly before I moved west, Larry had to take a semester off due to liver problems. We exchanged several e-mails, and talked on the phone a couple of times during the year after I moved.

Not hearing back from him, I returned to the day-to-day routines of my life. After not hearing from him for slightly over a year, I called yesterday. Larry's mother in-law informed me that Larry had died last winter. Hanging up the phone, I felt a deep sense of shock and shame. Shame was my dominant feeling; shame that I was not a better friend, that I did not try harder to stay in touch. Cleary, he was very sick for a long time, and I did not make the extra effort. Now, I have no chance to reconnect, no chance to be there for him as a friend. Now, I have to mourn the death of someone who was an important person in my life. I have to contend with more than his loss—the concomitant feelings that are triggered by the loss of meaningful friendships. I present this poem, written several months before his death, in honor of Larry. While traditional academic articles usually end with a conclusion, I will end with this poem. The loss of friendship is a little-understood phenomenon. Subsequent research is needed to clarify individual differences regarding how people respond to the loss of a friend, as well as the social construction of friendship loss. For now, just this:

Respect
A hairdresser before, he traveled the globe following lines of powder and pills with his wife, his assistant, his model. That was before his liver blew like a truck tire slamming down the interstate, maybe too much speed, or just poorly made material. Perhaps fate slammed her foot on the brakes moments before certain wreck. Now fifty, he pops more pills than ever before, tranquilizers to keep his ever rejecting liver silent. Jaundice skin melting easily in the sun, we watch a lot of movies. Mostly, juvenile comedies, gentiles in apple pie gags, awkward sex in backs of minivans with the PTA moms, stupid flip lines that we repeat incessantly. Of course, the ubiquitous teenage flaccidity. The more inane, the fulfilled. The fifty year old ex-hairdresser, his unsteady gait and orange din, and his college professor. Also ate kennels of heart attack chilidogs, grilled with grease and onions, covered in sauerkraut jalapenos and quasi cheese spread. Spicy food is poison to his liver. But we do not speak of this, instead gossip about the women in my class. We speak of breasts we cannot have, legs we would not want, and mouths we are glad only speak to us in sentences few. They tell him things I am not meant to hear—he loves to watch me blush. We have not spoken often since I moved west, and he was too weak to fly out for my wedding. A stroke late last summer, he has death on his mind. After speaking to him on the phone, I am driven by my car, find myself at the nearest fifty's style diner. Two chilly dogs, lots of peppers. I power down the first in seconds. The second more slowly, let the cheese drip off my face. Close my eyes as I sense the chilies working their way into my body. For dessert, order a slice of apple pie, watch it sit perfect in the middle of the table. Take a bite, let memories wash over me. Just out of respect.

References

Baumeister, R. F., & Leary, M. R. (1995). The need to belong: Desire for interpersonal attachments as a fundamental human motivation. *Psychological Bulletin, 117*(3), 497–529.
Brearley, L. (2000). Exploring the creative voice in an academic context. *The Qualitative Report, 5*(3/4).

Constas, M. A. (1992). Qualitative analysis as a public event: The documentation of category development procedures. *American Educational Research Journal, 29*(2), 253–266.

Creswell, J. W. (1998). *Qualitative inquiry and research design.* Sage.

Gee, J. (1991). A linguistic approach to narrative. *Journal of Narrative and Life History, 1*(1), 15–39.

Finley, S., & Knowles, J. G. (1995). Researcher as artist/artist as researcher. *Qualitative Inquiry, 1*(1), 110–142.

Furman, R. (2003). *The fence.* Aiga.

Goldstein, H. (1990). The knowledge base of social work practice: Theory, wisdom, analogue, or art? *Families in Society,* Winter, 32–43.

Hutter, H. (2001). On friendship. *Contemporary Sociology, 30*(6), 579–581.

Padgett, D. (1998). *Qualitative methods in social work research.* Sage.

Patton, M. Q. (2001). *Qualitative research and evaluation methods* (3rd ed.). Sage.

Percer, L. H. (1992). Going beyond the demonstrable range in educational scholarship: Exploring the intersections of poetry and research. *The Qualitative Report, 7*(2).

Poindexter, C. C. (2002). Meaning from methods: Re-presenting narratives of an HIV-affected caregiver. *Qualitative Social Work, 1*(1), 59–78.

Richardson, L. (1994). Nine poems: Marriage and the family. *Journal of Contemporary Ethnography,* 23(1), 3–13.

Part II:

Poetic Inquiry: Poetry and Research

Chapter 9

Poetic Forms and Structures in Qualitative Health Research

The arts and humanities have become increasingly important in the treatment practices of health professionals (Begel, 1998; Donohoe & Danielson, 2004; Genova, 2003). Not only have music, poetry, dance, and art become aids in patient care, each has become a valuable tool in qualitative research. Poetry in particular has become a valuable tool for qualitative researchers. For example, Oiler (1983) utilized published poetry written by nurses as a source of qualitative data. Other researchers have used poetry as a means of data representation by arranging data from qualitative interviews into line and stanza breaks. By so doing, these researchers use poetic devices as a means of highlighting important themes from research.

Text presented in this manner has been referred to as "poetized verse," (Willis, 2002) or "poetic transcription" (Glesne, 1997; Carr, 2003) and consists of quasi-poetic forms that do not adhere to any particular standard poetic construction. In other words, while some poetic devices are used, the power of formal poetic structures has not been utilized in social science and health research. The overarching question of this study addresses this issue: How would structured poetic forms impact the presentation of data? In this article, I will explore the use of multiple poetic forms as vehicles for data representation, utilizing a poem itself as data. Differing from a previous article by Carr (2003) published in the "Pearls, Pith, and Provocation" section of *Qualitative Health Research*, this article utilizes poetry throughout the research process, not solely for data representation. As my source of data, I will use a personal poem about an experience I had as a patient in an emergency room. I analyze data thematically and use the themes that were derived to create research poems in two forms: the Pantoum and the Tanka. Prior to presenting these forms, I will explore the uses of poetry in, and as, social research.

Poetry as Research

Over the past several decades, qualitative researchers have begun to utilize various artistic media as both sources of data and for the purposes of data representation. Willis (2002) describes how the arts are congruent with the expressive research agenda. This is contrasted with the analytical tradition of research, in which experience is reduced into compressed numerical forms that often strip the essence and important meanings from the experience or phenomenon being explored. Expressive research:

> does not grasp an object to analyze and subdue it. It attempts to hold it in consciousness, to allow its reality and texture to become etched on the mind. It holds back from closure and returns again and again to behold the object, allowing words and images to emerge from the contemplative engagement. (Willis, 2002, p.4)

This notion is congruent with Denzin's (1997) conception of utilizing alternative forms of data to evoke deep and powerful emotional reactions in the consumer. The expressive and creative arts seek to expand understanding, present subtle ideas that may even be paradoxical or dialectic, and lend themselves to the study of that which is difficult to reduce. This is particularly important in qualitative health research. For example, researchers and practitioners wanting to understand the health-seeking behaviors of those from historically oppressed communities, must use methods which facilitate the expression of powerful emotions that may not always be easily expressed in a clear or linear fashion. The arts, which allow for the expression of feelings that may not have previously been clear even to research participants, create a space for an interactional process of discovery. As such, engaging participants in arts-based research should not be a top-down process of gathering data but a reciprocal relationship in which insights are developed and shared.

Poetry is a particularly powerful tool for achieving this aim. For thousands of years, poets have utilized the medium to explore and express the important truths of their hearts and their experiences of existence. Poetry often has the capacity to penetrate experience more deeply than prose. For instance, in his classic and haunting poem *Howl*, Ginsberg (1956) proclaimed: "I saw the best mind of my generation destroyed by madness." When reading the poem, one does not doubt his perceptions, or the intensity of the madness that he observed. His words penetrate the experience profoundly.

The compressed nature of the poem forces the author to make decisions about what is essential. This is analogous to the data-reduction process in both qualitative and quantitative research. The compression of a poem allows text to powerfully and evocatively express affect and context, or affect-in-context. Also, the compression of a poem makes it more consumable than longer, less "cooked" narratives. Poems are built on concrete, real-world images that engage the reader through various senses. Successful expressive poems are based upon empirical data that is sensory and evocative in nature. Imagistic language allows the reader to enter a work and develop their own personal relationship with it; the images are transformed into knowledge pertaining to both the poem and the reader. Having had a visual, image evoked, the reader of a poem is allowed to explore the currency and relevance of the poem to their own life. It is through the image that poetry can become "metaphorically generalizable" (Stein, 2003, 2004). While a poem addresses a particular person or situation, it seeks to communicate more universal truths. It is for this reason, perhaps, that Hirshfield (1997) refers to poetry as "the clarification and magnification of being."

Researchers who utilize poetry in and as research typically utilize it in one of two manners. First, researchers from various disciplines use poetry as a means of data representation (Poindexter, 2002). These researchers begin with traditional qualitative research methods, and form poems from their data. While the use of poetry may have been intended from the onset of the inquiry, poetry is used only after data has been collected. Poetry does not seem to be imbedded within the structure and processes of such studies. Other researchers have utilized poetry as an integral component in their inquiry (Chan, 2003; Richardson, 1993; Stein, 2003). In such studies, poetry is not viewed solely as a means of data representation, but as a tool that gives shape to the research design as a whole. For instance, in his autoethnographic research of his father's bout with cancer, Furman (2004) utilizes poetry as a source of data and reflective narratives as a means of adding additional layers of meaning. Poetry and writing become both data and data analysis. In reflecting critically upon his own words, and through presenting his own biases, the reader is invited to explore their own sense of the limitations and potential reliability of the data.

As a means of data presentation, different poetic forms may have different effects on data re-presentation. Langer and Furman (2004) utilized a 700-year-old Japanese poem as a means of reducing traditional qualitative interviews into a compressed form. The Tanka, from which the more familiar Haiku originated, consists of five lines and forced the researchers to capture the essence of their clients' words into a highly succinct form. By reducing the more lengthy interviews, the authors hoped to maintain the depth and richness of the interviews yet also achieve the data reduction so prized by quantitative researchers. Besides this work, there is little indication that traditional poetic forms have been utilized in qualitative health research. This study experiments with such forms as a means of impacting the presentation of data.

Method

Several poems are presented based upon different poetic forms that explore the same heath care-related event. The original poem was written approximately one month after I was taken to the emergency room for what I thought, at the time, was a heart attack. As it turns out, the event was due to respiratory distress from nearby forest fires. There were three goals for writing this poem: 1) to faithfully represent the salient affective and psychosocial issues; 2) to create an aesthetically satisfying poem; and, 3) to act as a means of self-exploration and even self-therapy. While the explicit aim was not research per se, the above-stated goals are congruent with the expressive research agenda (Eisner, 1981; Finley & Knowles, 1995). In many regards, the poem may be viewed in much the same way as a qualitative interview—as an exploration of the lived experience of the research subject/participant.

The subsequent poems each were derived from using the first poem as data. Treating the poem itself as text, I analyzed it for themes using traditional open and axial coding methods. A five round method of coding was utilized in the data analysis phase. During the first round of coding, I read the poems without the intent to develop codes or themes. The goal was to familiarize myself with the text. During the second round, general impressions were noted and written in the margins of the text. The third round of coding consisted of a line-by-line analysis of the text. During the fourth round of coding, general themes were induced from the identified codes. A fifth round of coding was conducted two weeks after the last round, utilizing the identical method. Congruence was found in nearly all identified themes. The following themes were identified: fear of dying, fear of medical procedures, concern about the meaning of my life, humor as a defense. the desire to live.

Once these themes were identified, I undertook the process of representing various themes in different poetic forms to experiment with impact of the various forms. I posited that different poetic forms would highlight different aspects of the data. Too often, data re-presentation is seen as something separate from the research. Richardson (1992) suggests that methods of data representation are integral to the research process. By experimenting with representing this data in different forms, the author hopes to stimulate similar experimentation and attention to strategies of data representation. The original poem is presented first.

Emergency Room, Almost Thirty Seven

They force tubes through your nostrils
and roughly shave your chest
in uneven swatches like cornfields
plowed by psilocybin farmers,
hook you to machines you cannot see,
the nurses calm as you contemplate
a life without you.
Who will attend the funeral?
How long with they keep your website up at work?
You are almost calm too.
You stare at a container on a shelf
written in black marker, *diapers*.
The doctor asks you questions
but you keep thinking about diapers.
Are they one size fits all?
Unisex, or ones cut for muscular squat legs—
think of Sumo wrestlers dancing on your chest.
The doctor asks—*heart or lungs?*
How are you to know?
On a bike or making love
they always seemed to work together
flawlessly,
but now you're not so sure,
three days before turning thirty seven.
When your wife enters you
ask her if a blood pressure reading of

> 200 over 400 is high
> through feigned calmness and tearing eyes——yes dear it is,
> and you tell her it sounds high and
> thank god yours is nearer to normal,
> and through your laughter she knows you're ok,
> or as ok as you ever were,
> but maybe not,
> and tears mix with laughter
> thinking this could be your last night
> wishing to hear the sound of the wind
> or even your huge farting dog,
> tears, pouring down your lips.

The Pantoum is a powerful form that can create a haunting effect through the repetition of lines throughout the poem. The Pantoum is a French poem, based upon Malaysian forms (Unst, 2002). It was introduced to the west by the French poet Victor Hugo. The Pantoum gained popularity in the United States throughout the twentieth century. Colorado poet Jack Martin (2003) referred to the Pantoum as the poetry machine, in that the repetition of lines and energy in the poem can be almost contagious. It should be noted that since each of the following research poems are of a condensed nature, each of the identified themes are not contained in each poem.

> Tears, pouring down your lips
> through feigned calmness and tearing eyes
> they force tubes through your nostrils
> emergency room, almost thirty seven
>
> through feigned calmness and tearing eyes
> you contemplate a life without you
> emergency room, almost thirty seven
> How long with they keep your website up at work?
>
> you contemplate a life without you
> Who will attend the funeral?
> How long will they keep your website up at work?
> You are almost calm too.
>
> Who will attend the funeral?
> they force tubes through your nostrils

you are almost calm too.
tears, pouring down your lips

The following Tanka was crafted mostly using lines from the original poem, with some minor restructuring to help the poem fit close to the traditional form of the American Tanka. With origins tracing back to eighth century Japan, the Tanka is one of the oldest forms of poetry still widely being used (Waley, 1976). The Tanka is far older—and, in many ways, of more historical significance—than its cousin the Haiku. Traditionally, the Tanka was written in one long line of thirty-one onji, or sound units (Ueda, 1996). The rhythmic pattern of onji consisted of units of 5-7-5-7-7 sound and meaning units (Strand & Boland, 2000). The onji in Japanese is a different unit of sound than is the English syllable, yet the American Tanka has come to utilize the same pattern, corresponding to syllables instead of onji.

Tears, pouring down lips
who will attend the funeral?
Feigned calmness and tears

they force tubes through your nostrils
you contemplate life without you.

Discussion/Conclusion

Clear differences can be noted between the three different forms and their effect. The first poem, written for the purposes of self-expression and self-therapy, was treated as raw data from which the other poems were written. This original "free verse" poem is analogous to a more traditional qualitative interview or other "uncooked" data. It is expansive and at times narrative. While it expresses the fullness of my affective state, it also contains details that may not contribute to elucidating the most salient aspects of the experience. This is the weakness of presenting data in unanalyzed forms: While the data preserve the full "livedness" of the author's experience, the consumer may not easily construe the most salient information. The two other poems were created to by including only data that was uncovered by thematic analysis.

The Pantoum is long enough to contain a great deal of the original "data," yet through repetition it creates a haunting emphasis on key affective aspects of the original work. It moves away from a narrative or linear portrayal of the experience toward a more metaphorical, lyrical treatment. The Tanka, as a highly compressed form, forced me to make specific choices and seek to explore the essence of the experience. The Tanka is more direct in its treatment, yet creates a sense of mystery through what is omitted and implied. While I sought to rely on the data and the subsequent thematic analysis, intuition certainly played a key role in the creation of the Tanka. As Reason (1988) suggests, interpretative research processes often push researchers to trust their own intuition and "gut" sense of their data. One of the implications of this research is that qualitative tools and techniques borrowed from the humanities can have powerful effects on qualitative research. Qualitative researchers who utilize the arts and humanities in their inquiry can uncover insights that are multi-sensory in nature, thus portraying more completely many aspects of the human condition that do not lend themselves to numerical reduction or even portrayal through traditional narrative and naturalistic methods.

The inquiry presented here is situated at the intersection between the humanities and social sciences. As disciplinary boundaries continue to be transcended, qualitative health researchers may find the insights of both lend richness and depth to their work. Research based upon the "logical" of the humanities, which is metaphorical, image and intuition, is meant to illuminate experience and can complement research paradigms that can subsequently test the generalizability of such arts-derived insights.

References

Begel, A. (1998). The family conference: A jazz jam. *Families, Systems & Health,16*(4), 437–441.

Carr, J. M. (2003). Poetic expressions of vigilance. *Qualitative Health Research, 13*(9), 1324–1331.

Chan, Z. C. Y. (2003). Poetry writing: A therapeutic means for a social work doctoral student in the process of study. *Journal of Poetry Therapy, 16*(1), 5–17.

Denzin, N. K. (1997). *Interpretive ethnography: Ethnographic practices in the 21st century.* Sage.

Donohoe, M., & Danielson, S. (2004). A community approach to medical humanities. *Medical Education, 38*(2), 204–207.

Eisner, E. W. (1981). On the differences between scientific and artistic approaches to qualitative research. *Educational Researcher, 10*(4), 5–9.

Finley, S., & Knowles, J. G. (1995). Researcher as artist/artist as researcher. *Qualitative Inquiry, 1*(1), 110–142.

Furman, R. (2004). Using poetry and narrative as qualitative data: Exploring a father's cancer through poetry. *Family, Systems & Health, 22*(2), 162–170.

Genova, N. J. (2003). Expanding our concept of the medical literature: The value of the humanities in medicine. *Journal of the American Academy of Physician Assistants, 16*(3), 61–64.

Ginsberg, A. (1956). *Howl.* Harper & Row.

Glesne, C. (1997). That rare feeling: Re-presenting research through poetic transcription. *Qualitative Inquiry, 3*(2), 202–221.

Hirshfield, J. (1997). *Nine gates: Entering the mind of poetry.* HarperCollins.

Langer, C., & Furman, R. (2004). The Tanka as a qualitative research tool: A study of a Native American woman. *Journal of Poetry Therapy, 17*(3), 165–171.

Martin, J. Personal communication. Fort Collins, CO.

Oiler, C. (1983). Nursing reality as reflected in nurses' poetry. *Perspectives in Psychiatric Care, 21*(3), 81–89.

Poindexter, C. C. (2002). Meaning from methods: Re-presenting narratives of an HIV-affected caregiver. *Qualitative Social Work, 1*(1), 59–78.

Reason, P. (1988). *Human inquiry in action: Developments in new paradigm research.* Sage.

Richardson, L. (1992). The consequences of poetic representation. In. C. Ellis and M. G. Flaherty (Eds.), *Investigating subjectivity: Research on lived experience* (pp. 125–173). Newbury Park: Sage Publications.

Richardson, L. (1993). Poetics, dramatics, and transgressive validity: The case of the skipped line. *The Sociological Quarterly, 34*(4), 695–710.

Stein, H. F. (2003). The inner world of workplaces: Accessing this world through poetry, narrative, literature, music and visual art. *Consulting Psychology Journal: Practice and Research, 55*(2), 84–93

Stein, H. F. (2004). A window to the interior of experience. *Families, Systems, & Health, 22*(2), 178–179.

Strand, M., & Boland, E. (2000). *The making of a poem: A Norton anthology of poetic form.* W. W. Norton.

Ueda, M. (1996). *Modern Japanese Tanka.* Columbia University Press.

Unst, Q. (2002). The Pantoum verse form. http://baymoon.com/~ariadne/form/Pantoum.htm

Waley, A. (1976). *Japanese poetry.* University of Hawaii.

Willis, P. (2002). Poetry and poetics in phenomenological research. *Indo-Pacific Journal of Phenomenology, 3*(1), 1–19

Chapter 10

Autoethnographic Poems and Narrative Reflections: A Qualitative Study on the Death of a Companion Animal

To Belinda, 1993–2004

The death of a companion animal can be a devastating emotional experience, as companion animals are often perceived as integral members of the modern family (McCutcheon & Fleming, 2002; Noonan, 1998). Researchers, theorists, and practitioners have found that relationships with companion animals can be as significant as relationships with other human beings (Archer & Winchester, 1994; Cowles, 1985; Cusack, 1988; Gosse & Barnes, 1994; McCutcheon & Fleming, 2002; Planchon et al., 2002; Ross-Baron-Sorensen, 1998). The pain and grief triggered by the death of a companion animal may be exacerbated by the society's devaluation of such relationships (Sharkin & Knox, 2003).

Within the context of a complex, post-industrial society, traditional family relationships may not meet all of people's needs. Indeed, many people report that their companion animals provide them with as much, if not more, support than their human family or friends (Gosse & Barnes, 1994). Relationships with companion animals have been shown to help people meet many psychosocial needs (Hart, 2000). For example, companion animals often prevent loneliness and can help people recover from illness or disease (Gunter, 1999). Companion animals hold a significant place in the lives of many people at each stage of the life cycle (Sable, 1995). Companion animals may be conceptualized as integral members of many families. Not viewing companion animals as potential family members privileges one form of life over another (Best, 2004), an ethical position that does take into account the affective and social bonds that exist for many families. The profession of social work has long advocated for an inclusive view of what constitutes a family, preferring a constructionist perspective where families are self-defined entities. In accordance with this position, pets are conceptualized as family members by those who view them as such.

Autoethnographic data is a valuable methodology for exploring the lived experience of intense human events (Alsop, 2002; James, 1999). It is particularly valuable for studying subjects that have previously been neglected in the literature or that deal with subjects that may be difficult or painful for research participants to address (Reed-Danahay, 1997). Autoethnographic research of difficult topics focuses attention on notions central to post-modern research, such as authenticity and empathy. Researchers striving for authenticity must be willing to be at least as vulnerable and open as their clients. By making themselves the subject, researchers can develop increased empathy and sensitivity to research participants in subsequent studies. Autoethnographic poetry previously has been used to explore loss and disease (Furman, 2004a & 2004b).

Based upon this previous research, the author of this article posited that this method would be valuable for exploring his experiences surrounding the death of his dog. The purpose of this study is to explore the meaning of the loss of a pet through the use of autoethnographic poetry in conjunction with narrative reflections. Narrative reflections expand the depth and scope of poetry in qualitative research. The author will meet the objectives of this article in several ways. First, an exploration of autoethnographic poems is presented. Second, a brief account of the life of Belinda, the companion animal who was a vital member of this researcher's life for eleven years, is described. Third, the methodology is explicated. Lasty, autoethnographic poetry and narrative reflections are presented.

Autoethnographic Poems as Sources of Data

> What artistically crafted work does is to create a paradox of revealing what is universal by examining what is particular. (Eisner, 1995, p. 3)

Methods of social research must be consonant with the subject under consideration (Morgan & Drury, 2003. Loss is a highly personal, complex phenomenon. In order to study its intricacies, a medium is needed that captures the subtleties of affect and its cultural expression. Feminist and post-modern researchers have long advocated for means of knowing that attempt to capture the complexity and richness of human experience, eschewing positivistic methods that reduce emotion to over-simplified numerical expression (Finley & Knowles, 1995; Richardson, 1992). Such researchers advocate for research methods that transcend disciplinary boundaries and the traditional schism between the arts and sciences (Richardson, 2000).

The creative and expressive arts have increasingly become important in social science research (Begel, 1998; Donohoe & Danielson, 2004; Edwards, 1990; Frank, 1998; Genova, 2003). Eisner (1981) has advocated for art and artfulness as a means of exploring the human condition. He also posits that the artist and scientist actually have much in common; both need to ground their work in careful observation of the empirical world, have the capacity to reflect upon their work, and have the ability to reflect upon their experience and understand the impact that their own subjective understanding has upon their subject.

Poetry has become a particularly valuable tool of qualitative researchers in various disciplines. Richardson (1993), a sociologist, utilizes poems in the presentation of data about the lives of unwed mothers. She compresses traditional qualitative interviews into lyrical poems to present their "lived experiences." Scholars in social work have also begun to utilize poetry in social research. Furman (2003) utilizes autoethnographic poetry as a means of exploring the complexities of step-fatherhood. He utilizes poetry to explore the impact of his father's cancer on his own life (Furman, 2004a), as well as the importance of friendships to psychosocial well-being (Furman, 2004b, 2004c). Poindexter (2002) utilizes the research poem as a means of exploring the relationship between HIV-infected people and their caretakers. Borrowing techniques from anthropology and linguistics, the author crafts research poems from traditional qualitative interviews. Langer and Furman (2004) utilized two types of poetry in their study exploring the identity of Native Americans: the research poem and interpretive poems. By incorporating poetry crafted from the exact words of research participants, as well as interpretative poems that integrate their own subjective understanding of research data, the authors bridge the divide between social science research and the creative/expressive arts. Such methods affirm the valuation of the subjective experience of the researcher, and stress the importance of reflexivity and researcher awareness (Brew, 2001), and lead to the questioning of the privileged, power position of an objective, detached researcher (Ellis & Flaherty, 1992).

What accounts for poetry's ability to express the human experience? The compressed quality of poetry is central to its utility. Poetry derives its power from its brevity, while prose relies upon expansion and elaboration. Metaphor is also central to the evocative nature of poetry. Experience that has been accurately captured through a method increases the likelihood of its being remembered. Poems are often remembered for longer periods of time than are works of prose (Rowe, 2000). The metaphors within poems are analogous to themes and codes within qualitative research. Poems also tend to be full of concrete, observable images. Unlike photographic images, images conjured by the mind that are triggered by the written word may be attributable as much to the receiver as to the source. The images inspired by a poem engage the reader in a creative relationship that moves beyond passivity to co-creation.

Poetry has the capacity to simultaneously express affect and context, or more accurately, affect *in* context. Through the juxtapositioning of emotion within the life narrative of the writer, emotions occurring within the life space and life span of the author. When adolescents are encouraged to write poetry from their own experience, in their own words, and in their own styles, what emerges are sociocultural artifacts that document their own personal experience. In this sense, poetry can be thought of as an affective, sociocultural microchip.

This is not to say that poetry written by the author is necessarily generalizable. The relationship between the reader of the poems and the author is different than in traditional research, where the reader is assumed to take a passive, consumptive, yet critical role. Poetry encourages a more reciprocal relationship, where the reader is encouraged to understand the poetry through the lens of their own personal experiences (Kaminsky, 1998). Therefore, the success of a poem is not measured by the degree to which the reader learns about generalizable patterns or trends, but by the evocative capacity of the poem itself. Was the poem able to inspire reflection and insight within the reader? Was the poem able to portray emotions and experiences that the reader understood? Poetry then can be viewed as data that penetrates deeply into the human condition. For these reasons, poetry is a valuable source of data for helping human service professionals (Raingruber, 2004).

Poetry has previously been utilized to explore, document, and heal the experience of loss. Hodges (1993) explores the uses of art and poetry with terminally ill patients. Robinson (2004) demonstrates how she uses poetry in nursing practice to help her process issues involving the complex and difficult feelings triggered in palliative and hospice care. It is with her words that I began my research:

> I believe that poetry has the ability to speak of and confront the great issues in life, such as terminal illness, loss and bereavement that confront us all. Poetry can give comfort, humor and expression not only to the writer but also to the reader. Through poetry feelings can be expressed that otherwise may never surface. (p. 34)

The Life and Death of Belinda

Belinda was a lovely, playful, grouchy, wonderful American Bulldog. She was an incredibly social dog, demanding the love and attention of all who met her. Belinda was special to me in many ways. She was my first dog. She was my present to myself upon graduating with my masters of social work degree. She was the "child" in my first truly long-term relationship. After the relationship ended, I kept custody of her and our other American Bulldog, Buster. When I married, the dogs came across country with me, and Belinda become became the "twin" of one of my step-daughters (both born on the same day, the same year). Until I married, when she shared her love equally amongst the family, Belinda was my constant shadow. She slept with me, stayed by my feet when I was eating, and cuddled with me on the sofa while I read and wrote. I worried that when she was no longer around, I would not be able to produce any scholarship.

Several months before her tenth birthday, Belinda was diagnosed with lymphoma. We were going to move to Omaha several months later; our mantra became, "just make it to Omaha, 'Fly'" (one of her many nicknames). True to her tenacious, bulldoggie spirit, Belinda made it to Omaha, and lived two months after her eleventh birthday. Belinda helped ease our adjustment to our new lives. She took turns sleeping with my wife and me, or each of the children, helping to make our new house a home. As she became progressively more ill, she remained strong and brave, and never stopped loving her family with all of her heart. Belinda always reminded us of the importance of living, and loving fully. It was the most painful decision of my life when we decided to euthanize her once her tumors were clearly causing her pain. On June 14, 2004, Belinda was euthanized and died in my arms.

Methodology

In this study, poetry is presented along with narrative reflections. Using two different methods allows me to present different voices of the self that help present a more complex, full account of my experiences. Shapiro (2004), in a recent commentary on an article utilizing the same methodology, observed that narrative reflections on previously written poems helped turn me into "the archeologist of my own experiences." This aptly captures my experience of the process, which was at times heart wrenching and painful. Often, I had to stop the process of combing through the poems. At other times, writing the narrative reflections served as research and therapy. In this sense, the process was akin to action research (Reason, 1994), with the end goals of emotional healing and the in-depth portrayal of my grief and loss.

Several days after Belinda died, I gathered the poems that I wrote concerning her illness and imminent death, cut and pasted each of the poems into a Word document, and began to write the introduction to this article. For the first two weeks, I read the poems sporadically. I was not yet ready to respond. I felt too sad and raw, unable to process my emotions. After two weeks, I began to reread each poem and write narrative reflections triggered by the work. In total, I wrote forty-seven narrative reflections. Unlike previous studies where I wrote narrative reflections for a specific time frame, I choose to keep this process open-ended. I realized that the nature of the reflections would change over time as my sense of loss and grief shifted. The reflections that are presented here date from July 1 to September 2, 2004. The reflections I chose were those that seemed to most powerfully and evocatively convey the emotions I was experiencing.

The Poems and Reflections

I Most Certainly Would be Dead

Nobody needs to tell me
that she is a bad dog.
I have raised her for nine years.
Yet without this maddening beast,
I most certainly would be dead.

Do I really want to reveal this? Yet, I promised that I would take chances in this work, that I would be willing to reveal my truths. Also, if these were the words of a research participant other than myself, I would find this level of sharing important. It is so easy to want to expose others, but difficult to expose the self. Ok, enough qualifying, what else does this poem trigger for me? Well, I am thinking of her death. I can share that as I held her, as the vet injected the lethal dose of barbiturates into her, the words I repeated over and over to her were "thank you, I love you, thank you, I love you." What was I thanking her for? Perhaps it was that in those years, many years ago, when I felt lost and hopeless, she tethered me to the earth. That there were things about love I did not learn from my family of origin, that I learned these things with her; through loving her, and through being loved by her. That she helped me through my doctorate, through working full-time and going to school full time, through lonely winters. Mainly, for loving me.

And Nobody Will Care but I

She is not a good dog.
Growls maniacally
as we prepare to leave.
Now and then snaps at
the kids or wife, never biting
but a worrisome scare.
Thinks she owns the bed.
Farts.
Does little.
Moody, grouchy.
More like I
than I care to admit.
And as her days wind down
tender in tuck of my arm,
where many have been
and many have left,
she too will leave
and nobody will care but I.

I am stuck with the sense of how true this poem is for me on so many different levels. How I identified with this dog so much, how it felt that her fate and my fate were truly wrapped together. Somehow, I think I believed that if I could learn to love and accept her for who she was, with all her foibles, that somehow I could possibly be accepted for who I am. Whether or not any human truly does accept us totally, I am not sure, but I am certain that our dogs accept us for who we are. They love us unconditionally, and we struggle to love them in a similar manner. What a gift dogs give us; what a gift this dog gave me. By simultaneously being so loving and so difficult, she pushed the envelope that is my capacity to love. She forced me to look at myself, to work on my limitations, to stretch my ability to love and be present.

Prehumous

Will you be my dog when I am dead?
And I am not speaking of religion.

There is more than this, as I watch you
sleep with the step daughter we have adopted.

It is not that you saved me from the beyond.
There is more than this.

Your bent teeth bucking out of your mouth,
your discolored graying face melted

like old vinyl records through high heat summer window,
trying to futilely play its maddening warped song.

That mouth, resting on my chest as I write the poem
and contemplate my end.

Others will read this, banal words of soon to be dead dog.
There is more than this.

You cellular thing,
you have invaded all.

I am reminded that I have not yet picked up her ashes. In the first line, will you be my dog when I am dead? Is that why I asked for her ashes in the first place? I hope that she will somehow in death live on with me. Is this denial? Two weeks after, somehow having them seems less important than it did to me the day after. The day after, thinking about not having any part of her, I felt dead. I felt as if not having her ashes would somehow be a betrayal, an abandonment. Abandonment has been a theme in my relationship with my dogs for years. Somehow, I always saw it as a moral no, a spiritual obligation to never abandon them, to care for them "always." What did, does that "always" mean? Perhaps my own fantasy about my own mortality, that somehow by wishing to be with them always, I pretend that there will be an always for me. Yes, her death makes me feel closer to my own.

Living

Living in the belly of death
watch *Rainman* with my kids
take turns cuddling close
on the fading couch dirtied by dogs
living in the belly of death
watch the five year old
tickle the nose of the dog
dying of lymphoma
living in the belly of death
tears taste like shadows
tears bleed like never
tears bend to catch retreating winter
living in the belly of death
drinking last night with my pal Jim
words like time standing on its head
words like pigeons in Venice
words like tears in the belly of death
living in the belly of death
ingest chelated minerals
sip porcelain cup of *dragon well*
bike three times a week
hit the weights until bulging
watch my dog's breathing ribs
pushing up the torn blue blanket
knitted for my wedding
waiting for each other
to move closer
waiting for endings
none of us understand.

Why does eating a chocolate chip cookie today seem like a sinister act? This loss has put me more in touch with my own mortality then I have felt since my father's successful battle with lung cancer. This morning I lay on the floor with Buster, wondering when he would die. The realization hit me that perhaps I would die before him, that nothing is guaranteed. When we are not faced with death, we are able to deny its existence just enough to go forward—wash the dishes, take out the trash, work on course preparations. Faced with death, I alternate between fear and the desire to live, to create, to be vital. I long to not waste a single moment, to find some way of living each day, each second, as a precious gift. Yet, how much pressure this is! Perhaps this is why those more sensitive, more existential than myself struggle with feelings of futility and hopelessness.

Caught

by the bloody talon of god
the vicious meat hook of faith
of existence,

my head, resting on my dying dog's rear,
her life picked apart by the vultures of time
she moans in pain,

sucked from us by the vacuum
of that bastard janitor,
petty custodian of it all,

throwing her life into his infinite waste can,
my head, maybe something also
building up and breaking down,

or somewhere an unknown organ poisoned, rotting,
that bastard's talon, his hook,
slowly spreading me apart as well.

The vet says some medicine, maybe more time,
but only playing hide and seek,
cowering behind the washing machine,

he can see us, smell us, taste us,
the bastard vulture will pluck us at will
uncaring that I barely believe

> this Jewish Easter
> ending later then sundown
> earlier than lies.

After I read this poem, I look at a picture of Belinda. It is clear to me that I have moved from the overwhelming profound grief to a sense of sadness and loss. Tonight, I just miss her being part of my life. As I type this, Buster is lying asleep on the small couch, the opposite one where Belinda usually slept. He is a quiet dog. Even though he is twice as large as Belinda was, he takes up less space. She had such a large, often intrusive presence. I find that I can start to speak about her faults more easily now. I no longer feel angry and defensive when my wife makes a comment that is not wholly positive about her. Yes, the house is quieter now. As I type in my chair in the living room and look to the larger couch, it is empty. When I wrote in my chair when she was alive, her eyes never left me. I gave over to the spot where she would be. There is nothing left to write now.

Other reflections
The following entries are reflections that I wrote not in response to a particular poem but written after reading several poems and while reflecting upon Belinda's life and its meaning to me.

> Yesterday, I saw an old boxer that reminded me of Belinda, slightly gray face, the same enthusiastic expression, similar size. I practically sprinted to the dog, and asked the owner if she is friendly. I start to pet her, fighting back the urge to tell this complete stranger about Belinda, how much I loved her, how precious she was to me. I fight back the urge to implore him to enjoy his time with his friend, to say that time and life are fleeting. He is a stranger on a walk with his dog, and as much as I feel in this moment, I keep my feeling private.

*

> This morning I feel I turned the corner somewhat. I woke up thinking of the prayer/song I sang to Belinda moments before she was put to sleep. A smile immediately came to my face. I felt a sense of joy from her being my dog, from having been able to love her and raise her for all these years. Joy from a sense of

gratitude from what I learned in the process of loving her, that somehow so much of what I have become and become capable of doing was given to me by our shared love. For the first day, perhaps, I am truly feeling the joy of her life in her death. My pain and mourning have not ended, but somehow today I feel more connected to living, and to her. As I type these words, I start to cry. Today will be a good day.

*

Today while working out and listening to music, I feel a deep sense of Belinda being gone. Not only that she is gone from my life but gone from the world, that there is so little trace of her. I look outside the window; of course, life continues. Nothing stops for my grief; there is no marker other than the pain in my own heart. Somehow, I feel guilty, as if somehow the world should know how big an impact this dog had on me. Perhaps this is why I am writing this article. I look over at Buster, sleeping on the floor, listen to the children upstairs playing. I know I am allowed my moments of grief. These two weeks I have written so little but have allowed myself moments of private grief and loss. Perhaps, for fifteen minutes or a half hour, once or twice a day. I think I would feel too guilty to not cry for her.

*

I try to work on the section of this article describing Belinda, her life. I cannot do it today. Sitting in my writing chair next to the couch where she would watch me, I feel her absence today more so than for some time. I feel the long shadows of death, close. With school starting this week, I have had so little time to feel, but I still miss her. It is there. Sometimes is a part of me believes this is not permanent, like being temporarily separated from a loved one who takes a job in another state. But, she is dead, and I will never see her again. She is dead, and her death is still a reminder that each day I am one day closer to death. What a powerful gift her dying can be if I can live a little more fully, slightly more aware that my time here is so finite. The tragedy, and miracle, of life.

*

It is six weeks after her death. I am watching Saturday morning cartoons with the kids. In one of the cartoons, a seventh grader's goldfish died. He is not able to talk about it, is not able to grieve. Everyone gives him goldfish, but he is not ready to take one yet. Finally, one of his friends gives him a book on grief. As he reads from it about the sadness and loss of losing a pet, I start to cry. I wonder when I will stop crying, or at least stop crying daily. Usually, I go into the basement, spend a few minutes by myself, look at her pictures. I want to model to the children that it is human to feel, to cry, that crying is part of being fully alive. Yet I am also supposed to be steady for them. I cannot be steady for them now, however. Their mother will have to be the one this time.

Conclusion

What is research, but an exploration that leads to the truth? What are the truths that social workers need to know? Helpers need to understand the depths of the human soul, their pains and joys, their dreams and aspirations (Dass & Gorman, 1999. Autoethnographic methods may be extremely valuable tools in accessing these existential issues. In a very real sense, poetry lies in the domain of the heart: writing poetry is the research of soul.

Is this study generalizable? Can this be utilized by social workers in any real way? Stein (2003, 2004) observed that poetry can be what he called metaphorically generalizable. It may speak *about* one, but it speaks *to* many. In a very real sense, we are all simultaneously unique and the same. Practice must take into account our inherent uniqueness and idiosyncraticness (Gilliland & James, 1997). Poetry has the capacity to fully express this dialectical relationship. Studies such as this may be viewed as exploratory in nature. Insights and issues discovered from autoethnographic studies may be further explored and tested by other research methodology, or utilized by clinicians to sensitize them to potential practice issues.

Engaging in this autoethnography has impacted me in several ways. First, it has helped me to appreciate how difficult it is for research participants to share vulnerable and personal information. This realization has encouraged me to increasingly view those whose lives I explore as participants and partners rather than as subjects. Those who share with me personal and vulnerable aspects of their lives are giving me a profound gift. By viewing the research process in this manner researchers can be more sensitive to the needs and stories of their collaborators. It seems logical that this would only help the trustworthiness of data. Second, while the goal of this study was not therapy, it was very therapeutic. Writing my narrative responses helped me to come to grips with my feelings of grief and loss. Having this article published feels like a tribute to a life that gave so much to me.

In closing, I would like to end with a stanza from a poem taken from a children's book about a boy who came to *learn* to love poetry, but *naturally* loved his dog.

Sharon Creech (2002):

> Love that dog
> Like a bird loves to fly,
> I said I love that dog,
> like a bird loves to fly...

References

Alsop, C. K. (2002). Home and away: Self-reflexive auto/ethnography. *Forum: Qualitative Social Research, 3*(3).
Archer, J., & Winchester, G. (1994). *Bereavement following death of a pet. British Journal of Psychology, 85*(2), 259–272.
Begel, A. (1998). The family conference: A jazz jam. *Families, Systems & Health, 16*(4), 437–441.
Best, S. (2004). *Terrorists or freedom fighters? Reflections on the liberation of animals.* Lantern Books.
Brew, A. (2001). *The nature of research: Inquiry in academic contexts.* Routledge.
Cowles, K. V. (1985). The death of a pet: Human responses to the breaking of the bond. Special issue: Pets and the family. *Marriage and Family Review, 8*(3–4), 149–161.
Creech, S. (2002). *Love that dog.* Scholastic, Inc.
Cusack, O. (Ed.) (1988). *Pets and mental health.* Haworth Press.
Dass, R., & Gorman, P. (1999). *How can I help?* Alfred A. Knopf.
Donohoe, M., & Danielson, S. (2004). A community approach to medical humanities. *Medical Education, 38*(2), 204–207.
Edwards, M. E. (1990). Poetry: Vehicle for retrospection and delight. *Generations, 14*(1), 61–62.

Eisner, E. W. (1981). On the differences between scientific and artistic approaches to qualitative research. *Educational Researcher, 10*(4), 5–9.

Eisner, E. W. (1991). *The enlightened eye. Qualitative inquiry and the enhancement of educational practice*. Macmillan.

Eisner, E. W. (1995). What artistically crafted research can help us understand about schools. *Educational theory, 45*(1), 1-6.

Ellis, C., & Flaherty, M. (1992). *Investigating subjectivity: Research on lived experience*. Sage.

Finley, S., & Knowles, J. G. (1995). Researcher as artist/artist as researcher. *Qualitative Inquiry, 1*(1), 110–142.

Frank, A. W. (1998). Just listening: Narrative and deep illness. *Families, Systems & Health, 16*(3), 197–212.

Furman, R. (2003). Exploring step-fatherhood through poetry. *Journal of Poetry Therapy, 16*(2), 91–96.

Furman, R. (2004a). Using poetry and narrative as qualitative data: Exploring a father's cancer through poetry. *Family, Systems & Health*, Summer.

Furman, R. (2004b). The prose poem as a means of exploring friendship: Pathways to reflection. *Journal of Poetry Therapy, 17*(2).

Furman, R. (2004c). Exploring friendship loss through poetry. *Journal of Loss and Trauma, 9*(1), 181–187.

Genova, N. J. (2003). Expanding our concept of the medical literature: The value of the humanities in medicine. *Journal of the American Academy of Physician Assistants, 16*(3), 61–64.

Gilliland, B. E., & James, R. K. (1997). *Crisis intervention strategies*. (3rd ed.). Brooks/Cole.

Gosse, G. H., & Barnes, M. J. (1994). Human grief resulting from the death of a pet. *Anthrozoos, 7*(2), 172–187.

Gunter, B. (1999). *Pets and people: The psychology of pet ownership*. WhurrPublishers.

Hart, L. A. (1999). Psychosocial benefits of animal companionship. In A. H. Fine (Ed.), *Handbook on animal-assisted therapy: Theoretical foundations and guidelines for practice* (pp. 59–78). Academic Press.

Hodges, D. (1993). For every season: Art and poetry therapy with terminally ill patients. *The Journal of Poetry Therapy, 7*(1), 24–44.

James, P. (1999). Rewriting narratives of self: Reflections from an action research study. *Educational Action Research, 7*(1), 85–103.

Kaminsky, M. (1998). Voicing voicelessness: On the poetics of faith. *American Journal of Psychoanalysis, 80,* 405–416.

Langer, C., & Furman, R. (2004). Exploring identity and assimilation. Research and interpretative poems. *Forum: Qualitative Social Research, 5*(2), 205-211.

McCutcheon, K. A., & Fleming, S. J. (2002). Grief resulting from euthanasia and natural death of companion animals. *Omega, 44*(2), 169–188.

Morgan, A. K., & Drury, V. B. (2003). Legitimizing the subjectivity of human reality through qualitative research. *The Qualitative Report, 8*(1).

Noonan, E. (1998). People and pets. *Psychodynamic counseling, 4*(1), 17–31.

Planchon, L. A., Templer, D. I., Stokes, S., & Keller, J. (2002). Death of companion cat or dog and human bereavement: Psychosocial variables. *Society & Animals, 1*(10), 93–105.

Poindexter, C. C. (2002). Meaning from methods: Re-presenting narratives of an HIV-affected caregiver. *Qualitative Social Work, 1*(1), 59–78.

Raingruber, B. (2004). Using poetry to discover and share significant meanings in child and adolescent mental health nursing. *Journal of Child and Adolescent Psychiatric Nursing, 17*(1), 13–20.

Reason, P. (1994). Three approaches to participative research. In N. K. Denzin & Y. S. Lincoln (Eds.), *Handbook of qualitative research* (pp.324–339). Sage.

Reed-Danahay, D. E. (1997). *Auto/ethnography. Rewriting the self and the social*. New Berg.

Richardson, L. (1992). The consequences of poetic representation. In. C. Ellis and M. G. Flaherty (Eds.), *Investigating subjectivity: Research on lived experience* (pp.125–173). Sage.

Richardson, L. (1993). Poetics, dramatics, and transgressive validity. The case of the skipped line. *The Sociological Quarterly, 34*(4), 695–710.

Richardson, L. (2000). Writing: A method of inquiry. In N. K. Denzin & Y. S. Lincoln, (Eds.), *Handbook of qualitative research* (2nd ed.; pp.923–948). Sage.

Robinson, A. (2004). A personal exploration of the power of poetry in palliative care loss and bereavement. *International Journal of Palliative Nursing, 10(*1), 32–38.

Rowe, R. C. (2000). Poetry and verse: An ideal medium for scientific communication. *Drug Discovery Today, 5*, 436–437.

Ross, C. B., & Barron-Sorensen, J. (1998). *Pet loss and human emotion*. Accelerated Development.

Sable, P. (1995). Pets, attachment, and well-being across the life cycle. *Social Work, 3*(3), 443–342.

Shapiro, J. (2004). Can poetry be data? Potential relationships between poetry and research. *Families, Systems, & Health, 22(*2), 171–177.

Sharkin, B. S., & Knox, D. (2003). Pet loss: Issues and implications for the psychologist. *Professional Psychology: Research and practice, 34*(4), 235–248.

Stein, H. F. (2003). The inner world of workplaces: Accessing this world through poetry, narrative, literature, music and visual art. *Consulting Psychology Journal: Practice and Research, 55*(2), 84–93.

Stein, H. F. (2004). A window to the interior of experience. *Families, Systems, & Health, 22(*2), 178–179.

Chapter 11

Poetry and Narrative as Qualitative Data: Explorations into Existential Theory

The principles most important to existential psychotherapy are difficult to explore through the traditional lenses and methods of logical positivism. In-depth qualitative methodologies that present people's lived experiences have become a valuable means of exploring existentialism (Moustakas, 1994). As existentially oriented therapies evolve, new methods of inquiry have been developed that demonstrate how existential themes emerge within the context of people's lives. The purpose of this paper is to contribute to this growing body of work through an exploration of autobiographical poems and narrative reflections as vehicles of inquiry into existentialism. Informed by a growing body of literature on expressive arts research and inquiry (Eisner, 1981, 1991; Finley & Knowles, 1995), poetry has been utilized by many post-modern researchers (Brearley, 2000; Gee, 1991; Richardson, 1992, 1994).

In this article I discuss poetry and narrative as vehicles of social inquiry and describe how they are appropriate tools for exploring existential themes. This is followed by short descriptions of several key principles in existentially oriented practice. In each section one or two poems are presented that explore how I have grappled with each theme. Along with each poem, I present two narrative reflections that contextualize, explore, or expand each poem. As I will discuss later in this article, the narrative reflections simultaneously function as data and data analysis. This methodology has been utilized in previous studies to explore complex psychosocial processes such as coming to terms with a father's cancer (Furman, 2004a), the death of a companion animal (Furman, 2006) and depression (Gallardo & Furman, in review). Finally, implications of this type of work are explored as they apply to therapy itself, and therapists' own growth and development.

Poetry and Narratives as Inquiry

In her often quoted assertion, Hirshfield (1997) notes that poetry has the capacity to clarify and magnify existence. Poetry may be thought of as the emotional microchip in that it may serve as a compact repository for emotionally charged experiences. Poet James Smith (Smith, 2003) observed that poetry is the "distillation of the essence of being." At its best, poetry honors the subjective experience of the individual and presents it in a manner that is "metaphorically generalizable" (Stein, 2004). The notion of metaphoric generalizability is not the same as it is in the traditional sense of the term, but instead it refers to the relationship between the author of a poem and their audience. A poem that expresses an author's emotional "truth" can elicit a powerful empathic reaction in its reader. The reader recognizes him- or herself in the poem, and learns to view him- or herself in a novel way. The relationship between the poem and the experience of the reader can be understood through Bakhtin's (1982) concept of multivoicedness; meaning resides neither in the speaker nor the receiver but is created through the interaction between the two.

In this way, poetry is an excellent tool for exploring existential themes. Existentialists posit that individual human emotions are by nature subjective and highly idiosyncratic (Krill, 1978); each of us experiences anxiety, dread, joy, and other key emotions in their own way (Jourard, 1968). Our life context and histories, and the meanings we ascribe to them, are complex and varied. They are not easily studied through research methods that seek clear and tidy reductionistic categories.

Poetry is not based upon linear cause and effect logic; a poem does not need to "make sense." In this manner, the poem may be a particularly valuable means of exploring emotions (Mazza, 1999). Through the use of metaphor, the poem allows for interplay between the external and internal worlds of the person that are often complex, contradictory, and even dialectical (Harrower, 1972).

Further, through the device of imagery, a poem can convey the essence of an emotion by evoking images that often transcend the schism between the experience of an emotion and its expression in language. For instance, in a poem about a close friend, I describe her depression as her "Auburn void." In another poem, I refer to my own depression as "a two hundred pound rodent squatting on my chest." Such metaphors and images do more for depicting the quality or tone of an emotion than does a score on a standardized test. Important in existential practice, the poem allows for an assessment of the *meaning* of depression in a person's life, not merely the intensity or strength of the mood (May, 1979). It is through an in-depth exploration of the meaning of clients' feelings and experiences that they are helped to make sense of their feelings as they relate to their needs, dreams, and values.

It is for these reasons that social scientists have begun to utilize the research poem as a means of data reduction and presentation. For instance, Richardson (1993) utilized poems in the presentation of data about unwed mothers. She compressed thick narratives about research participants' lives into lyrical poems that powerfully presented their "lived experiences." In a similar manner, Poindexter (2002) utilized the research poem as a means of exploring the relationship between people infected with HIV and their caretakers. Also, Langer and Furman (2004) utilized the poem as a means of exploring issues related to Native American identity. Their methodology consisted of utilizing three types of data: the presentation of traditional qualitative data in narrative form, a research poem utilizing the exact words taken from the subject's narrative, and interpretive poems written by the researchers that expressed their analysis of the original data. This method was found useful for expressing the subjective experience of the researchers in the data analysis process. By presenting their developing perceptions about the data and their own biases and judgments, the researchers sought transparency, thus leading to an increased sense of trustworthiness.

Chan (2003) utilized poetry as inquiry into the study of her emotions and life context as a doctoral student. Her work holds two distinct yet complementary purposes: as inquiry and as self-therapy. Her poetry simultaneously is a document of consciousness and of the process of working toward the creation of meaning and health.

It would be fair for the reader to ask about the epistemological assumptions implied by, and the limits of, utilizing autobiographical poems as data. Those schooled in the tradition of logical positivism might wonder about the quality of such studies. Positivists often note that even traditional qualitative studies are unscientific and biased, and are not the proper method for studying important social and behavioral phenomena (Morgan & Drury, 2003. To what degree are such studies valid and reliable? Are assumptions and interpretations gleaned from autobiographical poems generalizable?

The answer is probably not. Yet not all research must have as its ultimate goal the generation of knowledge that is generalizable.

Phenomenological research seeks knowledge that accurately and faithfully reflects processes and experiences of complex social phenomenon (Swingewood, 1991). Case studies explore in-depth experiences and meanings of individual subjects for the purposes of uncovering meaningful patterns that are not possible to reduce into numerical form (Stake, 1994). Such methods are congruent with the needs of practitioners, who develop practice wisdom and skills based on an intuitive synthesis of personal, empirical, and theoretical knowledge (Goldstein, 1990). Richardson (2001) suggests five potential criteria to assess a monograph: substantive contribution, aesthetic merit, reflexivity, impact, and expression of reality. The author encourages the reader to assess the merits of this inquiry by these criteria.

Methodology

This method has been previously utilized in other autoethnographic studies that I have conducted (Furman, 2004b & 2006). As Shapiro (2004) noted, the method is useful for being the archeologist of one's own experience. That is, through writing narrative reflections about my own poems, and in exploring how the poems present my lived experiences of existential themes, I simultaneously present additional layers of data and narrative analyses of the poems. The poems were selected from a body of work written over a twenty-year period. Each poem was chosen for its relationship to the existential themes explored.

Each day for two weeks, I read the poems and wrote narrative reflections. While I was free to write whatever came to mind, I attempted to focus on the specific existential theme explored. Given that the poems themselves were autoethnographic in nature, I attempted to contextualize my personal insights into broader cultural issues. This method follows from the post-modern tradition that views writing itself as a method of inquiry (Richardson, 1992).

Narratives are presented in their original form, save for the most basic editing. I want to present them in the rawest form possible to allow readers to have as close access to my actual thought processes as possible. I chose approximately one third of the narratives that I wrote, selecting those that best explore and/or amplify the meaning of the poems.

Existential Issues Explored

The issues that are considered core to existentially oriented therapy depend upon various factors, including the discipline of the therapist and the significant issues of their time. In this section, I will explore several key existential issues including death, meaning and identity, nothingness, dread, and what I refer to as existential resolve. A brief discussion as to how each of these issues fits into existential practice precedes the presentation of the poetry and narratives.

Death and Dread

In discussing the work of Martin Heidegger, van Deurzen-Smith (1997) states: "In spite of the ineluctable anxiety that is triggered by the potential loss of all we care for, we nevertheless tend to take the essentials of life for granted" (p.36).

The specter of death is simultaneously the source of existential anxiety as well as a potential source of energy, creativity, and vitality (Frankl, 1959). Attempts to deny death are found in a variety of symptoms such as compulsive behavior, substance abuse, and depression (Krill, 1969). Facing death leads to anxiety. The pain of this anxiety is difficult to bear, and demands a deep sense of courage to face. But in confronting the reality of death deeply and personally, one may come to appreciate the finite nature of the life we are given. Facing death each day can become an urgent quest toward self-discovery and revelation. Giving into fear and anxiety leads to escapist behaviors of even the most benign (yet insidious) sort—for example, watching television for hours a day. The following poems document the process of confronting death and all that it entails. Dread occurs when the reality of death is present, yet is feared deeply as one avoids the call of death: to live each day as fully as possible.

Speaking with Death on Wednesday

Nothing
that should not

peer at its center
laugh

even
when cancer devours

the IRS levies
the mind whispers

brutal acts
the hands

contemplate obeying
I examine my hands

tan ridged scars
crossing blue green veins

and look at death
with challenging glance

across my aging face
spit in the eye of time

bark at beckoning winds.
I will wait for you

in this rooted space.

This poem speaks to me of how trivial so much of what we worry about really is when juxtaposed with death. At times, it is hard to know exactly what to do with this insight. Do I not worry about trivial things and focus only on what is important? How possible would this really be without driving myself crazy? Also, how often can we really face death and not be paralyzed? Like much of life, the answer seems to be in finding balance, of finding a way to be aware of the *specter* of my own death, of using it for my benefit, but in being able to not be overcome with fear. Sometimes, I think about the death of others more easily than I do my own. Sometimes my friend Gil comes to mind, dead over two years; sometimes I use his death as motivation. Motivation to do what— to create a life for myself, to live to the fullest.

Today I felt very clearly the relationship between death and anxiety. Thinking about this poem and death, I began to feel a great sense of fear. The whole day I have felt ill at ease, nervous, almost desperate to do things, to make things right. The choice at times seems between being oblivious to the realities of our existence, or a nervous tension.

Awaken and Save

Eyes drench nothingness
deep through
the throws of the bowel.
Awaken to this:
Your children dead.
Dogs gone.
Wife a long shot ghost of the heart.
You, only aware of the sand and silt
filling your mouth, maybe the feel
of bugs feasting.
Who has time for television?
Those lost to false hopes
of eternal salvation, baby fools
suckling the breast of sorrow.
Let me just taste the breath of wind
the lonely howl of time.
TV Guide and fresh bodies be damned.
All pulled off the air by
the final network's final end.
(Furman, 2003)

I read this poem several times and find multiple meanings to it. On one level, it seems to be a battle between resignation and hope. On another level, it is another call to be motivated by death, by the finite quality of our lives.

It took me longer to write what feels like meaningful reflection for this poem. I had to actually lie down and visualize myself dead, in a box, with no contact with those I love. I was helped by attempting to feel the distance I actually experience with those who have long been dead. Our relationship to death in the West is based upon detachment and fear. We are taught to deny death, to do whatever it takes to avoid it, and certainly to avoid thinking about it. Yet, death can be the ultimate motivator. Existential thought posits that only when we have a constant awareness of our own death can we truly live. How true this feels to me, yet so exhausting.

Meaning and Identity

Meaning, and a person's ability to construct a meaningful life, lies at the heart of existential thought (Bugental, 1978). People are thought to possess the capacity for creating meaning and fulfillment even within the most dire social contexts. According to Sartre (1965), life has no inherent meaning and purpose other than what we ascribe to it through the process of being. Essentially, man/woman was born alone and will ultimately die alone; each individual must come to terms with developing their own personal mission and purpose. Mullan (1992) observed that at the core of existentialism is men/women's "quest for a reason for existing without recourse to religion or outside authority." Existential novels such as Camus' (1942) *The Stranger* and Sartre's (1938) *Nausea*, each written as an intimate, first-person account, highlight the centrality of the conscious, self-creating individual. Both highlight the importance of choice, meaning, and responsibility. These poems reflect the process of coming to understand the ways in which I ascribe meaning to my own life.

Creepers

Misnamed   indelicate   plodding,
but with the right pair of jeans,

my feet grin fungal-smiles,
they remember for me.

The knobby rubber sole
that squealed even on carpet,

the clumsy metal buckle
I fumbled with when fleeing

faces on the brink   can barely recall
the edge of dorm-room beds,

an eighteen-year-old boy
pretending he was a man,

wrestling crusted dishes   ramen dignified with shallots,
and the Infinity avoided like statistics,

and lips like whispering hammers on girls ready for love.
And now   I forget most of the details,

jeans faded from dancing thighs and sun,
clunky crimson *zapatos*   courage.

As I read this poem, I think about the complex relationship between personal identity construction and the social roles and masks that were worn. I watch my teenaged daughter now. She wears her clothes as both a uniform to fit in with her peers, but she has a style all her own, a way about her that is all hers. This is the dance of creating meaning in life, perhaps. We find ways of making life personally meaningful within the constraints of social expectations. At least, that is the way it appears to me now, forty-one-years-old, married with children. Each day I balance my own sense of destiny, my own desires, with my responsibly to others. I am not sure this is congruent with many existential authors, who often stress the tension between society and the individual. Yet, I feel this tension myself, I feel the pull of what the external world wants me to do and be. It is perhaps for this reason I feel so invested in articles such as this, that attempt to bring my whole self into the academic endeavor.

To the existentialist, identity is largely about allowing yourself to be who you are, in spite of the social pressures. This contradicts what I said above, to some degree. Sure, social responsibility is important, but existentialism pushes us to ask ourselves at what cost? This is on my mind tonight. Tonight my wife and I went out to dinner with some new acquaintances. They are nice, good, and kind people. In the restaurant, they were very loud and drank a great deal. I felt uncomfortable with people looking at our table; it was clear they were bothering others. It was difficult to be social and cordial and still honor my own needs and wants, my own values. I excused myself early and went home. Now, sitting here typing this, I feel at home with myself for the first time in hours. Part of me wishes I were easy in such social situations, that I could "go with the flow" and have fun. Yet, the older I get, the more I need my quiet, my solitude, and prefer less social contact in groups. I knew beforehand that I needed my time alone but did not honor this. And what does this have to do with the poem? Perhaps not a great deal, other than reading it before I wrote this passage reminds me of the importance of not only understanding who you are, but of being true to it.

Nothingness or the Void

In many ways related to death, the notion of nothingness, or the existential void, is important. The void is the experience that one is profoundly aware of the deep silence and emptiness of the existence of the universe, which is often faced during meditation practices. For many, coming face to face with this emptiness creates the experience of dread (discussed in an earlier section); from which they quickly run. It is facing and coming to terms with the void that allows us to be free; if we can face the void, we can face death, and ultimately life. It is from this void that true creativity can arise.

But One Time in Ten

I hold the void
but one time in ten,
pretend the roll of the dice
will never stop.

The last touch of my child.
The emperor falls again.
The armies, faded.
The dogs, past.

Burning of ice, freezing of fire
the rules of being reversed.
All you hold in worry
and pretend to fear.

Like the tears wasted.
Moments neglected as
chamomile in the cracks
of city sidewalks.

The possibilities,
the sleeping lives you
cannot remember,
but only to hold the void.

This poem could easily have been placed in the section about death. In fact, it occurs to me that each of the poems could be placed in other sections; there is so much cross-over in existential themes; they are so intertwined. This poem speaks about loss and the relationship between nothingness and loss. One of the things that is hard, at times, about writing narrative responses is that sometimes it feels like a poem says it all, or works on a level that is more metaphorical than logical. That is what I experience reading this poem now. It works on an emotional level, for me; it makes me want to accept the things I have, appreciate the connections between myself and others, and also accept how tenuous life really is. I am very privileged, and very lucky. I sit in silence reading this poem, for this is the only way to appreciate nothingness.

Holding the Void
*inspired by the statue of the same name
by Alberto Giacometti*

The name of the sculpture,
nature of the life we all lead.

At minimum, he was honest, in bronze
faceless and nameless, incandescent glowing alone.

They do not gaze for too long,
must not face that break between his fingers cupped,

the expanse of invisible, a field of giants
to be crossed with iron webbed feet drunken,

a tower to be scaled in gripless gale and ice,
a map to be read ragged and stained, the marked spot vanished.

I stare at the abyss, long to pry bronze hands apart,
wrench in between, the connections attached,

melded to knowing seer, into that void.
Perhaps it is time to close your hands.
(Furman, 2002)

One of the hardest things for me about family life is the lack of quiet. To me, silence is that space where I can get in touch with the void, with the splendor of the planet. This poem speaks to me about that vast nothingness that exists when we are alone, when there is nothing to do, nowhere to go. It is the emptiness that you find when there is no cell phone, no e-mail, no work. Just this morning, I was talking to my daughter about how her generation has become so dependent on technology for their own happiness; I hope they find ways of encountering the void so they do not fear it so.

I used to walk in nature so much more than I did. I once believed God lived in the woods, that God was the silence that existed between the trees, between my breath and the sky.

Poems of Existential Resolve

That existentialism is often considered a dark philosophy is a reflection of where it starts (e.g., death, dread), not where it ends. We start with death and end with life. The ultimate purpose of grappling with death, nothingness, and dread is that to do so means to face life and live authentically. To seek, to know, and live out one's own special meaning is to develop a deep sense of satisfaction with life and to learn to live fully in the moment of the unfolding drama that is our existence. The following poems are those that express movement beyond struggle to resolve. It is understood that struggling with existential issues is a lifetime process, not an event to be "worked through" in the classical Freudian sense of the word. However, there are moments when having bravely encountered life on life's terms leads to an inner sense of satisfaction and wholeness. These poems reflect varying degrees and aspects of such sentiments.

Like We Do

She tells you of her theories
of the moths'
sinister reproductive cycles,
how they flatten out and

hide in the windowsills
in her bras
inside the mattresses.
Wants to know
where they go
when they prepare to die?
Wonders if she will
need to vacuum corpses.

Or will they slowly decay
hidden on the oriental rug
or in our sweaters and boots.
She chatters to be close

will come back soon
more questions
theories
something essential about

the structure of existence,
or the moths, wonders if
they make love hard
like we do,

slither flat against each other
desperately taking hold of the nights,
before they will die,
like we do too.

The lives of moths seem so simplistic, mindless, determined. Maybe I merely fail to understand their world, but it is hard to know. Yet, there is a simple elegance that comes from having your purpose predetermined. Choice is painful, the process of creating meaning and moving toward it day in and day out is painful. The struggle of knowing, also, that in the end all that mattered was this very struggle. The value was in the way we lived our lives, the way we loved, the manner in which we treated others, the manner in which we created our lives. Slick, my ten-pound dog, is resting on a blanket on the couch next to my chair. He rests easily; he seems deeply at peace. How long can humans truly be at peace? Is it our nature, when we have this internal desire to live so fully? Complex lot we are, creatures with complex cognition.

It Was Meant To Be

The hail falling hits the May earth hard. We laugh at
the absurdity of such cold in spring. We refuse to submit
with t-shirts, girls with tummies naked. It is like this.
We surrender to the infinite way like a child takes to medicine.
Rebelling choking struggling the inevitability

> lost to the madness of will. Over a beer, we fret over the details,
> marvel at the wonders. Taxes, baseball, stiffening joints, time,
> the young bodies that will spoil as sure as sharp cheese in the sun,
> the minds that will ruin with redundancy, the fall of cherished idols.
> We open our mouths, catch the sky one time in every ten.
> This is the way it was meant to be.

It may not be very meaningful to say, but I miss the snow. There is something powerful about winter weather, something cleansing to the soul. Perhaps it is that you are powerless against it, like the will of the world, and that your choice is to be resolute, to transcend, to overcome. Winter teaches you to push, to push on. Spring will soon bring fresh hope; you just have to be present for it.

Conclusion

Mullan (1992) contends that the existential therapist's development as a clinician is predicated on their own ability to have faced dread, meaninglessness, and other existential dilemmas. It is important that therapists find ways to face these issues for themselves. In existentially oriented practice, the therapist must cope with the intensity that comes from engaging people about powerful existential concerns. As such, self exploration into existential themes is essential for the therapist. The writing of poetry and narrative reflections is one way of developing awareness about these issues.

In the work presented above, the process of self-reflection occurred on several levels. The poetry served as an initial exploration of the related themes. Reading the poems years after they were written forced me to reflect upon what the poems mean to me now, and what they meant to me when they were written. I was compelled to explore how I changed in my relationship to these key concepts, how I have changed as a professional helper, and as a person. Writing the narrative reflections allowed me to continue this process; I have come to appreciate my own growth and change.

It is the hope of this author that readers who are interested in existential therapy may attempt to utilize poetry, narrative, or other creative means, as a way of engaging in self-reflection. This can be done through creating poems or other works of art that focus on therapists' own experiences or those of their clients. For those readers who are new to reflective forms of writing or expression, you may wish to write narrative responses to the poems and narratives that are presented here.

References

Bakhtin, M. M. (1982). *The dialogic imagination: Four essays.* (reprint ed.). Austin, TX: University of Texas Press
Brearley, L. (2000). Exploring the creative voice in an academic context. *The Qualitative Report, 5*(3–4).
Bugental, J. F. (1978). *Psychotherapy and process: The fundamentals of an existential-humanistic approach.* Random House.
Camus, A. (1942). *The stranger.* Alfred A. Knopf.
Chan, Z. C. Y. (2003). Poetry writing: A therapeutic means for a social work doctoral student in the process of study. *Journal of Poetry Therapy, 16*(1), 5–17.
Eisner, E. W. (1981). On the differences between scientific and artistic approaches to qualitative research. *Educational Researcher, 10*(4), 5–9.
Eisner, E. W. (1991). *The enlightened eye. Qualitative inquiry and the enhancement of educational practice.* Macmillan.
Finley, S., & Knowles, J. G. (1995). Researcher as artist/artist as researcher. *Qualitative Inquiry, 1*(1), 110–142.
Frankl, V. E. (1959). *Man's search from meaning.* Pocket Books.
Furman, R. (2002). Holding the void. *13th Warrior Review, 5*(3).
Furman, R. (2003). Awaken and save. *Crimson Feet, 2.*
Furman, R. (2004a). Using poetry and narrative as qualitative data: Exploring a father's cancer through poetry. *Family, Systems & Health, 22*(2), 162–170.
Furman, R. (2004b). Exploring friendship loss through poetry. *Journal of Loss and Trauma, 9*(1), 181–187.
Furman, R. (2006). Autoethnographic poems and narrative reflections: A qualitative study on the death of a companion animal. *Journal of Family Social Work, 9*(4), 23–38.
Gallardo, H., & Furman, R. (in review). Explorations of depression: Poetry and narrative in autoethnographic qualitative research: *International Journal of Qualitative Studies on Health and Well-Being.*
Gee, J. (1991). A linguistic approach to narrative. *Journal of Narrative and Life History, 1*(1), 15–39.
Goldstein, H. (1990). The knowledge base of social work practice: Theory, wisdom, analogue, or art? *Families in Society: The Journal of Contemporary Human Services*, Winter, 31–42.
Harrower, M. (1972). *The therapy of poetry.* Charles C. Thomas.
Hirshfield, J. (1997). *Nine gates: Entering the mind of poetry.* HarperCollins.

Jourard, S. (1968). *Disclosing man to himself.* Van Nostrand Reinhold.
Krill, D. (1969). Existential psychotherapy and the problem of anomie. *Social Work.* April. 24–31.
Krill, D. (1978). *Existential social work.* Free Press.
Langer, C., & Furman, R. (2004). The tanka as a qualitative research tool: A study of a Native American woman. *Journal of Poetry Therapy, 17*(3), 165–171.
May, R. (1979). *Psychology and the human dilemma.* W. W. Norton.
Mazza, M. (1999). *Poetry therapy: Interface of the arts and psychology.* CRC Press.
Morgan, A. K., & Drury, V. B. (2003). Legitimizing the subjectivity of human reality through qualitative research. *The Qualitative Report, 8*(1).
Moustakas, C. (1994). *Phenomenological research methods.* Sage publications.
Mullan, H. (1992). Existential therapists and their group therapy practices. *International Journal of Group Psychotherapy, 42*(4), 453–458.
Poindexter, C. C. (2002). Meaning from methods: Re-presenting narratives of an HIV-affected caregiver. *Qualitative Social Work, 1*(1), 59–78.
Richardson, L. (1992). The consequences of poetic representation. In. C. Ellis and M. G. Flaherty (Eds.), *Investigating subjectivity: Research on lived experience* (pp.125–173). Sage.
Richardson, L. (1993). Poetics, dramatics, and transgressive validity: The case of the skipped line. *The Sociological Quarterly, 34*(4), 695–710.
Richardson, L. (1994). Nine poems: Marriage and the family. *Journal of Contemporary Ethnography, 23*(1), 3–13.
Richardson, L. (2001). Getting personal: Writing-stories. *International journal of qualitative studies in education, 14*(1), 33-38.
Sartre, J. P. (1938). *Nausea.* New Directions
Sartre, J. P. (1965). *Essays in existentialism.* Carol Publishing.
Smith, J. (2003). Personal communication. Boulder, Co.
Stake, R. (1994). Case studies. In N. K. Denzin & Y. S. Lincoln (Eds.), *Handbook of qualitative research* (pp. 236–247). Sage.
Stein, H. F. (2004). A window to the interior of experience. *Families, Systems, & Health, 22*(2), 178–179.
Shapiro, J. (2004). Can poetry be data? Potential relationships between poetry and research. *Families, Systems, & Health, 22*(2), 171–177.
Swingewood, A. (1991). *A short history of sociological thought.* St. Martin's.
van Deurzen-Smith, E. (1997). *Everyday mysteries: Existential dimensions of psychology.* Routledge.

Chapter 12

Poetry as Qualitative Data for Exploring Social Development and Human Experience in Latin America

Quantitative analysis is an important aid in understanding the nature of social problems in Latin America. Quantitative data can help development specialists understand the scope of social problems and provide evidence that may serve as a rationale for funding and support. Yet, to what degree do statistics aid in helping prepare those who work directly with poor and vulnerable people? Can social development indicators help line-level professionals understand the lived experiences of those they are charged to serve? Can such data lead to an increased capacity to form empathic connections and an understanding of complex psychosocial processes? While valuable in understanding the range of social dilemmas, quantitative data provide little assistance to practitioners when it comes to developing the *capacity* to work collaboratively with diverse and often oppressed people. What are needed are data that help portray the lives of people as they are lived and experienced—the raw emotions that form the text and textures of existence.

Typically, this informational need has been met by traditional qualitative data such as ethnographic accounts or phenomenological studies. However, traditional qualitative studies, which are often characterized by long narratives and thick descriptions, may not be easily or frequently consumed by line-level workers, or may be too impersonal or dense and leave readers unmoved (Francis 2002). More useful would be methods that organically convey the complexities of human emotion and cultural context yet reduce data into consumable forms.

Over the last two decades, researchers have demonstrated the value of the creative, expressive, and even performing arts in social science research for presenting data in just such a manner (Allen 1995; Blumenfeld-Jones 1995; Cole & Knowles 2001; Barone 2001; Barone &

Eisner 1997; Eisner 1981 & 1991; Finley & Knowles 1995; McNiff, 1998; Prosser 1998; Stein 2003; Willis, Smith & Collins 2000; Wong 1999). The purpose of this paper is to explore the uses of one such art form, poetry, as a means of exploring social problems and issues in Latin America. Poetry has been shown to be a valuable tool in illuminating complex social phenomena (Furman, 2004; Richardson 1993, 1994). This paper presents poems that document the lived experiences of those embroiled in various social problems, as well as the perspective of this author on his experience encountering these people and their social problems.

These poems serve to demonstrate the role of poetry as research in the social sciences. First, the role of poetry in social research will be explored to familiarize the reader with epistemological and methodological issues implicated in the use of poetry as research. Second, two sets of poems will be presented. The first set of poems is from a manuscript by the author of this article about his experiences traveling, working and conducting research in Mexico and Latin America over a several-year period. These poems were not originally conceived of as research and were written primarily with an expressive agenda in mind. The second set of poems was recently crafted specifically for the purpose of this project. Differences between these two sets of poems will be explored. Last, implications for social development research will be briefly explored in concluding comments.

As stated by Sanders (1982): "Social development as a movement embodies the philosophy of positive, humane, people-oriented development in societies" (p. x). Therefore, the ultimate aim of this article is to present a means of examining social situations that is humanistic and provides relevant data for those working in social development. In this sense, an applied form of humanistic research is advocated.

Poems as Documents of Human Reality

The purpose of research and knowledge acquisition is to document the essence of an object or experience. Regardless of the epistemological underpinnings of particular methods, the goal of social research is to explore social life in a manner that illuminates the phenomenon under investigation (Creswell 1998). Simply, the goal of research is to increase understanding (Eisner 1995). Social research methods are the vehicle through which this illumination occurs, with each method casting light upon different aspects of that which is being explored. What is needed in international social development research is a means of investigation capable of capturing the richness and complexity intricate social relationships and personal experiences. The goal of this type of research is to discover *many truths*, and not one definitive *truth*. The arts can help researchers get "more in touch" with the experiences of those they seek to explore (Stein 2003), and allow for ambiguity, complexity, and paradox.

For the past quarter century, Eisner (1981) has been exploring the possibility of a synthesis between research methodologies of the arts and the social sciences. Eisner posits that the role of the artist and the scientist are actually more similar than they are different. For instance, both seek to encounter truths about the world and communicate these truths to others. They build upon careful observation, and must make decisions about what to include and exclude (subject and variables), and careful, imaginative interpretations of data. The relationship between the researcher and the research participant is central to arts-based inspired inquiry. Willis (2002) addresses the nature of this relationship:

> In expressive writing, the mind does not grasp an object to analyze and subdue it. It attempts to hold it in consciousness, to allow its reality and texture to become etched on the mind. It holds back from closure and returns again and again to behold the object, allowing words and images to emerge from the contemplative engagement. (p.4)

The above passage is analogous to the methodological approaches used by feminist and post-modernist analysts, which have become increasingly important in research with culturally diverse populations (Chan 2003; Eisner 1981, 1991; Irwin, Mastri and Robertson 2000; Morgan and Drury 2003; Percer 1992; Poindexter 2002) Post-modern and social theorists concerned with multicultural and culturally sensitive inquiry assert that methodological principles and methods associated with logical positivism replicate unequal relationships that are imbedded in sexism, colonialism, imperialism, and neoimperialism (Ellis and Bouchner 2000; Ellis and Flaherty 1992; Lum 2000; Turner 1982). Too easily, those seeking to foster social change and empower the poor, unwittingly adopt methods that replicate relational patterns characterized by oppression (Boal 1974). This tendency is embodied in the very language of positivistic research. For example, one speaks of the *subject*, or one who is subjugated. Data, which pertain to the subject, must be *controlled*.

For development practitioners in Latin America, research methods must be in unison not merely with the nature of the investigation, but must model relational patterns that they seek to foster. Even fields such as medicine that gave birth to the biomedical model and its reliance on quantitative methods has turned to poetry as a means of understanding the social world (Donohoe & Danielson 2004; Genova 2003; Hannay and Bolton 1990; Mazza 2003). In addition to being used as a means of fostering understanding, medicine has turned to poetry and the arts as therapies for conditions that have been seen historically as biomedical in nature, such as Alzheimer's and dementia (Edwards 1990). Stories and narratives have been used by those working with clients suffering from chronic and life-threatening diseases (Frank 1998).

Poetry has become an important tool for qualitative researchers due to its capacity to facilitate in-depth and penetrating inquiry. The research poem is based upon principles of qualitative research and the fundamentals of social science. Research poems are a means of presenting data that have been empirically gathered. The purpose is to present the lived experience of those being studied. In expressive poems, the researcher/poet utilizes their own observations and self-reflection as derived insights to craft works that attempt to metaphorically penetrate the essence of an experience. Various social scientists have begun to embrace the value that the arts and humanities place upon the insights of a trained, skilled observer (James 1999; Morse 1998; Morgan & Drury 2003). For these reasons, social scientists have used the research poem, as well as interpretative poems, to explore complex social relationships. Furman (2004) utilizes autoethnographic poetry to explore his own experience of dealing with his father's cancer. He relies upon poetry written for self-therapy and self-expression as entry points into his inquiry. Through exploring the poems as data ten years after they were written through narrative reflections, he becomes "the archeologist of his own past" and his poetry is "transformed into the stuff of research" (Shapiro 2004, p. 171).

Langer and Furman (2004) utilized two poetry-based methodologies to explore the sense of self-identities of Native Americans and their development of biculturality. Working from traditional qualitative interview transcripts, they crafted research poems, a compressed form utilizing the most essential words of research participants derived from axial coding, and interpretative poems, which allow for the infusion of the researcher's own subjective understanding of the data. Through these methods, they were able to deeply and holistically capture what has been referred to as the "lived experience" of their research participants. Others have utilized poetry in a similar manner. For instance, Poindexter (2002), utilizing methods borrowed from linguistics (Gee 1991), presents research poems of HIV patients and their caretakers. Her sensitive reduction of their stories, also derived from qualitative interviews, uses line breaks, capitalization and other grammatical devices to portray the experiences, beliefs, and emotions of her participants. Through this process, she successfully portrays the tone of her interviews without needing to rely on footnotes and other explanatory methods. Such methods lead to a sense of compression whereby the essence of the data comes through quickly and evocatively. Academics who traditionally rely upon methods based on logical positivism or reductionism will certainly question these methods on traditional criteria such as reliability, validity, and generalizability. Yet, several scholars have observed that these criteria, as traditionally utilized, serve as gatekeeping devices that preserve the hegemony of quantitative methods and its associated knowledge (Lincoln and Guba; 1985; Patton 1999). Aguinaldo (2003), in a social constructivist reconstruction of the concept of validity, suggests that researchers should no longer ask "is this valid?" but instead ask "what is this research valid for?" In so doing, the author repositions validity as a discursive guide that forces us to grapple with the appropriate uses of various types of knowledge and unpacks unspoken power assumptions embedded within any investigative endeavor. Therefore, it is not that research is valid or invalid but that data sources are representations of reality that can inform not only about the phenomena itself but the social rules and implications underlying research. Further, Stein (2004) suggests that good poetry and art, while not generalizable in the traditional scientific sense, is metaphorically generalizable. That is, poetry begins with specific examples, and through the use of metaphor, the reader is able to "gain access to the breadth and depth of human experience" (Stein 2004, p. 179). To Richardson (2001) part of the value of such inquiry is that it "frees us from trying to write a single text in which everything is said at once to everyone, a text where the complete life is told. The life can be told over and over again, differently nuanced" (p. 36).

Methodology

Two different sets of poems are presented. The first set of poems is purely of the interpretative variety. They were not written as research, yet may be judged by the degree to which they capture the essence of the experiences they explore and are metaphorically generalizable. Do the poems sensitize the reader to the issues at hand? Do they stimulate self-reflection and understanding in the reader? The second set of poems was written more specifically with a research agenda in mind. The first four poems in this collection were written about an orphanage in Managua, Nicaragua. This orphanage, other social institutions, and phenomena were observed with the intention of exploring them through poetry.

Field notes were taken, and then coded through open and axial coding methods, through which themes were elicited. Once themes were elicited, poems were crafted, utilizing data from field notes as well as interpretation and reflective impressions. These works, to varying degrees, move beyond the research poems in the strictest sense, as they do not merely reposition and re-represent data, but are a synthesis of the observed data and interpretations of data. Data collection, analysis, and implications are interwoven into the works. It is for this reason that the poems are allowed to stand alone, without any contextualizing comments. Also, the second set of poems is less aesthetically crafted than the first set. The primary goal was not to create aesthetically mature works, but to present the use of the methods as a means of illustration.

Poems [1]
Poetry Group One

Lying in Wait (Furman 2002a)
Written in the voice of a prostitute in Mexico City

I sit on this bench, filth,
outside the hotel, more filth
rent by the night, if I am paid.
Wait for men to want, not me,
but the skin, the flesh, the folds

---

[1] Many of these poems, along with other poems the authors experience in Latin America, are also included in *Trotting Race of Time* (2020, University Professors Press).

they lie into, but do not touch,
my eyes to the ceiling and
mind other places. My body open,
things they never will force out, mine.
I will lie there and wait. They will finish.
They will dress quickly, our eyes will not meet.
They think about their wives,
or wonder about my health. I will wash.
I will scrub many times. I read in a magazine,
that if one touches you, their cells stay
with you for years. No matter, I will
scrape with rough soap and rinse. They will be gone, almost.
But not from my mind. Memories last
longer than sweet first kisses
I can hardly remember.
But for now, I will wait, and worse if they
do not come, do not tell me what they want,
do not pay me for what will sadden us both.
Worse to sit here painted, starched to the bench,
hours pass the bones ache and muscles sore.
The boredom is nearly as bad as the act.
Here comes one now. Asks me to use my mouth.
I will promise him this, but will only use my hand.
He may hit me, he may not. This one looks timid.
He will be scared of my distant gaze and wide-eyed smile,
    teeth.
He will leave quickly, like most of the rest.
He will not hit me. Christmas, only five months away.

Que Que
Alone in the gray soft shadows
the scowl of caverns haunted
arms crossed silent,
and what nine year old
folds her arms in anger, but those
abandoned by death some roadside
or in shanty shacks baking alone?
She waits for voices hurled between fragile ears,
her only communication a sound or
maybe a word, no one knows.
Que que, what what. Does she intend

her yearning calls to compel us to know?
She follows me around the courtyard
and tilts her head to shoulder whispering, que que,
what, what, phonics and eyes begging us to not fail.
I wonder how come not, why why?
Perhaps not yet ready,
never ready
to comprehend the reasons
for being thrown away
like littered, scavenged bones
to the scrap-heap

Por Que (Furman 2002b)

We eat tacos and meats on the street
by the metro station market,
breaded meat *milanesa*
tender flaky pork in green mole.
Suck on the bone to not miss a drop.
Beaded dull colored beef,
tropical soda pink and pulpy.
The waitress, harried, smiling,
brings them out one by one,
slowly, for those who must learn to wait.
A begging couple enters,
his legs thinner than the bones on my plate,
head cocked to the side with eyes
pleading, a look prepared for our guilt.
His shoes too large wagging like truck mud flaps.
we turn attention to tortillas
to soak up last drops of sauce.
A guitar player strolls in full of songs,
Sappy in any language. We give him some pesos,
Finish our plates to the rumble of stomachs filled.

The Next Open Door (Furman 2002c)

1
An amplifier strapped to his back
he belts out blind songs of desire
in the subway for centavos.

His change cup held forward,
He waltzes down the crowded aisle smiling,
Lips parted, his hands raised with the microphone
Like an excommunicated lounge act priest.

2
Selling candy for a peso is a rough way to go,
no one buying,car after car.
Awake at five to ride by six until midnight.
Why not grab a knife
and do things right?
But he belts his jingle in rhyming hawker song
the locals and tourists look away, stare at their feet.
He leaves downtrodden, dead for some seconds,
Rejuvenated as he walks though the next open door
to live small dreams that quickly fade.

We Supply the Dead (Furman 2003)

*They supply the weapons,
we supply the dead*

   Salvadorian archbishop Rivera y Damas

Rusty crowbars pry
marble smooth tires
recycling rubber each time
to the less fortunate,
but still more so
than some.
The death squads hold our hands
and walk us across the road
to freedom. Lack of beans do not bother
the rotting lips of traitors
and the less stomachs to be fed
the less angry mouths to scream.
Summers have become peaceful
here in the hillsides.

Tegucigalpa, Honduras

Is a bus cutting through the night,
rumble and exhaust spent and disregarded,
graffiti painted wall pleading and begging and raging
for Gringos to leave with their assassins and AIDS,
secluded airfield for cocaine and *Contras*
for slaving import and murdering exports,
Comeaguela sex tour drunken madness for Marine advisors
the smell from the river and markets squabble shooting
 desperation,
dollar sign whore or a skinny dog limbless in the gutter
 squalor,
an abused child that wants no more,
the hopeless screams in the night echoed through walls in
 homeless hotels
and a stabbing that goes bad for both and a desert mirage flesh
 smelling.
Kafka without angst, Hemingway with simple lines,
ice cream cone fallen to dirt with a bitter cherry dripping,
a deaf god in the face of desperate supplication,
a banana child with failure to thrive in bondingless distance,
a scream of vocal cords cut, wavering through moonless night.

Of Conquests Dreamt

Mariachis lounge in the square,
hauling their horn cases,
eating tongue tacos,
praying for five dollar gigs
to pay for rents back due.
Men peer over corral doors
as drag queens flirt and dance
with others who can pay for their drinks, for them.
Strip bar neon lights flash unsteady,
hours sagging, silent girls peer out the doors
to temp with fantasy so thinly veiled.
A mother holds her naked toddler,
vagina pointed towards the street,
urine spouting forth, flowing past the tourists
who blind, flip through guidebooks
for the next attraction to be crossed off their lists,
accountants of borrowed existence,

hash marks in the wooden beds of conquests dreamt.

Alone

What do you do but beg?
Abandoned beneath the doorway
face like the moon, beaten, alone?
The pastel colonial elegance.
The sway of lovely ignoring skirts.
The blistering sting. The shrapnel cuts. We are all alone.

La Zona Rosa

The children begging place their empty paper cups between
the ropes of outdoor café, of the tequila sipping gold clad
   crowd,
they watch lips and laughter, smell treats sealed,
homeless dogs rolled in sad balls kicked in
cruel soccer practice by feet in leather and lizard,
Indigenous women sell dolls for near nothing
by the dance club line, the lovely powdered faces,
poise their legs just so, music, thumping, western,
electronic, the threads of her brilliant blouse frayed,
cyber cafes, padded couches and cappuccinos.

Trolls (Furman, 2002d)

In front of the auto shop, the sign that reads,
multi-health services for your car,
the one legged man in the Frankenstein rickshaw wheelchair,
begs for change in the center lane
of the highway that leads out of town.
He itches legs real and missing,
the spot where the pant leg sewn shut with cord and dirt,
the exhaust that coughs, the unconcern of the cars,
his hand trolls for change like a lure skimming the top of
   frozen pond.

Morning in Morelia (Furman, 2002e)

He wakes each morning at three,
grinds fresh corn by hand,
rolls the dozens of tamales,
salsa roja, verde, dulce,
queso y especial.
Places the fifty pound pot,
on the rack of his bicycle,
with the missing left petal and slumping frame,
and rides down the mountain dark road
in the moonlight hiding the edge so near,
to take his place in the market.
In his faded torn shirt,
American designer made in prior life,
the belt tightened to its final, yearning hole,
his hair slicked carefully to his scalp,
he calls his goods to the crowd.
To the bent old women shaping the perfect tortilla,
to the blind boy peeling fruit with razor knife
swirling around fingers like foam on high seas,
to the ribwide sleeping dogs of shallow breath,
to each, faithful, purified, a nun behind monastery walls,
the results of prayer second to the faith, words lonely
placed into the crisp forgotten air.

San Simon (Furman, 2002f)

They bring offerings of roasted chicken and grain liquor,
cigars and cigarettes, to the saint so human viceful failed.
Drop to their knees, ask for miracles for their sick or dying,
relief from card game debt or to sway fantasy love heart.
From his decaying wooden thrown above, black tuxedo plastic
   wry grin,
granting wishes for sinners who can do no right.
These are the ones he favors, derelict saint beloved
part Mayan, part Catholic, Guatemalan holy mutt,
yet shared by all, the parish priest in conforming red robe,
the Quiche holy men outside, their swaying supplication
and burning mirth and fires flailing to the above,
the lover who held the waist of thin isthmus dancing for all

times.
They pray and rebel so softly, trampled by giants always,
the Spanish armored knights, the moguls of dollar bitter fruit,
dictator death squads, failed coup after failed coup.
Better to bring lean pork and smooth rum to the wicked saint,
who quietly conjures his magic, the other saints long fast
asleep.

84 days (Furman, 1993)

84 days
from hell to hell from death squads'
black hand neverness
to liberty's branding cattle prods
blue suits and steel
safeguard the indelible line
between us and them
between our separate
forms of misery
84 days
form Huehuetenagno
its streets of indigenous brightness
the markets of peppers screaming
campesinos working Shangri-La
emerald hillsides of coffee
to Los Angeles
pools filled with rocky dreams
air thick enough
to roller skate on
shattered hopes
stuffed into working sacks of denial
84 days
to walk they said
across the frontier
of the disappeared
greening genitals
stuffed into mouths
that could not confess
fast enough by roadside's rotting heat
across the Sierra Madres
where Guatemalan bones

turn to Mexican earth
to Tijuana's human coyote
rivers polluted death
children with no arms
drinking in next generation's
children with no arms
or worse
it took you five days
and with your plastic freedom
six hours back
now in front of silicon
wondering how
you will rationalize this one

Poetry: Group Two

Emilio

What to say to you, words? These you do not understand. Or perhaps I sell you short. Perhaps we all do. I am sorry your tortures are your triumphs. That each bite of food that finds its way to your stomach is matched by two that trickle into your lungs. That at seven your limbs are brittle, useless, that your brain was drained before you had a chance. I am sorry that I obsess about the ten extra pounds I carry around my middle, when you can carry nothing. Mostly, I am sorry, perhaps, that even if I read these words to you, it would mean little, and certainly would help even less than that.

Hangs

how my own sadness
hangs above this room
like a blind prince holding court
in a land of misunderstanding

Pain and Hope

She gurgles her excitement
at a photograph.
at her love of a shoulder

at a wayward ray of sun.
she follows each with
the bent curl of broken hands
bent and crooked,
useless threats are her fingers.

Gladys

your cupped hands open
they strain, brittle
your eyes are all that
do not betray you
trapped
behind a body
broken and unworkable
secrets
that only you know
your lips are turncoats
we are all frail of spirit
and love is imperfect

What to Do?

1
Why this small hand
reaching toward me?
supplication
for what?
What is it that I will give
or not?
Pennies, not
a future or love.
what is this love we speak of
when scraps suffice?
life is a whip,
the future, blistering skin.

2
read that 30% of the children
leave school before age ten,
this explains these small hands

selling gum,
or the teenagers in the park,
selling their ripened flesh
and innocence never owned.
My pink skin cremated
in the sun of shame.
Revolution?

1
In the collective taxi
I ask if things were better now
or during the revolution
when I was last here.
now he says, there are more cars,
jewels, ropa Americana,
things,
more loans, more work,
more work to work off loans,
and more knives late at night
petitioning their way into affluence.

2
how to ask someone
if fifty cents is too much to pay
for a cab ride?

3
the emerald green parrot
outside the museum
of the heroes and martyrs,
museum of the revolution,
killed off by what?
a gringo blockade, this blistering heat,
inevitable greed, a fault of philosophy?
but this parrot, squeaks his *Hola.*
I wait, listen for history. El dolor del pueblo.
Nothing. Nada.
Solo Hola. Hello.
My breath is short. Life.
My hand upon the crumbling stucco wall,
this vertical earth, this heart that listens

throughout time.
O' this sun is wicked.
but worse, the incineration
of hope never realized.

4
How to sing to you
of corrugated metal
thrusting from a ruined edifice,
maybe an unworthy church,
or an enemy—
but pastels fade from blue to orange,
from the sun's sweeping brush of destiny,
these words are not my heart,
my heart is a fluttering monkey,
dancing to the organ grinder's
favorite song,
my heart is unknowable,
my heart is a prison of humor,
my life a fluttering monkey,
a flickering speak in time,
my heart is Bukowski's cheap red wine—
he is dead.
My heart the florescent dream
of a kindly spring,
or the wipe of sweat from my brow.

5
In the voice of a 48 year old man met in the park
I graduated 12 years ago,
but what jobs are there now?
See that building there? Before,
three hundred worked, now twenty.
Here, in this town square,
there are friends of mine,
accountants, lawyers, professionals all,
they do as I, we sell what we can,
for bread, to live, but we feel shame
from those who forgot our
past positions. My children?
Now they are part of the police,

all they could find after college.

Conclusion

Skeptics of the role of poetry and the arts will argue that insights gleaned from such accounts are too highly subjective to be of value. Yet, why should the personal insights of social scientists be deemed unimportant? Such insights are the manifestation of one of the most important types of knowledge: practice wisdom—the synthesis of years of training and the absorption and integration of theory, facts, and values (Goldstein 1990). Artistically inspired research may not be capable of analysis or explanation in the positivist or modernist sense, but is able to express complex social phenomena and lived experience (Reason 1998).

Poetic reflections encourage self-reflexivity by the researcher. Such reflexivity can help guard against research being a colonial, ethnocentric undertaking (Alsop 2002). By evaluating their own experiences of being *with* people, as opposed to merely documenting them, researchers are encouraged to explore and unpack their own biases. The reflexive process in which creative arts researchers must engage may help researchers explore the relevance and potential meaning of their work. This process may be of particular value to social development practitioners who can use these techniques to develop increased insight, empathy, and compassion.

References

Aguinaldo, J. P. (2003). Rethinking validity in qualitative research from a social constructionist perspective: From 'Is this valid research?' to 'What is this research valid for?' *The Qualitative Report 9*, 1: 127–135.

Allen, P. (1995). *Art is a way of knowing.* Shambala Press.

Alsop, C. K. (2002). Home and away: Self-reflexive Auto/ethnography. *Forum Qualitative Social Research* 3 (3).

Barone, T. 2001. "Science, art and the predisposition of educational researchers," *Educational Research* 30(7), 24–29.

Barone, T. & Eisner, E. (1997). Arts-based educational research In R. M. Jaeger (Ed.), *Contemporary methods for research in education.* American Education Research Association.

Blumenfeld-Jones, D. (1995). Dance as a mode of research representation. *Qualitative Inquiry*, 1(4), 391–401.

Boal, A. (1974). *Theater of the oppressed.* Pluto Press.

Chan, Z. (2003). Poetry writing: A therapeutic means for a social work doctoral student in the process of study. *Journal of Poetry Therapy, 16*(1), 5–17.

Cole, A. L., & Knowles, G. (2001). *Lives in context: The art of life history Research.* Altamira Press.

Creswell, J. W. (1998). *Qualitative inquiry and research design.* Sage.

Donohoe, M., & Danielson, S. (2004). A community approach to medical humanities. *Medical Education, I*(2), 204–207.

Edwards, M. E. (1990). Poetry: Vehicle for retrospection and delight. *Generations, 14*(1), 61–62.

Eisner, E. (1981). On the differences between scientific and artistic approaches to qualitative research. *Educational Researcher, 10*(4), 5–9.

Eisner, E. (1991). *The enlightened eye: Qualitative inquiry and the enhancement of educational practice.* Macmillan.

Eisner, E. (1995). What artistically crafted research can help us understand about schools. *Educational Theory, 45*(1), 1–5.

Ellis, C., & Bouchner, A. (2000). Autoethnography, personal narrative, Reflexivity. In N. Denzin & Y. Lincoln (Eds.), *Handbook of qualitative research.* (2nd ed.; pp. 733–768). Sage.

Ellis, C., & Flaherty, M. (1992). *Investigating subjectivity: Research on lived experience.* Sage.

Finley, S., & Knowles, G. (1995). Researcher as artist/artist as researcher. *Inquiry, 1*(1), 110–142.

Francis, M. D. (2002). *Interpretations of development: Critical research and the development encounter in KwaZulu-Natal.* Paper presented at the 8th annual qualitative/critical methods. http://criticalmethods.org/p98.mv.

Frank, A. W. (1998). Just listening: Narrative and deep illness. *Families, Systems & Health, 16*(3), 197–212.

Furman, R. (1993). *84 days.* Free Lunch.

Furman, R. (2002a). Lying in wait. *Steel Point Quarterly* (Spring).

Furman, R. (2002b). Por que. *Poor Mojo's Almanac* 86.

Furman, R. (2002c). The next open door. *Ascent* (May).

Furman, R. (2002d). Trolls. *Wild Velvet.*

Furman, R. (2002e). Morning in Morelia. *Steel Point Quarterly* (Spring).

Furman, R. (2002f). San Simon. *Nasty* (March).

Furman, R. (2003). *We supply the dead. Thorny Locust* 2.

Furman, R. (2004). Using poetry and narrative as qualitative data: Exploring a father's cancer through poetry. *Family, Systems & Health, 22*(2), 162–170.

Furman, R. (unpublished manuscript). Poetic explorations of adolescent identity: Authoethnographic poems.

Gee, James. (1991). A linguistic approach to narrative. *Journal of Narrative and Life History, 1*(1), 15–39.

Genova, N. (2003). Expanding our concept of the medical literature: The value of the humanities in medicine. *Journal of the American Academy of Physician Assistants, 16*(3), 61–64.

Goldstein, H. (1990). "The limits and art of understanding in social work practice. *Families in Society, 80*(4), 385–395.

Hannay, D., & Bolton, G. (1990). Therapeutic in primary care: Feasibility study. *Primary Care Psychiatry, 5*(4), 157–160.

Irwin, R., Mastri, R., & Robertson, H. (2000). Pausing to reflect: Moments in feminist collaborative action research. *The Journal of Gender Issues in Art and Education, 1*(1), 43–56.

James, P. (1999). Rewriting narratives of self: Reflections from an action research study. *Educational Action Research, 7*(1), 85–103.

Langer, C., & Furman, R., (2004). Exploring identity and assimilation. Research and interpretative poems. *Forum: Qualitative Social Research, 5*(2).

Lincoln, Y., & Guba, E. (1985). *Naturalistic inquiry.* Sage.

Lum, D. (2000). *Social work practice and people of color: A process-stage Approach.* Wadsworth.

Mazza, N. (2003). *Poetry therapy: Theory and practice.* Brunner-Routledge.

McNiff, S. (1998). *Arts-based research.* Jessica Kingsley Publishers.

Morgan, A., & Drury, V. (2003). Legitimizing the subjectivity of human reality through qualitative research. *The Qualitative Report, 8*(1).

Morse, J. (1998). *Critical issues in qualitative research methods.* Sage.

Patton, M. (1999). *Qualitative evaluation and research methods* (2nd ed.), Sage.

Patton, M. (1999). Enhancing the quality and credibility of qualitative analysis. *Health Services Review, 34*(5),1189–1208.

Percer, L H. (1992). Going beyond the demonstrable range in educational scholarship: Exploring the intersections of poetry and research. *The Qualitative Report* 7(2).

Poindexter, C. (2002). Meaning from methods: Re-presenting narratives of an HIV- affected caregiver. *Qualitative Social Work, 1*(1), 59–78.

Prosser, J. (Ed.) (1998). *Image-based research: A sourcebook for qualitative research.* Falmer.

Reason, P. (1998). *Human inquiry in action: Developments in new paradigm research.* Sage.

Richardson, L. (1993). Poetics, dramatics, and transgressive validity: The case of the skipped line. *The Sociological Quarterly, 34*(4), 695–710.

Richardson, L. (1994). Nine poems: Marriage and the family. *Journal of Contemporary Ethnography, 23*(1), 3–13.

Richardson, L. (2001). Getting personal: Writing stories. *Qualitative Studies in Education, 14*(1), 33–38.

Sanders, D. (1982). *The developmental perspective in social work.* The University of Hawaii.

Shapiro, J. (2004). Can poetry be data? Potential relationships between poetry and research. *Families, Systems, & Health, 22*(2), 171–177.

Stein, H. F. (2003). The inner world of workplaces: Accessing this world through poetry, narrative, literature, music and visual art." *Consulting Psychology Journal: Practice and Research, 55*(2), 84–93.

Stein, H. F. (2004). A window to the interior of experience. *Families, Systems, & Health, 22*(2), 178–179.

Turner, V. (1982). *From ritual to theatre.* Performing Arts Journal Publications.

Willis, P. (2002). Poetry and poetics in phenomenological research. *Indo-Pacific Journal of Phenomenology,* I(1), 1–19.

Willis, P., Smith, R., & Collins, E. (2000). *Being seeking telling: Expressive Approaches to qualitative adult education research.* Post Pressed.

Wong, L. (Ed.). (1999). *Shootback: Photos by kids in the Nairobi Slums.* Booth-Clibborn.

Chapter 13

Autoethnographic Explorations of Researching Older Expatriate Men: Magnifying Emotion Using the Research Pantoum

Introduction

Jane Hirshfield (1997) observed that poetry magnifies and clarifies life. The notion of research magnifying the lived experience is an important one that at times has been lost in the positivist discourse about the aims of social research (Eisner, 1981; van Manen, 2006). Expressive researchers and scholars have flung aside the shackles of false objectivity and detachment (Ellis & Bouchner, 2000), and have sought to value the depths of the lived experiences of research participants and researchers alike (Francis, 2002). Researchers' capacity to use their own humanity to connect with the humanity of others is essential; increasing our own capacity for emotional depth and insight is certainly a prerequisite to our producing research of emotional depth and sophistication (Denzin, 2003). Many research methodologies have been developed that seek to explore and represent the lived experiences in evocative, passionate ways that can help inform various "consumers" of research (Finley & Knowles, 1995).

While traditional ethnographic data, thick descriptions, and other evocative methods do have the ability to present people's emotions in context, they are at times too dense and long to be of value to people who are not likely to read research studies (Cahnmann, 2003). Additionally, the lack of compression and immense density in most in-depth qualitative studies can often obscure the most salient affective messages and themes that researchers wish to communicate. Evocative as they are, they often do not implement means of data reduction and presentation that allow for readers to connect to the core messages and insights of the researchers.

Many of these concerns have contributed to what has often been referred to as the "crisis of representation" (Denzin, 1994; Richardson,

2000). Those responding to these dilemmas have experimented with writing and data representational methods that present the lives of others in evocative and creative ways (Poindexter, 2002; van Manen, 2002). The strength of these diverse means of data presentation rests in their privileging the creativity of their authors in exploring methods that are most congruent with their own sensibilities, talents, and understanding of the data. One such tool that has been developed by researchers from various disciplines has been referred to as the research poem or poetic inquiry (Faulkner, 2009). In poetic inquiry, researchers use various methods to present data in creative and evocative ways. As such, it has highlighted the spirit of creativity that has typified what Hemmingson (2008) posited as a needed antidote to various scholars positioning their methods, experimental as they may be, as "the right way."

Yet, what of the scholar who wishes to experiment with such approaches, yet finds him/herself without the artistic sensibilities (or confidence in such sensibilities) to engage in such work? Might not some forms or structures assist them, without being overly prescriptive as to hinder their experimentation?

The purpose of this article is to explore how the research poem is a valuable tool for qualitative researchers who wish to highlight powerful emotions in evocative ways that seek to create a sense of "emotional resonance" with their audience. More specifically, as a means of providing a potential method and one structure to those interested in experimenting with poetic inquiry, this article will explore how the poetic form of the Pantoum is a powerful vehicle for focusing on and magnifying human emotion. In a previous study, the author demonstrated how different poetic forms and structures lead to different data representational effects (Furman, 2006).

The Pantoum is a useful form for researchers, as its use of repeating lines can create an evocative and haunting "ringing" of emotional content discovered through various data collection methods. In this paper, autoethnographic research poems are presented based upon the author's field notes of his research with older expatriate men. The poems are autoethnographic in that they explore the researcher's connections to broader socio-cultural issues implicated in the process of conducting research with his respondents (Reed-Danahay, 1997).

The paper will meet its aims in the following ways. First, it will explore how poetry can be used as a tool in expressive research and can be a valuable vehicle for focusing and magnifying emotion and meaning. Second, it will explore the use of autoethnography in research, and situate autoethnographic methods as a tool for social research. Third, the form utilized for data representation in this article, the Pantoum, is described. Finally, four research pantoums are presented that explore key themes that the author grappled with in his research with older, expatriate men. I end with these poems and not traditional concluding comments, in the spirit of the poetic tradition's call to "show don't tell." The poems should speak for themselves.

Poetic Inquiry

Arguments that pit one methodology over another often neglect to account for the multiplicity of needs for various forms of data. An important use of research is to help practitioners from many professions (i.e., education, social work, nursing, counseling, etc.) understand and develop empathy for the lived experience of others (Witkin, 2014). Research methods that focus on the powerful emotions of people may be useful in sensitizing practitioners to how people experience various affective states; such data may better prepare them for contending with powerful and even extreme emotions than other types of data.

To be an effective portrayer of emotion, methods should amplify or magnify the affective experience. Magnification does not connote alteration; when a biologist peers into a microscope, thereby magnifying a specimen, they are more able to view essential aspects of their subject and their details more clearly and with minimal distractions. So too, in applying or magnifying emotions, they are highlighted and enlarged, or brought from a background consisting of a multitude of information to the foreground of awareness.

One means of magnifying meaning in research is through the use of literary and artistic means of data (re)presentation. Such methods are often grouped under the broad classification of arts-based or expressive arts research (Leavy, 2008). Expressive arts research uses various artistic genres such as poetry, music, art, and dance to present data in a way that may preserve the "lived experience" of research subjects (Finley & Knowles, 1995). According to Willis (2002), research that incorporates or relies upon the expressive arts is looking not to analyze or constrain meaning, but to elaborate and enhance it.

Poetic inquiry, or the research poem, has been used throughout the research process. For instance, researchers have conceptualized poetry itself as a form of highly condensed affective data (Furman 2004a; 2004b; 2006; Furman, 2006; Furman, Lietz, & Langer, 2006). Poetry has even been used in research for the generation of research questions (Leung & Lapum, 2005). Perhaps the most common means of utilizing poetry in research is as a method of data (re)presentation (Prendergast, 2009). Research poems can be written from data as a way of presenting the results of research implementing various data- collection strategies. One of the first researchers to utilize research poetry was Richardson (1992), who used research poems drawn from interview data to more fully capture the "lived experience" of women's family life.

Poindexter (1997) crafted research poems based on her work with HIV-affected caregivers. Later, Poindexter (2002) used the linguistic work of Gee (1991) to help her standardize the process of creating a research poem. By using Gee's work, Poindexter was able to develop procedures that provide structure for her crafting of research poetry. The notion of structure is essential, as it allows for researchers to explore the strengths and weaknesses of various techniques.

Furman and others have also adopted various methods for crafting research poetry (Furman, 2006, Furman, Lietz, & Langer, 2006; Langer & Furman, 2004). By utilizing existing poetic forms, research poetry helps provide a container to highlight essential themes found in the data, regardless of the method of data analysis. Langer and Furman (2004) explore two main ways of crafting research poetry. The first method uses only the words of the subject from narratives, interviews, or other types of rich qualitative data that have been analyzed thematically. When using this method, only exact words from the original or transcribed text are placed into the poem. The words can be rearranged or juxtaposed in order to highlight themes, or to convey complex or conflicting ideas. A second method of crafting poems in research is writing interpretive poems based upon the researcher's sense of the data. Interpretive poems differ from research poems in that they can use words and ideas that may not be found explicitly in the data itself. An interpretive poem can explore anything from the actual lived experience of the research participant, to the relationship of the researcher to participants, or even the research process itself. In writing interpretive poems, the researcher must be reflexive, aware of their own positionality, and have a deep understanding of the strengths and limitations of their data.

Depending upon the impact the researcher wants their work to have, different poetic forms may be utilized. Different poetic forms and structures possess different features that create various possibilities (Furman, 2006). For example, the Tanka, due to its highly condensed five-sentence line structure of limited syllables, was found to be useful in capturing the essence of the data being analyzed (Furman 2006). The Pantoum, on the other hand, was useful for highlighting affective aspects of original data through the use of repeating lines that move throughout the poem's form (Furman, 2006).

Through the use of poetry and poetic forms, lengthy and complex data can be presented in a shorter form than traditional ethnographic accounts and narratives. These ethnographic accounts, while providing thick descriptions, may be unwieldy or hard to digest for consumers of research. They may also at times be too impersonal to move readers to really understand research participants' lived experience (Francis, 2002). For these reasons, research poetry is a powerful tool that seasoned and new expressive researchers can use to enhance the affective magnitude of their work.

Autoethnography/Autoethnographic Poems

Autoethnography is a method and methodology of research that seeks to explore sociocultural phenomena by using the self as a vehicle of research (Chang, 2008: Pelias, 2003; Philaretou & Allen, 2006). Richardson (2000) observed that autoethnography is "Highly personalized, revealing texts in which authors tell stories about their own lived experiences, relating the personal to the cultural (p. 935).

Autoethnographies vary in the degree and manner in which they focus on the self (auto), on a cultural group (ethno) and in the tools they use to engage in inquiry (graphy) (Reed-Danahay, 1997; Foster, McAllister, & O'Brien, 2006). However, all autoethnographers engage in a process of casting the gaze of the researcher on themselves, using these insights as a means through which to explore the larger world. How this is done, to some degree, depends on the goals, methods, and epistemological orientations of the researcher.

In this sense, it has been suggested that autoethnographies may be classified into two subtypes, evocative or expressive (Ellis, Adams & Bochner, 2011) and analytical (Anderson, 2006). Evocative or expressive autoethnographies utilize methods from the humanities, the arts, and narrative-based inquiry. The focus of such research is on the ways in which people's lived experiences, as told through evocative and powerful narratives, can provide insights into the explored phenomena. Ellis and Bochner (2000) privilege the power of emotion and empathic resonance as a means of contextual, personal truth telling. Expressive autoethnographers may or may not always "bend" their narratives consciously and expressly back to larger social issues. Some expressive autoethnographers allow their narratives to become unanalyzed, "lived" exemplars of larger social issues. Such researchers do not view the role of the expressive researcher to reduce their story to easy-to-comprehend generalizations, but instead to create an evocative, emotional resonance with their audience (Willis, 2002).

Analytical autoethnographies, less common in literature, are less influenced by the humanities and arts-based traditions and more by the social sciences (Anderson, 2006). Analytical autoethnographers tend to utilize methodologies that are more congruent with various qualitative approaches that use triangulation of methodology, often beyond the lived experience of the self into collecting data from and about ethers (Chang, 2008). Additionally, analytical autoethnographies tend to (but not always) utilize more explicit theoretical lenses by which to understand the data.

Autoethnography is a recent form, and as such, it is still under development; insights and strengths from various types of autoethnographies should be used as they meet the aims of a particular study. For example, while expressive autoethnographers tend to privilege complete narratives, they certainly can utilize methods that are evocative and powerful yet not privilege long and complete narratives. For instance, Furman (2005) used poetry and reflective memos to explore the personal and sociocultural meaning of the death of his companion animal. Further, analytical autoethnographies most certainly can rely on powerfully evocative text and may at times use privileged insights into the self. I would argue that taken together these two stands of autoethnography actually can be viewed as various strategies and tools of the thoughtful and methodologically evolving autoethnographer. As the approach is relatively new, it is important that researchers utilize various tools whereby they can explore the individual as a means of speaking of larger group and social truths.

Methods

The Pantoum

Prior to exploring the methods of this study, a brief description of the poetic from used in this study, the Pantoum, is presented. In the 15th century, the pantoum originated in Malaysia as a simple folk poem. Originally, it consisted of two rhyming couplets, but as it was introduced into Western countries, its form has evolved and has become more structurally variable. The pantoum now is a poem consisting of any number of stanzas, whose second and fourth lines become the first and third lines of the next stanza. Typically, the last line of a pantoum is the same as the first line. The repetitive nature of the pantoum presents an almost haunting quality. Pantoums are emotionally evocative, and have been ideal for the expression of intense topics. I present this poem, written by me not for research purposes, as an example. Notice the effect of repetition, and how starting or ending stanzas with certain lines can create powerful emotional responses. While the intentional use of line positioning is essential, the author of a Pantoum is often surprised and challenged by the juxtapositioning of lines in future stanzas. The evaluation of position and its effect compels the author of a Pantoum to contend with various layers of meaning and consciousness that are essential in autoethnographic exploration (Ellis and Bochner, 2000; Humphreys, 2005).

Pantoum for Her

Brains leaking through my ears   my years with you,
pawned to prisons,   priests,
we traded clubbings between whispering songs,
and in the end, vacuous.

Pawned to prisons,   priests,
dog rectal tumors, rent, chigger orphans   the rest,
in the end, vacuous,
faded photos chucked into the sea.

Dog rectal tumors, rent, chigger orphans   the rest,
saddled with the shit of space   you crawled away,
fading photos chucked into the sea.
Spent love like cholesterol, battery acid, phlegm.

And taking stock of our years? What's left?
We traded clubbings between whispering songs,
spent love like cholesterol, battery acid, phlegm,
Brains leaking through my ears   my years with you.

The following pantoums were written from field notes I have taken while conducting research with older expatriate men. For the last several years, I have conducted in-depth interviews with men 55 and older who have expatriated to Costa Rica, Thailand, Mexico, and the Philippines. In addition to my interviews and interview transcriptions,

I have taken dozens of pages of field notes focusing on my emotional reactions to the research participants, their lives, social conceptions about them, and observations about my own life. While I have learned a great deal about their lives, I have also learned a great deal about myself, my own sense of identity, aging, and masculinity. While such insights have at times been denigrated as constituting "navel gazing" (Holt, 2003), this type of self-reflection and reflexivity is invaluable for those of us who not only are researchers but who teach and practice within the helping professions (social work, in my case). I do not view this as either an analytical or an expressive autoethnography, but one that is influenced by and consists of both traditions yet consciously seeks methods that best meet its aims. It begins with traditional qualitative interviews and field notes, yet is represented through a specific poetic form and structure, not a traditional narrative. I am also conscious of my own use of theory(ies), in this case from masculinities studies, as a primary set of lenses that focus me on various aspects of my participants' experiences, as well as my own. In this sense, I use analytical lenses both in my creation of field notes and in my understanding of them. Through the use of theory, a traditional method of thematic coding, and an evocative, expressive vehicle of data (re)presentation, this study is influenced by both the analytical and expressive autoethnographic traditions.

For a two-week period, I read my research notes and made interpretive codes in the margins of printed copies. After this initial coding, I waited for two weeks as a cooling-off period before I approached the text again. This was done to allow for a bit of distance from which to view the text with fresh eyes. I then re-coded the data without looking at the first set of analytical codes. Two days later, I compared the two sets of codings and wrote reflective notes to understand any discrepancies between the two sets of codings. After several hours of reflecting on these codes, I developed final themes that reflected my sense of the meaning of the data. Given that I was both researcher and researched, my use of self-reflection and multiple coding sessions helped ensure the trustworthiness of the data (Leitz, Langer & Furman, 2006). Still, while trustworthiness is an essential consideration for all qualitative researchers, I make no pretense about themes being dispassionately or objectively induced; the purpose of inquiry such as this is to present one's lived, emotional experience. Themes were selected for inclusion here not for their representativeness or generalizability, but for their representation of what I, the subject and "researcher," believe to be a core, emotionally relevant theme. Therefore, while themes were systematically discovered, their inclusion was based on my own values and emotional resonance.

Research Pantoums

Research Pantoum One
Themes: Social perceptions, my own biases, role of researcher

These are the words they use against them:
Sexpats. Misogynists. Failures.
And I, the researcher?
I am supposed to be objective, observe, code data.

Sexpats. Misogynists. Failures.
I feel their tears inside of me, light tears, trying to hide.
I am supposed to be objective—observe, field notes, code data.
First. We are all human.

I feel their tears inside of me, light tears, trying to hide.
I feel my own—what am I to do?
First. We are all human.
Must I report my heart to the Human Subjects Committee?

I feel my own—what am I to do?
Put down the notebook, the pen—touch a bony shoulder.
Must I report my heart to the Human Subjects Committee?
My hand here, now, more ethical than any form.

Put down the notebook, the pen—touch a bony shoulder.
And I, the researcher?
My hand here, now, more ethical than any form.
These are the words they use against them

Research Pantoum Two
Themes: Resilience, ability/disability, transcendence, aging

His limp does not define him.
His shuffling to the right, the dragging motion.
I see myself, thirty years from now.
My trifecta of arthritis defining me.

His shuffling to the right, the dragging motion.
He triumphs each day, refuses to submit.
My trifecta of arthritis defining me.
I have much to learn.

He triumphs each day, refuses to submit.
His girlfriend of thirty, smiles at his tenacity.
I have much to learn.
Oh, to let go of unrelenting infallibility

His girlfriend of thirty, smiles at his tenacity.
A new kind of power as his sun slowly sets.
Oh, to let go of unrelenting infallibility.
Almost eighty, he holds dear each day.

A new kind of power as his sun slowly sets.
I see myself, thirty years from now.
Almost eighty, he holds dear each day.
His limp does not define him.

Research Pantoum Three
Themes: my experiences with death, men and emotions, researcher's use of self, masculinity and research

I do not feel safe in my skin.
I think of all the tubes, his moaning in pain
I really just want to go home.
I just think about the night my dog died.

I think of all the tubes, his moaning in pain.
I try to listen. I am the researcher.
I just think about the night my dog died.
Supposed to be selfless here, focus on collecting.

I try to listen. I am the researcher.
I must be stoic. They must not know of my pain.
Supposed to be selfless here, focus on collecting.
When I held him as he died, I felt so close to death.

I must be stoic. They must not know of my pain.

He is 70, he tells me his girlfriend of 23 is great in bed.
When I held him as he died, I felt so close to death.
Stuck. I play researcher. I play masculine, nodding, silent.

He is 70, he tells me his girlfriend of 23 is great in bed.
I really just want to go home.
Stuck. I play researcher. I play masculine, nodding, silent.
I do not feel safe in my skin.

Research Pantoum Four
Themes: Isolation, men and social work, care

Who cares about them?
Alone, drinking and lost, a world away.
Funders love the innocent: children, the abused, the vulnerable.
My profession ignores them, ignores me.

Alone, drinking and lost, a world away.
I minimize and overemphasize, as guilty as most.
My profession ignores them, ignores me.
Better than rotting in assisted "living."

I minimize and overemphasize, as guilty as most.
Sadness. Joy. Pain. Pleasure.
Better than rotting in assisted "living."
Millions spent, but nothing on them.

Sadness. Joy. Pain. Pleasure.
The choices we make are ours alone.
Millions spent, but nothing on them.
We will not die public heroes, only in our own stories.

The choices we make are ours alone.
Funders love the innocent: children, the abused, the vulnerable.
We will not die public heroes, only in our own stories.
Who cares about them?

References

Anderson, L, (2006). Analytic autoethnography. *Journal of Contemporary Ethnography, 35*(4), 373–395.

Cahnmann, M. (2003). The craft, practice, and possibility of poetry in educational research. *Educational Researcher, 32*(29), 29–36.

Chang, H. (2008). *Autoethnography as method*. Left Coast Press.

Denzin, N.K. (1994). Evaluating qualitative research in the poststructural moment: The lessons James Joyce teaches us. *Qualitative Studies in Education, 7*, 295–308.

Denzin, N. K. (2003). *Performance ethnography: Critical pedagogy and the politics of culture*. Sage.

Eisner, E. W. (1981). On the differences between scientific and artistic approaches to qualitative research. *Educational Researcher, 10*(4), 5–9.

Eisner, E. W. (1991). *The enlightened eye. Qualitative inquiry and the enhancement of educational practice.* Macmillan.

Ellis, C., Adams, T. E., & Bochner, A. P. (2011). Autoethnography: An overview. *Forum: Qualitative Social Research.*

Ellis, C., & Bochner, A. P. (2000). Autoethnography, personal narrative, reflexivity. In N. K. Denzin & Y. S. Lincoln, (Eds.), *Handbook of qualitative research* (2nd ed.; pp. 733–768). CA: Sage.

Faulkner, S. L. (2009). *Poetry as method*. Left Coast Press.

Finley, S., & Knowles, J. G. (1995). Researcher as artist/artist as researcher. *Qualitative Inquiry, 1*(1), 110–142.

Foster, K., McAllister, M., & O'Brien, L. (2006). Extending the boundaries: Autoethnography as an emergent method in mental health nursing. *International Journal of Mental Health Nursing, 15*, 44–53.

Francis, M. D. (2002). *Interpretations of development: Critical research and the development encounter in KwaZulu-Natal.* Paper presented at the 8th annual qualitative/critical methods conference. Retrieved January 4, 2015: http://criticalmethods.org/p98.mv

Furman, R. (2004a). *Exploring friendship loss through poetry. Journal of Loss and Trauma, 9*, 181–187.

Furman, R. (2004b). Using poetry and narrative as qualitative data: Exploring a father's cancer through poetry. *Family, Systems, & Health, 22*(2), 162–170.

Furman, R. (2005). Autoethnographic poems and narrative reflections: A qualitative study on the death of a companion animal. *Journal of Family Social Work. 9*(4), 23–38.

Furman, R. (2006). Poetic forms and structures in qualitative health research. *Qualitative Health Research, 16*(4), 560–566.

Furman, R., Lietz, C., & Langer, C. (2006). The research poem in international social work: Innovations in qualitative methodology. *International Journal of Qualitative Methods, 5*(3), Article 3. Retrieved January 2, 2015 from http://www.ualberta.ca/~ijqm/backissues/5_3/pdf/furman.pdf

Gee, J. (1991). A linguistic approach to narrative. *Journal of Narrative and Life History, 1*(1), 15–39.

Hemmingson, M. (2008). *Here come the naval gazers—Definitions and defenses for auto/ethnography.* SSRN. Retrieved March 14, 2015 from http://papers.ssrn.com/sol3/papers.cfm?abstract_id=1099750

Hirshfield, J. (1997). *Nine gates: Entering the mind of poetry.* HarperCollins.

Holt, N. L. (2003). Representation, legitimation, and autoethnography: An autoethnographic writing story. *International Journal of Qualitative Methods, 2(*1), Article 2. Retrieved April 18, 2015 from https://www.ualberta.ca/~iiqm/backissues/2_1/pdf/holt.pdf

Humphreys, M. (2005). Getting personal: Reflexivity and autoethnographic vignettes. *Qualitative Inquiry, 11*(6) 840–860.

Langer, C. & Furman, R. (2004). The Tanka as a qualitative research tool: A study of a Native American woman. *Journal of Poetry Therapy, 17*(3), 165–171.

Leavy, P. (2008). *Method meets art: Arts-based research practice.* Guilford.

Leitz, C. A., Langer, C. L., & Furman, R. (2006). Establishing trustworthiness in qualitative research in social work: Implications from a study regarding spirituality. *Qualitative Social Work, 5*(4), 441–448

Leung, D. & Lapum, J. (2005). A poetic journey: The evolution of a research question. *International Journal of Qualitative Methods,* 4(3), Article 5. Retrieved January 10, 2007 from http://ualberta.ca/~ijqm/backissues/4_3/pdf/leung.pdf

Pelias, R. J. (2003). The academic tourist: An autoethnography. *Qualitative Inquiry 9*(3), 369–373.

Philaretou, A. G., & Allen, K. R.(2006). Researching sensitive topics through autoethnographic means. *The Journal of Men's Studies, 14*(1), 65–78.

Poindexter, C. C. (1997). Poetry as data analysis: Listening to the narratives of an HIV-affected caregiver. *Reflections: Narratives of Professional Helping,* 4(3), 22–25.

Poindexter, C. C. (2002). Meaning from methods: Re-presenting narratives of an HIV-affected caregiver. *Qualitative Social Work, 1*(1), 59–78.

Prendergast, M. (2009). Poem is what?: Poetic inquiry in qualitative social science research. In M. Prendergast, C. Leggo, & P. Sameshima (Eds.), *Poetic inquiry: Vibrant voices in the social sciences.* Sense Publishers.

Reed-Danahay, D. E. (1997). *Autoethnography. Rewriting the self and the social.* Berg.

Richardson, L. (1992). The consequences of poetic representation. In C. Ellis & M. G. Flaherty (Eds.), *Investigating subjectivity: Research on lived experience (*pp.125–173). Sage.

Richardson, L. (2000). Writing: A method of inquiry. In N. K. Denzin & Y. S. Lincoln, (Eds.), *Handbook of qualitative research* (2nd ed.; pp. 923–948). Sage.

van Manen, M. (2006). Writing qualitatively, or the demands of writing. *Qualitative Health Research, 16*(5), 713–722.

van Manen, M. (2002). *Writing in the dark: Phenomenological studies in interpretive inquiry*. Althouse.

Witkin, S. (2014). Narrating social work through autoethnography. Columbia University Press.

Willis, P. (2002). Poetry and poetics in phenomenological research. *Indo-Pacific Journal of Phenomenology, 3*(1), 1–19.

Chapter 14

The Tenderness and Vulnerability of Older Expatriate Men: A Poetic Inquiry of Research and Autoethnographic Poems

Men and masculinities is a growing area of study in the behavioral and social sciences, as well as in the humanities (Furman, 2010). Still, there is a paucity of research on non-"clinical" populations of men, or deficits and pathology within non-clinical populations (Mahalik & Cournoyer, 2000); most research focuses on the problematic behavior, criminality, or psychopathology of different male populations. When research is conducted on men's emotions, it tends to focus on clinical syndromes, or on anger or lust. This is lamentable, as it dehumanizes men and obscures our capacity to understand them well (Blundo, 2010).

For several years, I have engaged in a qualitative study, consisting of interviews and ethnographic field work, of older men who have retired in the Philippines, Thailand, Costa Rica, and Mexico. Little is known, and much is assumed, about the lives of these men. When I inform colleagues about this research, or at least before I explain the study and just merely mention the subject, their responses are fairly similar; the men being studied are viewed as caricatures and identified only by presumed pathology: drop outs, sexpats, those who could not make it in the Western world, and/or misogynists.

In truth, my sample—an awkward term for the real men who have honored me by sharing their stories and taking me into their lives—does contain men who, on face value, could be so labeled. Yet, such all-encompassing and uncritical labels conceal the humanity of these men and their deep and often touching vulnerability. A pathology focus fails to tell the whole story of many who have struggled to find their place post-marriage, post-careers, seeking to make connections in a post-modern, globalizing world that seems to hold little regard for them. And while the darker side of these men—indeed of all human beings—is perhaps a more compelling domain of inquiry, there is an important need to understand their strengths, their humanity, and even their tenderness. Men represent slightly less than half of the world's population yet are frequently ignored by the helping professions (Courtenay, 2000). Certainly, the focus on women and children is an important corrective to power distributions and abuses at the hands of men, specifically men in power, and patriarchy (Connell, 1998). Yet, a lack of focus on understanding the lived experiences and full spectrum of emotions may not only have deleterious consequences for men, but those in relationship with them (Furman, 2010).

One of the key areas helping professionals must understand is the "softer" emotions and vulnerabilities of men; to neglect to understand the full scope of their experiences will lead to misunderstandings and poor service delivery. Without understanding the real emotions of any population, it is impossible to provide clinical services to them (Kosberg, 2002). The stereotypes about men's emotions are powerful. This is especially true of older men, who are binomially viewed as powerful and privileged or bumbling and incompetent (Kosberg, 2005).

In this paper, I present research poems of one particular aspect of the experience of the men studied: tenderness and vulnerability. The research poem is a method of data compression that serves as a condensed poetic container for various types of qualitative data (Furman, 2004, 2006). In this brief paper, research poems are presented that represent important key examples of the tenderness and vulnerability of older expatriate men. This focus is not intended to deny many of the less socially accepted aspects of their lives, but to present an often-neglected aspect of the experience of older expatriate men that emerged from my data.

Research Poems

The following poems are research poems in that they are written from themes that I induced through traditional thematic qualitative analysis. My study, an ongoing longitudinal study with phenomenological and ethnographic components, has thus far consisted of interviews of over 50 men. These interviews have been transcribed and coded using a five-step method of qualitative analysis that seeks to induce themes from the data. For this study, I focus on the theme of tenderness and vulnerability that emerged from over half of my sample.

After I identified the themes, I mined the transcriptions of the interviews for the most representative passages that typify examples of tenderness and vulnerability. I then arranged these lines into several different poetic forms and structures. I played with several forms for each set of data, and selected ones that appeared to capture the tone and essence of the respondents' words. After this, I sent each poem to each respondent via email as a "member check" and elicited feedback. The notes following each poem describe if and how the poem changed from the original one sent to each respondent based on their feedback. Identifying information has been changed to ensure the confidentiality of respondents.

Haiku About Vulnerability

I used to be strong
now, my body fails me
and soon I will die

Billy made no changes to the above poem. He noted that seeing his words presented so directly and in such a compressed form made him feel not only sad but angry at himself for "giving up." Two weeks later, Billy, 82 years old, met three friends at the gym to begin to work out again.

Tanka of Sadness

Men don't ever cry
but I do, at night, alone
I turn, hide my tears.

Lost years, the bottle, regrets.
I would speak, but they would laugh.

I did not hear from Rick right away after I sent him his poem. I followed up a few days later to ask him if he received the poem, and to assure him that I would not share the poem if he did not want me to, and that I would not do so unless he said it was accurate. He wrote back the next day, saying that he wanted me to include it in my article but that I should include this sentence as a qualifier: "Men, either you cry too, are lying, or just don't give a crap about anything other than yourselves. Take the risk."

14. The Tenderness and Vulnerability of Older Expatriate Men

Never Too Late?

It has taken me almost seventy years,
admit that I feel sadness, loss, cry alone.
Why could I not have learned before?
Now my race is run.

Admit that I feel sadness, loss, cry alone.
Sometimes, I long to reach out, be known.
Now my race is run. Line 7
I am so afraid

Sometimes, I long to reach out, be known.
Why could I not have learned before?
I am so afraid
It has taken me almost seventy years

Charles made no changes to this poem. He said it captured his feelings well. In suggesting the current title of the poem, he asked me what I thought about it. I told him that I appreciated the honesty implied by the question mark, that sometimes it is easy to be "falsely positive" and dishonestly hopeful; a bit of doubt, I suggested, was healthy. Charles was pleased

Not So Crazy
Part 1

Flip is seventy three, his girlfriend, June, twenty seven
Flip is who we judge—sex tourist, misogynist, pervert.

Yes, they met in a bar. He pays for everything.
Does not work in the bar.

With his friends, he speaks as you would guess:
sex, young flesh, who needs older.......

On my third visit, June serves us lunch.
She knows my favorite, sour tamarind soup.

The house is a mess. June says she is sorry.
Flip tells her it means nothing, not important,

> he is sorry he has not been more of a help,
> he has not been well either.
>
> June's mother is sick, cancer.
> She tells me, it's not good, not good at all.
>
> Flip listens to her intently, his face softens.
> Under the table, he holds her hand.
>
> Flip says nothing. He does not try to fix her,
> does not try to make it better.
>
> He closes his eyes and squeezes her hand.
> As she begins to weep, he passes her a kleenex.
>
> *Part 2*
>
> Later, Flip and I speak alone.
> He tells me, he would never have done that before,
>
> listen to a women cry, without shaming her.
> She has been good to him, he to her.
>
> "It's a crazy thing, who we love and when."
> Not so crazy, I tell him, not so crazy at all.

I was able to share this poem with Flip in person. I interviewed Flip a second time, after I had conducted the original research. I was concerned that Flip would be angry, as it paints a less than flattering view of this life context. When I told Flip this, he told me "You are too sensitive Rich, but that's what I like about you." He suggested only one change; he had asked that the word "weep" be used in the last sentence of Part I of the poem instead of "cry."

Finally, I will end with a poem of vulnerability that is not taken from the words of my research participants but is a poem of my own. How can I expose the feelings of the men in my study without doing the same? Am I not a man as well, forced to contend with the same internalized rules and roles? The distanced stance that researchers are supposed to adopt does not always fit in the field; we can be human without "going native." Scholars in the helping professions, after all, are helping professionals first, and researchers second. In truth, we are first, second, and third, human. As such, I present an autoethnographic poem based upon my own field notes. Autoethnographic poems explore the lived experience of the researcher as a means of speaking about both self and culture (Furman, 2005).

Joe, 1932–1914

I head to the bar when everyone knows Joe.
It has been a year since I have been here,
they fill me in about their lives, their girlfriends, their health.

No one mentioned Joe. I sit in silence for a few, I want to ask,
I will ask, but sometimes the pregnant moments of silence are enough.

Maybe I was scared to know.

You knew Joe, right?
They know I knew Joe.

He died a few weeks ago.

I am the researcher; I am supposed to comfort them.
Again, silence.
Chuck, 300 pounds, biker jacket even in the Philippine sun,
moves two barstools over, sits next to me.

I look up at Chuck, his eyes well with tears. He does not wipe them.
I look down, scan the others.
They all are looking down, averting their eyes from Chuck and me.

I am crying now, not sobbing, but not merely tearing.
Chuck's huge right arm raises, moves to my shoulder, squeezes.

Ten minutes, fifteen minutes? Someone calls for a round of drinks
I don't drink anymore, the gout, but lift the beer in front of me, drink.

I owe them this.

References

Blundo, R. (2010). Engaging men in clinical practice: A solution focused and strengths-based model. *Families in Society, 91*(3), 307–312.

Connell, R. W. (1998). Masculinities and globalization. *Men and Masculinity, 1*(1), 3–23.

Courtenay, W. H. (2000). Engendering health: A social constructionist examination of men's health beliefs and behaviors. *Psychology of Men and Masculinity, 1*(1), 4–15.

Furman, R. (2004). Using poetry and narrative as qualitative data: Exploring a father's cancer through poetry. *Family, Systems, & Health, 22*(2), 162–170.

Furman, R. (2005). Autoethnographic poems and narrative reflections: A qualitative study on the death of a companion animal. *Journal of Family Social Work, 9*(4), 23–38.

Furman, R. (2006). Poetic forms and structures in qualitative health research. *Qualitative Health Research, 16*(4), 560–566.

Furman, R. (2010). *Social work practice with men at-risk.* Columbia University.

Kosberg, J. I. (2002). Heterosexual males: A group forgotten by the profession of social work. *Journal of Sociology and Social Welfare, 29* (3), 50–70.

Kosberg, J. I. (2005). Meeting the needs of older men: Challenges for those in the helping professions. *Journal of Sociology and Social Welfare, 32*(1), 9–31.

Mahalik, J. P., & Cournoyer, J. R. (2000). Identifying gender role conflict messages that distinguish mildly depressed men from nondepressed men. *Psychology of Men and Masculinities, 1*(2), 109–115.

Chapter 15

Extreme Data Reduction: The Case for the Research Tanka[1]

When it comes to data reduction, quantitative methods are normally far superior to qualitative procedures. Using basic descriptive statistics, valuable information can be conveyed quickly and easily with one or two numbers. In a fast-paced world where change occurs quickly, life occurs quickly, and data is needed quickly, simple, digestible information is desirable. However, when researchers or practitioners need to understand the lived experience of a human being, idiosyncratic perceptions and responses, and the ways people create meaning from their social worlds, numerical expressions may be of limited value. Such needs are the purview of qualitative methods, particularly constructivist and narrative approaches that present the lives of research participants fully and richly.

Yet, even academics with profound interests and dedication to their areas of research may have limited time for consuming long ethnographic accounts that they find of interest and of value. Traditional qualitative techniques, while able to capture the depth and richness of the human endeavor, may be at times too lengthy or dense, and may leave readers unmoved (Francis, 2002). This unconsumability is lamentable, as insights from important work may be neglected. However, a recent innovation in qualitative methods, the research poem, has helped rectify this dilemma. Characterized by compression, yet allowing for evocative and emotionally laden content, the research poem is a valuable means of condensing research data into its most elemental form (Faulkner, 2009). Furman (2006a) demonstrated how various poetic forms and structures can have different effects on readers when used as vehicles for data representation. The first author noted that the Tanka, consisting of five very short lines of a predetermined syllabic count, is compact yet allows

---

[1] Co-authored with L. Dill (2015).

for more context and depth than its more tightly condensed cousin, the Haiku.

The purpose of this article is to demonstrate how research Tankas can be used as a means of data representation. This study will consist of a secondary analysis of several research studies, and will also utilize this method with new textual data. The authors will meet this aim in several ways. First, we explore the nature of poetry in qualitative research. Second, we explicate our research methodology. Third, we present a research Tanka written from traditional qualitative narratives. Finally, we explore the implications of this work and final conclusions.

Poetry and Compression in Data Representation

Post-modern researchers have long advocated for means of knowing that attempt to capture the complexity and richness of human experience, eschewing positivistic methods that represent emotion as over-simplified numerical expressions (Finley & Knowles, 1995; Richardson, 1992). Such researchers advocate for methods of inquiry that transcend disciplinary boundaries and find commonalities between different ontological and epistemological positions (Richardson, 2000). The arts as research is an offshoot of what has been termed the "expressive agenda" in qualitative research. Expressive research has used numerous artistic means of data portrayal, such as art, dance, performance, theater, and creative writing (Becvar, 1996; Begel, 1998; Donohoe & Danielson, 2004; Edwards, 1990; Frank, 1998; Genova, 2003). Willis (2002) notes that expressive research seeks to expand meaning, not subdue or analyze it. He notes that in traditional, positivistic approaches, subtleties of human experience and encounter are lost in the transition from verbal to numerical form.

Utilizing various poetic forms, qualitative data can be reduced and compressed into a more consumable form. As previously noted, qualitative data is traditionally presented in long forms, like ethnographic accounts, that may be time consuming and hard to digest by consumers of research (Francis 2002). Also, these types of thick descriptions are often impersonal. Poetry allows for reductions in the text while still retaining the original meaning of the data. The use of poetic forms can allow data to be presented with more emotion so that consumers of research can feel a connection with not only the research itself but the research participants. Themes and patterns can also be explicated and written in poetic form, thus providing a summary of data that still retains some emotional quality.

Eisner (1981) has been a strong advocate of researchers integrating artistic methods in their research. He notes various similarities between the researcher and the scientist, including the need to ground work in empirical observation, the ability to use critical thinking to move from empirical data to theoretical formulations, and the importance of understanding the relationship that their own subjective understanding has upon the outcome of their inquiry.

Poet Jim Smith (2003) aptly expressed poetry's capacity to contain meaning when he stated that poetry is the "distillation of the essence of life." Poetry as an art form has historically been concerned with presenting powerful language without excess. Through various literary devices such as metaphor and imagery, poets present their individual accounts that become, in a very real sense, metaphorically generalizable (Stein, 2004). The poet attempts to show the reader through language that invokes images in the mind of the reader. In this sense, the experience of poetry is characterized by the construction of meaning between poet and reader. In the case of research poems, the co-construction is triangular between the subject, researcher, and the consumer of the research. Eisner (1991) expressed this notion well when he stated: "What artistically crafted work does is to create a paradox of revealing what is universal by examining what is particular" (p. 3).

The difference between common literary poetry and poetry as research is that research poetry is meant to be used as a tool to generate or represent data. Similarities between the two forms are that they both convey meaning and both seek to create an emotional response from the audience. They differ, however, by the author's position to the data. Research poems are written based on collected data and must remain true to the respondent, experience, or phenomenon being presented. Authors of literary poems do not have this constraint on them and can therefore explore fantasy, different perspectives, or alter an experience in a poem. When using research poetry and similar methods, researchers must discuss the methods they used in considerable detail, thereby allowing other researchers and consumers of research to assess the rigor of the representations and possibly replicate the methods (Leitz, Langer, & Furman, 2006).

Poetry can be used in qualitative research at many points throughout the research process. Poetry itself can serve as qualitative data and be analyzed. An example of poems being used as qualitative data is Furman's article exploring his father's cancer (2004a). In this article, the researcher took poems he had written 10 years ago about the experience of his father having cancer and analyzed them for meaning. Furman (2006b) has also used poetry as data to explore the death of a companion animal. Another researcher took published poetry by nurses to serve as qualitative data (Oiler, 1983). Two PhD nursing students, Leung and Lapum (2005), detail their use of poetry as a means to generate research questions. They write that by using poetry they are able to go beyond traditional, objective biomedical research to see "other truths" emerge (p. 2).

Another way poems are used in research is by utilizing poetic forms as a way of representing data. Various methods have been used to represent data using poetry. Richardson (1993, 1994) was one of the pioneers of the method, presenting the narratives of HIV caretakers in poetic form. Richardson (1993 & 1994) relied on her own expressive abilities and creative sense to arrange passages from her research participants into lyrical poems. Poindexter (2002) used more formal tools, methods borrowed from Gee's (1991) system of linguistic analysis, to present data that could express the pitch and tone of the original interview.

Furman and others (Furman, 2004b; Langer & Furman, 2004; Furman, Lietz, & Langer, 2006) have experimented using various formal poetic structures in the representation of data. Langer and Furman (2004) used research poems to represent the experience of a bi-cultural Native American woman. In this research, both research and interpretive Tankas were used to represent data. A research Tanka uses only words and phrases found in the original data, with unnecessary words removed to fit the form of the poem. In interpretive Tankas, the researcher uses their own feelings and thoughts on the data to create poetry that they believe captures the essence of the data. The researcher might also use interpretive poems as a means of reflecting on the relationship between the researcher and those being researched. These reflexive poems can then be used as field notes, commentary on the data, or as way of presenting compressed themes and ideas the researcher believes can be found in the data. The authors found that the Tanka was a valuable tool for exploring issues regarding identity, as the parsimony of the structure was not too confining but compelled the researchers to explore the tensions, contradictions, and complexities of their data. Based upon this prior research, the authors of this present study chose to use the research Tanka as a vehicle to experiment with a method of data compression in this research.

The poetic form of the Tanka originated in 8th century Japan and is still widely used today (Waley, 1976). It is related to the poetic form of the Haiku and has traditionally been written in one long line composed of thirty-one sound units, or onji (Ueda, 1996). The onji follow the rhythmic pattern of units of 5-7-5-7-7 for sound and meaning (Strand & Boland, 2000). The form of the American Tanka is similar to the original form, except that the sound units correspond with syllables as opposed to onji. This switch eases the writing of Tankas in English, but may cause the poem to lose some of its essential form since syllables are longer and convey more information than the onji. In its original form, the Japanese Tanka involves a good amount of compression of both sounds and data. The spirit of the Tanka is one of consolidation and abstraction. This is why Tankas may serve as a valuable research tool.

As noted, it is a valuable for researchers to find means of reducing the data in their studies to make presentation and reporting of results in a manageable and condensed form. In reducing their data, researchers need to take care to preserve the essence both of what those researched have to say and the emotional tone in which they say it. The Tanka is well suited for this because in a few words researchers can convey with emotional impact ideas or patterns present in the data. Researchers should carefully consider what data is left in and what is left out of research poems. This is not an idea that is unique to research poems, as any researcher must make these decisions when presenting qualitative data. Short poems are also easier for many consumers of research to digest when compared with long ethnographic accounts. By writing research poems, the researcher forms a close relationship with the data. Since one must be very familiar with the data in order to compress it accurately, researchers are forced to interact with the data on an insightful and emotional level.

Method

This study consists of a secondary data analysis utilizing data from two previous studies. The first author provided the first three data sets and the second author the second two sets. The actual method of this study constitutes not a traditional secondary data analysis but secondary data reduction and re-representation through the use of the research Tanka. The Tanka is used as the container for the data, as the organizing structure in which to fit data that best represent the themes that are identified. As such, the following method was used. Five qualitative passages were identified from two studies, each with clear themes that emerged from the data. Each passage was read by the author that did not provide the data and who selected themes that were most reflective of the essences of the work. Using the structure of the Tanka, the researcher who did not identify the themes (but who provided the data) arranged and juxtaposed words to reflect the theme that their research partner identified. Afterward, the researcher who identified the theme read the research Tanka and compared it to the original data and assessed the degree to which the theme was faithfully represented, as a means of increasing trustworthiness. If any discrepancies were identified, the researchers discussed the nature of their incongruence, and negotiated the meanings of the passage together and collectively made changes.

This type of methodological triangulation, termed triangulation by observation, was seen as an important means of establishing trustworthiness in this research process. Triangulation can be an important strategy for establishing rigor in qualitative work because opposing perspectives can bring an increased understanding of the data (Creswell, 1998, 2003; Li, 2004).

Data and Research Tankas

Except #1

The other week I wrote Louise and told her I was hurt she never called. I told her I understood how busy life gets, and that sometimes when we are down it is hard to find time, etc. She told me she would call the following week, that she was out of town. That week came and left, and I felt hurt, not knowing what to do. On one hand, friendships should not create more strain in a person's life; the last thing I want to be is some burden, to create a problem for someone I love. Friendships are about being easy and supportive, no? On the other hand, I have a difficult time reconciling the fact that as close as we have been, and as much as she says she "loves me," and as wonderful as it is when we do talk, can't I expect something from her once in a while? It is acceptable to speak with family about these things, but with friends, it somehow breaks the norm. It is as if we are supposed to accept friendships the way they are, or disengage. Or maybe this is just what I have learned. So little written about friendship, so little understood, it is like exploring a new wilderness with insufficient tools.

Themes: Friendship, Distress, Disappointment, Confusion

Research Tanka
Disappointment
hurt she never called
I expect something from her
she says she "loves me"

exploring new wilderness
with insufficient tools

Except #2

Jim came over and fixed my faucet. It took him maybe ten minutes, and he was glad to do it. Why did I feel the need to offer him an exchange? I told him I would read his poetry book for him, edit it. I was going to do this anyhow, but somehow that made my accepting help easier. He even had to minimize his helping, somehow lowering its significance. It is easier for me to give to friends than to be the recipient of help. Of course, I would tell someone else that we are all interdependent, that all of us need various types of support from friends and family. Yet, I suspect it is difficult for many men to be vulnerable to each other, to admit help is needed. We learn about friendship on the ball court, on the field, competing with one another. Feelings and vulnerability in those contexts were not acceptable. I must work at having them be more acceptable now.

Themes: Friendship, Reciprocity, Pride, Gender Norms

Research Tanka: Gender norm

Jim fixed my faucet
I had to offer an exchange
to accept his help

difficult for many men
to admit needed is help.

Research Tanka: Friendship

Vulnerability
not acceptable, learn,
compete with each other

feelings not acceptable
now, I must learn to accept

Except #3
The second year in row that I "missed" the high holidays. Over a year now, and we have only tried one of the two congregations in town that might provide us some Jewish community. Jill (my wife) really has a bias against reform. I also prefer the more progressive varieties, renewal and reconstructionism, but, even those I feel ambivalence about. So two years of no holiday celebrations, a couple of years of not being plugged into a community. Maybe this is why the student's question bothered me yesterday. Perhaps I am not sure of the answer myself. Until the last couple of years, I was comfortable and settled with my practicing Judaism my own way. I would attend services as I wanted, pray in Jewish song, and had a clear sense of the teachings that were important to my life. Now, what does it mean to be Jewish? What is my relationship to other Jews, other than as a common historical and cultural bond? Ok, what pops into my mind is Israel. This is always where I get stuck, feeling so different than mainstream Judaism in my response to, what I see, as the oppression of the Palestinian people. And where am I now, Omaha? Growing up in Los Angeles, living for years in San Francisco and Philadelphia, being Jewish never felt like something deviant. The schools I grew up in were very Jewish; being Jewish and Christian seemed to be part of the same family. Now, I hear comments; people want to save me. I feel distant from being Jewish, and angry at the judgmental brand of Christianity that some seem to want to force down my throat.

Themes: Faith, Religion, Confusion, Doubt, Rumination, Community

Research Tanka

Faith
feel ambivalence
what does it mean to be Jewish
pray in Jewish song

a common cultural bond
plugged into community

Except #4
Going into high school, I lost a lot of loved ones and, you know, it somewhat distracted me from my schoolwork, and my grades were dropping, and I didn't want to go to school. I lost uncles, my grandmother on my father's side. And I didn't want to talk to anybody. I didn't want to talk. I'd just be really quiet. If I did go to school, I wouldn't talk in class. I didn't want to participate. I just wasn't in a good mood to do anything. And the way I conquered that—I just looked at it as my loved ones, they were in a better place, and it was their time to go, and I just had to leave it in God's hands. And I couldn't beat myself up about it any longer, because it was just hurting myself, because I knew that my uncles and grandma wouldn't want me to be jeopardizing myself in school. So I just had to look at it from another perspective.

Themes: Loss, Faith, Transcendence, Tribute

Research Tanka-Theme: Loss

Loved ones lost a lot
Uncles, my Father's Mother
Didn't want to talk
Really quiet moody Blues
Better Place, it was their time

Research Tanka-Theme: Transcendence
And I conquered that
Had to leave it in God's hands
Not beat myself up
Not hurt myself, or my grades
Have another perspective

Except #5
I remember, I was in the 10th grade, and one of my "partnahs" from junior high was like, "do you remember so and so?" And I'm like, "Yeah, whatever happened to her?" They were like, "Oh, she on the track." I'm like, "Say what? What track?" "On the, you know, the ho stroll track." I'm like, "But she was the top student in our class, like the student that got the 3.0s, the 4.0s, on the honor…the scholarships." I'm like, "what the…what the…what?!" They were like, "You never knew that?" I'm like, "No. Like really?" A couple of my friends from junior high have got caught up in that and I've seen them and it was just like, they've done

so much drugs that you can't even recognize who they are no more and it hurts you because you know that person, you grew up with that person and…and it's just like, "what happened," and you wanna help them, but you can't help them because they don't want no help, or they be too scared because their pimp or their master is out of control, and it's like you really gonna let another dude control your every move? Like really? And they like, "what else am I supposed to do? I don't know. Everyone done gave up on me." And I give them advice, but that's all I could do.

Themes: Powerlessness, Loss, Hopelessness, Drug abuse, Wasted potential

Research Tanka - Theme: Powerlessness

Got caught up in that
Can't help them, they don't want help
Scared, out of control
What am I supposed to do
when everyone else gives up

Research Tanka - Theme: Wasted Potential

Whatever happened
to the Scholar with the Honors
Grew up together
She was the head of the class
Now, you can't recognize her

Discussion

The method presented here represents an experiment in data reduction and representation using a condensed form of poetry. While it may seem that the predetermined number of lines might be problematic for researchers, we actually found this structure extremely liberating. By using a predetermined "container," and not having to worry about the form and structure of the data presentation, we were able to focus on passages that were most reflective of the themes that were identified. Additionally, the extremely condensed nature of the form compelled us to think carefully about what words we used and what words we did not use. The parsimony of the structure leads to the creation of a dense product full of meaning, image, and emotion.

The process itself forced us to become more familiar, even intimate, with the data; it helps use rethink the potential meanings that were previously missed. We learned from each other's perceptions and were able to expand our analytical lenses. This method can be used as an exercise even for researchers who do not intend to use poetry forms and structures as their ultimate data representation system, as it helps the researcher become more immersed in their data. Such experiments may be of value to researchers who are more accustomed to working with computer software analysis systems and may not be as intimately connected to their data as researchers who use more "messy" manual methodologies.

The iterative process of reading, coding, and generating texts is informative to the nature of secondary analysis and to collaborative research. The research Tanka is able to evoke language and emotion from both the respondent and the investigator in a way that is easily translatable to the reader. In this sense, each aspect of the data analysis process, as well as the final products, represented the co-creation of research and meaning.

This method is congruent with other post-modern and expressive methods in which the researchers and their perceptions become part of the research text. It is also congruent with the assertion that writing in and of itself is a method of inquiry (Richardson, 2000), and helps add layers of depth and insight to "raw" research date.

References

Becvar, D. S. (1996). I am a woman first: A message about breast cancer. *Families, Systems, & Health, 14*(1), 83–88.

Begel, A. (1998). The family conference: A jazz jam. *Families, Systems & Health, 16*(4), 437–441.

Creswell, J.W. (1998). *Qualitative inquiry and research design: Choosing among the five traditions.* Sage Publications.

Creswell, J.W. (2003). *Research design: Qualitative, quantitative and mixed methods approaches* (2nd ed.). Sage Publications.

Donohoe, M., & Danielson, S. (2004). A community approach to medical humanities. *Medical Education, 38*(2), 204–207.

Edwards, M. E. (1990). Poetry: Vehicle for retrospection and delight. *Generations, 14*(1), 61–62.

Eisner, E. W. (1981). On the differences between scientific and artistic approaches to qualitative research. *Educational Researcher, 10*(4), 5–9.

Eisner, E. W. (1991). *The enlightened eye. Qualitative inquiry and the enhancement of educational practice.* Macmillan.

Finley, S., & Knowles, J. G. (1995). Researcher as artist/artist as researcher. *Qualitative Inquiry, 1*(1), 110–142.

Francis, M. D. (2002). Interpretations of development: Critical research and the development encounter in KwaZulu-Natal. Paper presented at the 8th annual qualitative/critical methods conference. Retrieved from http://criticalmethods.org/p98.mv.

Frank, A. W. (1998). Just listening: Narrative and deep illness. *Families, Systems & Health, 16*(3), 197–212.

Faulkner, S. L. (2009). *Poetry as method.* Left Coast Press.

Furman, R. (2004a). Using poetry and narrative as qualitative data: Exploring a father's cancer through poetry. *Family, Systems & Health, 22*(2), 162–170.

Furman, R. (2004b). The prose poem as a means of exploring friendship: Pathways to reflection. *Journal of Poetry Therapy, 17*(2).

Furman, R. (2006a). Poetic forms and structures in qualitative health research. *Qualitative Health Research, 16*(4), 560–566.

Furman, R. (2006b). Autoethnographic poems and narrative reflections: A qualitative study of the death of a companion animal. *Journal of Family Social Work, 9*(4), 23–28.

Furman, R., Lietz, C., & Langer, C. (2006). The research poem in international social work: Innovations in qualitative methodology. *International Journal of Qualitative Methods, 5*(3), Article 3.

Gee, J. (1991). A linguistic approach to narrative. *Journal of Narrative and Life History, 1*(1), 15–39.

Genova, N. J. (2003). Expanding our concept of the medical literature: The value of the humanities in medicine. *Journal of the American Academy of Physician Assistants, 16*(3), 61–64.

Langer, C. & Furman, R. (2004). The Tanka as a qualitative research tool: A study of a Native American woman. *Journal of Poetry Therapy, 17*(3), 165–171.

Leung, D., & Lapum, J. (2005). A poetic journey: The evolution of research questions. *International Journal of Qualitative Methods, 4*(3), Article 5. Retrieved from http://www.ualberta.ca/~ijqm/backissues/4_3/pdf/leung.pdf

Li, Defeng. (2004). Trustworthiness of think-aloud protocols in the study of translation process. *International Journal of Applied Linguistics, 14*(3), 301–313.

Lietz, C., Langer, C. L., & Furman, R. (2006). Establishing rigor in qualitative research in social work: Implications from a study regarding spirituality. *Qualitative Social Work: Research and Practice, 5*(4), 441–458.

Oiler, C. (1983). Nursing reality as reflected in nurses' poetry. *Perspectives in Psychiatric Care, 21*(3), 81–89.

Poindexter, C. (2002). Meaning from methods: Re-presenting narratives of an HIV-affected caregiver. *Qualitative Social Work 1*(1), 59–78.

Richardson, L. (1992). The consequences of poetic representation. In. C. Ellis & M. G. Flaherty (Eds.), Investigating subjectivity: Research on lived experience (pp.125–173). Sage.

Richardson, L. (1993). Poetics, dramatics, and transgressive validity: The case of the skipped line. *The Sociological Quarterly, 34*(4), 695–710.

Richardson, L. (1994). Nine poems: Marriage and the family. *Journal of Contemporary Ethnography, 23*(1), 3–13.

Richardson, L. (2000). Writing: A method of inquiry. In N. K. Denzin & Y. S. Lincoln, (Eds.), Handbook of qualitative research (2nd ed.; pp.923–948). Sage.

Smith, J. (2003). Personal communication. Boulder, Co.

Strand, M., & Boland, E. (2000). *The making of a poem: A Norton anthology of poetic form.* W. W. Norton.

Stein, H. F. (2004). A window to the interior of experience. *Families, Systems, & Health, 22*(2), 178–179.

Ueda, M. (1996). *Modern Japanese Tanka.* Columbia University Press.

Waley, A. (1976). *Japanese poetry.* University of Hawaii.

Willis, P. (2002). Poetry and poetics in phenomenological research. *Indo-Pacific Journal of Phenomenology, 3*(1), 1–19

Chapter 16

Poetry and Photography: An Exploration into Expressive/Creative Qualitative Research[1]

The multiple work responsibilities with which academics must contend make the creation and implementation of a research agenda difficult. Committee work and university governance, other service obligations, course preparation, teaching, and grading are all important faculty responsibilities. These daily obligations often compete with family and social responsibilities, frequently leaving scarce time for in-depth research and creative endeavors. Too often scholarship is driven by the need to "publish or perish" or to procure external funding for its own sake, in order to fulfill tenure requirements. Such pressures and obligations may dampen the motivation to find scholarly activities that enliven and enrich our professional identities, yet will not pad our resumes. For example, extended conversations between colleagues can be tremendous sources of growth and exploration. Such conversations become touchstones for creative research and inspiration, and may also counter alienating and isolating factors that often accompany the academic endeavor within the modern university (Dunlap, 1998; Lewis & Altbach, 2000). For the authors of this article, such traditionally undocumented experiences have had profound personal and professional impacts upon our development. Yet, it also has become clear that such conversations are neglected in the contexts of our busy lives; space and time must be carefully carved out for extended scholarly conversations and candid reflections. The authors also posit that accounts of such conversations might have value for other scholars both in terms of their process and content.

 This article explores one such conversation: an exploration of the uses of poetry and photography in social research. To explore the epistemological and applied research possibilities of these two separate media, and the possibility of their synthesis, two social work

---

[1] Co-authored with P. Szoto & C. Langer (2005).

researchers convened in Chicago for a series of conversations. This paper documents and expands this exploration in several ways. First, a discussion of the context of the conversation is explored. Second, a brief exploration of the role of expressive and creative arts research is presented. Third, the conversations are presented in their original, only slightly edited form. Fourth, the conversations were analyzed as data by another researcher as a means of independently eliciting the themes imbedded within conversations.

History and Context

In this article, we refer to each other as Peter and Rich, not author one and author two. In personal dialogues, it is important that authors not hide behind anonymity, but take ownership of their views and perspectives. We have known each other since the fall of 1991 when Rich was a first year student studying for his masters in social work at the University of Pennsylvania, and Peter was in his second year of the same program. Peter was the editor of the student journal *Forecaster*, for which Rich wrote two articles.

Over the years we kept in touch with each other to varying degrees. Over the last year, however, we communicated more frequently by way of e-mail and telephone to discuss our mutual research and teaching interests. Also, it became clear that Rich had the agenda of luring Peter to work at his university. It worked, as we are now both members of the faculty in the same school of social work.

Our conversation took place over the course of two days during hours of talk regarding the nature of using photography and poetry in social research. We engaged in the process of dialogue as a means of learning from each other about our respective work in expressive/creative arts research and as a means of exploring potential research collaborations. We discussed methodological issues as well as topics that held mutual interest.

Since our time together was limited, we decided that we were truly in an exploratory mode, and agreed that the subject matter of this short investigation would be less important than the process itself. Recognizing the importance of the notion of "person-in-environment" to social work, Peter suggested investigating a social phenomenon that occurs within public space. Further defining this, we explored potential activities and relationships that occurred in the public space of a large metropolitan downtown area. Upon considering Peter's work on the Tobacco-Free Michigan Board, Rich raised the possibility of investigating smoking outside office buildings. A relatively new social phenomenon, the notion of smoking in public place is tied both to individual factors and to social policy.

The outcome of this research is beyond the scope of this article; in this paper we present the content and process of this exploration as a means of illuminating such a process for other researchers. Conversations that seek to deepen and expand understanding such as this have been utilized previously as a means of exploring epistemological and methodological issues in qualitative research. Ellis and Bochner (2000) utilize a dialogue as a means of exploring the philosophy and methods of autoethnography. Through the use of dialogue as autoethnography, the authors are able to illustrate the processes of the method. Autoethnography, which traditionally has been utilized as a means of explicitly exploring cultural factors, has been recently expanded toward exploring more broadly defined psychosocial phenomena through the vehicle of the self (Furman, 2004a). Their lively, almost Socratic dialogue helps readers to understand not only the content of their deliberations, but the processes as well. In a very real sense, conversations about epistemology are conversations about culture; the way we understand and see knowledge is profoundly impacted by the many cultural factors that impact our construction of reality (Langer & Furman, 2004). Dialogue has been shown to be a valuable means of exploring differences in worldviews and cultural experiences (Schatz, Furman, & Jenkins, 2003).

Expressive and Creative Arts Research

Qualitative researchers in various disciplines have been utilizing expressive arts in research for several decades. Eisner (1981) postulated that both artist and researcher rely on accurate investigation of the social world to evoke an emotional impact on the audience. Both seek to present interpretations of the world that expand what is already known. Artists and the qualitative researchers both strive for authentic relationships with the external world based on the commitment to portray the experiences of others in an honest, accurate manner. They both explore the unknown and hope that such knowledge will lead to the betterment of personkind.

As with qualitative research, the arts have also been viewed as a valuable means for communicating complex social phenomena for which statistical means of representation is limiting (Finley & Knowles,

1995; Percer, 1992. These approaches are designed to *express* human experience, not *interpret* or *analyze* these experiences (Brearley, 2002). It is assumed that, as in the dissemination and consumption of all knowledge, the "consumer" will construct their own interpretations of data based on their own history, present social context, and needs. Such research seeks to present data in a manner congruent with the experience of research subjects.

Positivists and more traditional qualitative researchers may ask how and why the arts may be considered research. Babbie (2000) postulates that what separates research from other ways of knowing lies in its focus on empirical knowledge and the generation of theory. In their role as researchers, creative and expressive artists ground their work in the empirical world. They utilize their artistic medium—whether photography, painting, or words—as a means of capturing the essence of an experience, object, or phenomenon. As with traditional qualitative research, theory generation tends to be more inductive than deductive. It is true that the theory generated through artistic exploration may not adhere to the same standards of reliability and validity as traditional research paradigms. Stein (2003, 2004) observed that poetry and other arts, when they successfully capture the essence of experience, can be what he called "metaphorically generalizable." Research generated through poetry and the arts begins by investigating a particular case, yet seeks to penetrate the depths of that case to present more universal truths. To Willis (2002), this penetrative potential lies at the heart of the arts as a means of expressive research, which contrasts with more traditional analytic paradigms.

Poetry has been used in various ways as a tool of social investigation. Richardson (1992), a sociologist, used poetry to present data describing the life histories of unwed mothers. She compressed the essence of life narrative interviews into poems derived from key words and phrases of her subjects. She believes that presenting data as lyric poems—that is, poems that transcend the direct chronology of narrative—are extremely effective in communicating "lived experience." Poindexter (2002) used methodology developed by Gee (1991) in creating research poems utilizing subjects' own words to explore the relationship of HIV patients and their caregivers. Langer and Furman (2004) presented research and interpretive poems in the exploration of the identities of Native Americans. In their research poems, they utilize the poem as a means of data reduction, compressing thick narratives into tighter packets of meaning derived from the subjects' own words. In their interpretive poems, they allow for the presentation of their own subjective understanding of the experiences being studied. By so doing, they present not only the lived experiences of their research participants, but of themselves as researchers as well, thus exposing potential biases. This transparency helps the consumer of the research assess the trustworthiness of the data for themselves. Poetry has also been utilized in autoethnographic research as the vehicle for exploring the emotional dynamics of friendships (Furman, 2004b), the process of coping with a relative's cancer (Furman, 2004a), as well as the stress of doctoral education (Chan, 2003).

Photography has a more connected history with social research than poetry or other expressive arts as an explicit research tool. Since its discovery in 1839, photographers have explored the social function of the camera to capture, document, and express perceptions about the world. Frenchman Jean Eugene Auguste Atget (1856–1927) is the earliest known photographer to apply photography as a tool of social research. He recorded scenes of his beloved Paris in breathtaking black-and-white detail. His photographs proved beyond doubt that what he saw and experienced was everyday life in Paris. Atget demonstrated the power of the photograph to re-present reality in stark truthfulness. In America, Lewis Hine (1874–1940) recognized the analytic power of photographs to affect social change. Hine was an academically trained sociologist who used the camera as a tool of social work practice. The photograph's "inherent honesty" (Curtis, 1989) provided Hine a valid instrument to advance social justice. Distressed by children working under harsh factory conditions, Hine pointed his camera at these children to expose their miserable circumstances. His photographs of children were widely published and profoundly altered the public's awareness. As a result, debate over child labor laws ensued, followed by the passage of legislation to protect children.

Documentary photography continues to function as an important tool of social research. Its capacity to describe and analyze social problems is unprecedented in how it links the human condition to the viewer. For example, the act of looking is intensified through the emotive connection made by how the human mind perceives the external world through the photographic image. The high degree of correspondence between the external world and the photograph may help consumers of research connect more fully with the presentation of data, thereby making the data an indispensable tool for social research.

The Conversation

Our conversation was typed directly onto a laptop while it was occurring. It is presented in more or less original form, with a few words omitted when they appeared unintelligible or were unrelated to the discussion. We chose to leave the data—that is, our conversation—in its purist form to show the ebbs and flows of the process. A few editorial changes were made to help the narrative flow, and several parenthetical comments were added to help clarify points that the reader might otherwise not understand. The conversation is presented in two parts, with each of us alternating between the role of questioner and respondent. The roles we took were fluid and therefore our thought and inferences are tentative and not definitive. While we were tempted to go back and alter some of what we have said, we wanted to preserve the conversation as data.

Part 1

Rich: Why is photography research?

Peter: Why is it not? By its very nature it is research, it is writing with light. Whether you are writing with words or with light, you are writing. You are presenting an illustration of the world. Photography documents more accurately than statistics, it is a direct representation of reality.

Rich: While statistics are abstractions?

Peter: That's what inferential statistics are. They are estimations of reality. When you take a photograph of a mental hospital, for example, and you see the inhuman conditions, and you see the horror, the inhumanity, it is what it is. There is no extrapolation. It is not an approximation. And there are policy ramifications to this, since it is in front of you, you see injustice, and you must act. It is a tool, amongst other research tools. All tools have limits.

Rich: What are the limits of photography as a research tool?

Peter: It is still susceptible to manipulation. There is an interpretative component. I take a picture of you, and it is who you are, but we can manipulate it, just as we can manipulate statistics. You can leave out certain variables, motivated by ideology. I am not sure, some research is based on hypothesis testing, I am not sure photography has that experimental quality to it. But it does have a powerful sense of validating how things are. It is convincing. It reaches a wider audience, as it taps into a range of intuitive appeal that is broader. We all look at photographs; that is why advertising is powerful.

Rich: What about the ability to selectively take a picture of something in a biased manner. For example, a photograph of someone in poverty, in extreme pain, that may be only part of the story, selected to illustrate a point. It is not, perhaps, even the most salient part of the story. How is that research?

Peter: It happened. The Vietnamese kid who runs down the street [referring to a famous photograph taken during the Vietnam War of a child burned by Napalm], it happened. The photograph did not sensationalize the event, the event was sensational. Photographs are the eyes with a memory.

Rich: My question is this, you can photograph someone in a sad moment, the next moment they are happy. Choosing to photograph or present one or the other, biases the results, does it not?

Peter: No. This is about selection and presentation, not about the data itself. Isn't that done with all research? What and how we disseminate information is the choice of the researcher. The playing field is level, in the sense that is a valid question across the board, and it's not only about photography. And that is the function of education. You have to teach how to interpret the data. For social work and social research, you have to help people read the data. Is it overkill? Is it manipulative? If you teach people how to consume, that is half the battle.

Rich: So, in a sense, it is the researcher's responsibility regardless of the medium to collect data in a fair manner.

Peter: Well, and presentation as well. Why do I pick one versus the other?

Rich: So, in a sense, the reliability of the data is predicated on that "objectiveness" and fairness of the researcher. But what about research related to social action?

Peter: Yet, but there is also the aesthetic sensitivity of the researcher. There is a respect for subject matter that needs to happen.

Rich: And, taking a picture that does not capture a subject's reality is not respectful?

Peter: The photographer is an ethnographer in this sense. You try to capture the context. You have to take poetic license and select context.

Rich: You cannot take it all in.

Peter: Whether it is a pen and paper, or a tape recorder, you are still always telling a story. You are there. You have your perspective. And positivists have not overcome that, they think they do. But they still are subjective.

Rich: So, in a sense, the photographic researcher or creative arts researcher in general is just being more honest, hopefully, about their

subjectivity. Reflexivity is essential in qualitative and expressive arts research. How does the researcher using photography engage in reflexivity? How do you explore, not confirm?
Peter: It occurs before, during, and after. You have to think about subject matter and how you approach the subject matter. You have to decide what to focus on, and you have to think about it, and what it means, and how it inspires you. Within that frame, you allow for some spontaneity. If you want to take pictures of a homeless person, you photograph in a certain way. When you look at the picture later, you have to be open to things that are different. You have to respond to the data.
Rich: But, what about biases while photographing, how do you guard against just confirming your views about the matter?
Peter: In one sense, once you put your finger on the shutter, it captures that moment. But you can go back and pull out different layers of meaning. That is not confirming, it is learning from the documented event. So, in a sense, the photographer becomes a student, it is not only about recall. You have to be open.
Rich: Yeah, but what about before or during?
Peter: You have to keep shooting. You need to take a lot of pictures. In a sense, you have to just shoot, and not be biased, because you don't *know*. You have to shoot. You see a homeless person, and you have to just photograph what is in front of you, you just don't know.
Rich: What drives you to photograph in one moment rather than another? And not from an aesthetic perspective.
Peter: Let's say, it starts raining, you stop shooting. Or, you want to photograph the homeless, but there are none there, you have to go somewhere else. That is the discovery process. What drives the photography process is that you don't know, so you shoot more to discover.
Rich: So, in a sense, you are talking about a process, at best, of pure induction. And I agree, yet, for the purpose of credibility, in the academy we have to demonstrate how we deal with potential bias when we conduct research such as this. Otherwise, how will our work be accepted? How and when will it be published? We still must live in the world of traditional research, in a time when human behavior has been medicalized and quantified until they are reduced to often meaningless units. Since it is true that the social sciences are dominated by logical positivism, expressive arts researchers almost need to hold themselves to higher research standards than do other researchers. Quantitative

research studies rarely account for the bias of variable selection. Should we?

Peter: We need to be aware of this argument, yes. But, we must also guard against the false dichotomy of qualitative versus qualitative. It involves yin and yang, they are intertwined. The issues are different, so the standards are different.

Rich: So the expressive arts researcher must develop their own standards by which they are judged. Let's talk about the notion of photography as an expressive art or documentation. For example, poetry has a very expressive quality, in which the researcher utilizes poetic tools. For example, in making research poems, the poet/researcher takes a lot of liberties compressing thick narratives.

Peter: Photography is a one to one correspondence to the world, it *is* reality. Let's talk about the arts research, maybe all research, on a continuum. Expressive arts on one side, photography in the middle, and qualitative research on the end. They all do different things, your tool needs to match what you are trying to do.

Rich: So when would you specifically utilize photography in this sense?

Peter: When words are not appropriate. For example, I did a presentation of my photographs of a psychiatric hospital in China. The audience knew this was what it really looked like. Being there provided authenticity. In that sense, images might have been more powerful than words. We just saw the city, driving by; if we gave someone pictures of that experience, it would be more impactful than describing them. It takes out the imagination, there is only the image. Comparing it to words, it is more objective. Take ten people viewing a building, they all will describe it differently. But the photograph, even if it is taken under different lighting conditions, or different angles, we will still recognize the building as how it was perceived. But ultimately, we cannot achieve objectivity.

Now, thinking here about collaborating, it is about intersubjectivity. It's the dialogue between words and text, words and image, how they fit together. Hearing inter-subjective discourse, rather than about which is better than the other. In some ways, our line of conversation about bias was about justifying these interplays, and they don't need to be justified. So, part of the realization in talking about this is how we frame it. The goal is not objectivity. It's about what I was saying before, about the continuum. They are all legitimate, but historically, we have elevated experimental research over other avenues of gaining knowledge. When we think about social welfare policy, the WPA photographs were far more influential on Congress than statistics regarding poverty. Photographs are very influential, with lasting impact. Who really remembers NIMH research? Yet the photograph can be etched within the mind, and impact us long after statistics are forgotten. The question is where do poetry and photography fit, how do we show people how these methods are appropriate to help solve research problems, how they expand the possibilities? In one sense, statistical research does not impact treatment very much, but these other methods can.

Rich: So, how can you see poems and photography together in research?
Peter: If we are talking about the human spirit, there is something with both methods that resonates with the human spirit more than numbers, both in terms of expression and interpretation. I look at a painting, and I react. Someone produced it, and the audience reacts to it in a powerful way.
Rich: So, in a sense, what we are talking about is a possibly powerful way of impacting people?
Peter: Yes, that is one of the key criteria that we need to address when looking at these types of research.

Part 2

Peter: How do you see poetry on this continuum of social research?
Rich: I believe that there are many ways of knowing. There is not this clear distinction of knowledge, that is, no delineation between what we experience in the external world that can be broken down by method. The method of data collection and expression is what allows the world to experience what has been studied, in some fashion that, we hope, makes it more comprehensible. Poems allow for holistic understanding that transcends a logic that numbers cannot understand.
Peter: How so?
Rich: Poems allow for intuition, for emotion, which are important parts of the human experience that cannot be expressed numerically. Yes, you can have a numerical score for depression that in many ways is representative of the *strength* of depression. But what about the meaning of the depression, vis-à-vis the person's life, their context, their dreams, and goals? In working with people, therapeutically, we need to understand this in order for therapists and social workers to use their experience of depression for positive life transformations. The poem allows us to understand these subtle tones and textures. Poetry is also congruent with the ways many traditional people's experience of the world, so it is a good tool with culturally diverse populations.
Peter: What else can poems do in research?

Rich: One of the key aspects to poetry is compression, the reduction of many words into a few. In this sense, poetry allows for reduction of data; which we like about quantitative research, yet allows for the subtleties that we value in qualitative studies. It might be one means of reconciling these two traditions, which today can feel very far apart.
Peter: But aren't there different kinds of poetry?
Rich: Yes, there are, yet the differences may be less important than the similarities. Here is one of my aesthetic biases coming out: good poetry is characterized by three factors: compression, sensory imagery, and on some level, metaphoric language. Some wonderful poetry is abstract, yet when we really look at it, they are based on concrete images, things if you will, taken from the real world. Yet, they may have a dream-like quality or they may transcend formal logic and be more faithful to the logic of emotion, which is not very linear.
Peter: How about criteria for using poetry in research. You asked me about issues pertaining to validity and reliability with photography, what about poetry?
Rich: Well, in the role of researcher, the poet must engage in conscious and constant self-exploration. When he [or she] writes about a subject in front of himself [herself], or when he [she] is reducing data from narratives, he [she] has to be very clear to stay faithful to the data. His [her] notes serve as both data to be worked with, as well as ethnographic notes that explore their reactions. Many times, these biases should be presented so the reader can decide for themselves how to interpret the poem. The first allegiance of the researcher, as poet, has to be to the subject's experience. In a sense, there are two types of poems for the researcher. There are poems in which they attempt to merely present the subjects' experience as accurately as possible, hopefully utilizing their words, and there are interpretative poems, in which they deconstruct the meaning of the experience and consciously allow for interpretation.
Peter: How do you know when to use which mode?
Rich: Good question, again, back to the purpose of the research, and the means of using poetry in research. As data reduction in qualitative studies, you try to stay as close to the text as possible. It's good to utilize member checks and asking other researchers to check your coding, if you will.
Peter: What's the big hang-up in social work against poetry?
Rich: I think we're still affected by Flexner. Nearly eighty years ago, he challenged us to be more scientific. As we have sought professional recognition, we have tried to align ourselves with scientists, and this

has led to bias against the arts and humanities. I suspect this might be occurring in other professions as well. Yet, this is ironic, since we know that practitioners rely more on practice wisdom, i.e., intuition, synthesis of informed judgment and the totality of what we know. It is funny, that IS what a poem is. These are parallel processes, and social workers and others in the helping and educational professions would do well to pay attention to the poem of the poem.

Peter: What is the history of poetry?

Rich: Poetry's been utilized as a form of expression, and healing, in many societies throughout history. In ancient societies, healers used poetic incantations along with their tinctures and medicines. Many think it was the words as much as the medicine that was curative.

Peter: Define for me, poetry.

Rich: That is harder. I would say that poetry is language characterized by compression, image, and metaphor. Hirschfield say poetry is the clarification and magnification of being, through words. A friend of mine, Jim Smith, says poetry is the distillation of the essence of being, through language.

Peter: When is it appropriate to use poetry as social research?

Rich: When researchers want to capture the lived experience. They want to speak to the difficulties of existence, things that contain paradox and emotion. Again, it also depends on whether you are going to use a strict research poem for data reduction to compress traditional qualitative data into condensed lines, or whether you are going to go for an interpretative poem, in which the consciousness and judgment of the researcher/poet is evident, even valued.

Peter: What's the function of poetry?

Rich: Poetry can be used for both aesthetic means or in more utilitarian ways, as with poetry therapy, education or research. The function of art is complex, and who your viewer is depends upon your epistemology.

Peter: How is it social research?

Rich: Poetry is not social research, per say, but can be utilized as data or as data presentation. Poetry allows for social context, for contextualized meanings to occur. It also has value that is differential. For example, if we wanted to understand a homeless man, a social scientist could conduct an interview, and then reduce the data into a poem. Or, we could ask the homeless man for his experience of the world, have him write his own poem. What is social research but documenting social phenomenon? In using poetry as research, we can take certain measures to make sure we have accurate, faithful information. Notice I don't say valid or reliable, those concepts are steeped in logical positivistic notions that do not really apply. But, we must make sure it is trustworthy data. We can ask our subjects the degree to which their experience and emotion was accurately captured, and work collaboratively with them to change or fix our data when it falls short. We can work with colleagues to review interviews and give us feedback about the degree to which they feel we were true to the text. Most importantly, we can be reflexive and explore our biases and subjectivity, and make sure to present this as data also.

Data Analysis

Marshall and Rossman (1989) say that data analysis in qualitative research is a matter of "reduction" and "interpretation" (p. 14). Qualitative work yields a vast amount of information. The researcher should reduce that information to discover patterns, categories, or themes, and then interpret these using some scheme. Forming the categories of information to which analytical codes are attached has been called developing coding categories (Bogdan & Biklin 1992) or generating categories, themes, or patterns (Marshall & Rossman 1989). According to Berg (1995), there are three major procedures that are used to develop classes and categories in data analysis. The first of these is the common class. A common class occurs in the culture at large. Typical common classes include such things as age and gender. The second is the special class that is particular to the culture being studied and consists of terminology that might be used to generate in-groups and out-groups. An example of a special class would be the term "Wannabe." The third class is the theoretical class. This class emerges from the data analysis itself and is an overarching concept that links the data.

Conversation data was qualitatively analyzed using thematic analysis. Additional analysis of words used by particular speakers and overlapping themes is included. Four themes emerged from the data. The first theme emerges as a response to the question, "What is photography as research and what is poetry?" I call it the Descriptive theme. The second theme is the Differences theme. The third is the Biases theme, and the final theme is the Justification theme. Each will be presented using first-order constructs—i.e., the words of the respondents without interpretation or renaming by the researcher—as the titles of the categories.

Descriptive Theme

The first theme emerges as a definition of photography as research and from a definition of poetry. It is interesting to compare the different ways in which the respondents answer the question. Peter, the photographer, begins by describing what photography is.

"It is writing with light."

Peter uses the following words and phrases to describe photography:
- it is research
- it is writing with light
- an illustration
- documents (as in records)
- more accurate than statistics
- direct representation of reality
- it is what it is
- no extrapolation
- not an approximation
- a tool
- susceptible to manipulation
- interpretive
- validates how things are
- convincing
- taps into range of intuitive appeal that is broader
- reaches a wider audience
- photographs are the eyes with a memory
- photographer is an ethnographer
- photographer becomes a student
- it is a one-to-one correspondence to the world
- it is reality
- takes out the imagination; there is only the image
- resonates with the human spirit more than numbers
- it is a good tool

"Practitioners rely more on practice wisdom, i.e., intuition, synthesis of informed judgment and the totality of what we know. ...that IS what a poem is."

Rich says poetry is:
- a good tool
- compression

- the reduction of many words into a few
- compression, sensory imagery, metaphoric language
- (may have) a dream-like quality
- (may) transcend formal logic
- (may) be more faithful to the logic of emotion
- form of expression
- healing
- incantation(s)
- curative
- language characterized by compression, image, and metaphor
- clarification and magnification of being
- the distillation of the essence of being, through language
- capture(s) the lived experience
- speaks to the difficulties of existence, things that contain paradox and emotion
- complex
- not social research per se
- has value that is differential

One of the most salient differences in the friends' responses to the question regarding use of photography or poetry as research is that the photographer clearly states that his art is research while the poet says his art is not research but can be used as data or data presentation. Both agree that their chosen methodology is a good tool to capture and compress complex social sciences data. Hidden within some of their observations are representations of the core arguments about the differences between their chosen qualitative methodologies and traditional quantitative methods. A point that Peter might want to consider is that while he maintains the viability of photography as reality, he also says it is interpretive. This suggests an inconsistency that should be expanded upon.

Differences Theme
Peter seems to hold that photography is limited by the same restraints that limit quantitative methods yet argues that a photograph is not only more accurate than statistics but also is more powerful.

"I am not sure photography has that experimental quality to it."

Peter begins by explaining the nature of inferential statistics in contrast to photography.

- (they are) estimations of reality.
- ...not sure photography has that experimental quality to it.
- (in research) you have to help people read the data.
- (photography involves) the aesthetic sensitivity of the researcher.
- you have your perspective and positivists have not overcome that;
  they think they do.
- You have to decide what to focus on.
- You have to think about it, and what it means, and how it inspires you.
- You can go back and pull out different layers of meaning.
- You have to keep shooting.
- ...we must guard against the false dichotomy of qualitative versus quantitative (the article uses qualitative both times—Freudian slip?) They are intertwined.
- They are all legitimate, but historically, we have elevated experimental research over other avenues of gaining knowledge.
- ...the photograph can be etched within the mind and impact us long after statistics are forgotten.
- What drives the photography process is that you don't know, so you shoot more to discover.

In contrast, Rich seems to articulate that there are differences between quantitative methods, traditional qualitative methods, and the use of poetry as data analysis.
Examples of Rich's comments are:

- (there is) no clear delineation between what we experience in the external world that can be broken down by method.
- Poems transcend a logic that numbers cannot understand.
- You can have a numerical score for depression that in many ways is representative of the *strength* of the depression. But what about the *meaning* of the depression...

- ...poetry allows for reduction of data.
- It might be one means of reconciling these two traditions (quantitative and qualitative), which today can feel very far apart.
- ...the poet must stay faithful to the data.
- The first allegiance of the researcher, as poet, has to be to the subject's experience.
- Present subject's experience as accurately as possible.
- Deconstruct the meaning of the experience and consciously allow for interpretation
- Have sought professional recognition and tried to align with scientists.
- Bias against arts and humanities.
- (in an interpretive poem) the consciousness and judgment of the researcher/poet is evident, even valued.

The authors seem to diverge a bit at this juncture. Peter maintains that the photograph is research in its own right. In contrast, Rich says that poetry adds a dimension to our understanding that quantitative methods cannot. Further, Rich does not see poetry as data collection but as a qualitative tool that can be used to analyze data. This difference in perspective of the two authors is interesting and creates a bit of a quandary for this analysis. Peter maintains that teaching the consumer to read research can be done with photography (I'd be interested in seeing how this can be done), and photography as research is subject to the same biases as are other research methods.

Biases Theme
Both Peter and Rich explain some ways that the photographer/ researcher and the researcher/poet (note the order of the word "researcher" for each; does this mark importance for each?) must work to eliminate bias to the greatest extent possible.

"All tools have limits."
Peter says:

- All tools have limits.
- ...we can manipulate it
- ...leave out certain variables
- ...motivated by ideology

- The playing field is level in the sense that it is a valid question across the board, and it's not only about photography.
- If you teach people how to consume, that is half the battle.
- You have to think about the subject matter and how you approach the subject matter.
- ...you photograph in a certain way
- ...not be biased, because you don't *know*
- ...ultimately, we cannot achieve objectivity
- ...it is about intersubjectivity
- That is the discovery process.

"We can be reflexive and explore our biases and subjectivity and make sure to present this as data also."

Rich, however, maintains that the researcher/poet has specific obligations to guard against bias and to stay as true to the words of the subject as possible, even when using an interpretive poem.

- (the researcher/poet must undertake) conscious and constant self-exploration.
- Notes serve as both data to be worked with, as well as ethnographic notes that explore their reactions.
- ...these biases should be presented so the reader can decide for themselves how to interpret the poem.
- ...utilize member checks
- ...asking other researchers to check your coding
- ...make sure we have accurate, faithful information
- ...must make sure it is trustworthy data
- ...we can be reflexive and explore our biases and subjectivity and make sure to present this as data also

Rich maintains that if biases are present, it is important that the poet/researcher is aware of them, acknowledges them, and they even have the potential to become part of the process. In addition, Rich would utilize more traditional methods in order to eliminate as much bias as possible. Peter, on the other hand, maintains that all research is subject to bias and that it can never completely be eliminated. In order to control or account for bias, Peter would simply take more photographs. Peter seems to think that the photograph is both valid and reliable (to use quantitative terms).

Justification Theme
In this theme, the authors attempt to validate their chosen methodologies as important contributors to qualitative research endeavors.

"When words are not appropriate."
Peter believes that photography is a valid research methodology for the following reasons:

- (photography) documents more accurately than statistics
- (photography does not) sensationalize the event; the event (is) sensational.
- There is a respect for subject matter that needs to happen.
- You have to take poetic license and select context.
- You have to be open to things that are different.
- You have to respond to the data.
- It is not confirming; it is learning from the documented event.
- …allow for some spontaneity
- Peter would use photography "when words are not appropriate."
- (photography) provided authenticity
- images…more powerful than words
- …it is more objective
- …the photograph can be etched within the mind and impact us long after statistics are forgotten.
- …statistical research does not impact treatment very much, but these other methods can (both methods) resonate with the human spirit more than numbers, both in terms of expression and interpretation.

"There are many ways of knowing."
In conjunction with Peter's observations, Rich says:

- …there are many ways of knowing.
- Poems allow for holistic understanding that
- …transcends a logic
- Poems allow for intuition, for emotion…important parts of the human experience that cannot be expressed numerically
- …subtle tones and textures
- …is a good tool with culturally diverse populations

- ...allows for reduction of data
- ...aesthetic means
- ...utilitarian ways
- ...depends on epistemology
- ...can be utilized as data or as data presentation
- ...contextualized meanings

When comparing the two lists, it seems that Peter would create an image that may surpass words in power and longevity but would still allow people to try to put their own words to it. Rich would create, from words, an image that would also be more powerful than mere rhetoric. It is interesting that Peter uses the term "poetic license." Both agree that their method has the potential to resonate with the human spirit more than numbers.

Other Observations

Peter, as photographer, uses the word "frame" several times when speaking. This may be as a result of his skills or may belie a particular theoretical orientation—the social construction of reality. As researcher, I see the fit between his words, the method, and social constructionism, For example, using Berger and Luckman's (1967) major points: the most important reality is the everyday reality; reality has both a temporal and spatial component; knowledge is retained and disseminated in different ways by different people; and our everyday reality becomes routinized. It seems that Peter would try to understand everyday reality by taking as many pictures as possible of the moment. For him, then, he has created his reality. People who view the photographs will create their own realities based upon their life experiences and how they interpret the photographs. He maintains that he can teach people how to be consumers of research through pictures, but he doesn't articulate this. How can Peter share his reality with consumers of research with only one picture? He supposes that he can and that is the core component of photography: It is reality. Furthermore, this is consistent with the theoretical model.

If I were to use a theory to examine Rich's responses, I would use phenomenology, with a bit of existentialism. Rich is true to the subjective view of the respondent but maintains that the view of the researcher is also very important and neither can ever be fully understood; we can only try to understand. There are several words used in the manuscript that provide interest. For example, on page 14, the word "qualitative" is used once correctly and once where quantitative should have been used.

This could be passed off as an editing error, but it also may be an unconscious elimination of "quantitative" from the discussion. On page 19, the word "merely" appears before the phrase "present the subjects' experience as accurately as possible." One of Rich's primary concerns is that the poet/researcher should remain as close to the words of the subject as possible. This is not a "mere" attempt at accuracy; it is cardinal. Again, usage of this word might simply point out an issue of word choice, or it could indicate an unconscious understanding (bias) that interpretive work is much harder or more significant than research poems utilizing the subject's words. At least, this is food for thought and may lend itself to further study.

Finally, as would be expected, the Difference and Bias themes overlap. The authors set out to discuss the contrasts and comparisons of their work to quantitative methods. What emerged was more of a similarity between all methods. This is particularly interesting in view of the opinion that qualitative research is historically undervalued. This might tell the reader that these two individuals are committed to the research process, aware of the limitations of all methodologies, and see their works "through a different lens" and "in the words of the subject and their own stanzas."

Conclusion

The conversation between social workers explored the methodological and epistemological potential of poetry and photography for social work research. The discussion was personally satisfying as well as professionally beneficial. The authors found affirming the process of critically engaging one another in order to deepen ways of knowing and to better explain the social world. Questions and responses were motivated by a deep curiosity for gaining understanding and insight. The conversation revealed how poetry and photography offer expressive and creative opportunity for approaching knowledge-building beyond merely reducing the fullness of reality into bits and pieces. Meaning can be found between the conversants, the process if you will, as well as in the discrete representation of words.

The authors believe their conversation unveiled promising potential for qualitative social work research. Poetry and photography are valid means of collecting, organizing, and interpreting data. They recognize that the human experience occurs within natural settings and the importance of giving voice to situated events and perspectives. Such an approach to research resonates with social work's recognition of the vital relevance of person-in-environment. It is the hope of the authors to stimulate the engagement in and publication of similar conversations; such conversations are invaluable sources of knowledge to facilitate the growth and development of future qualitative researchers.

References

Babbie, E. (2000). *The practice of social research* (9th ed.). Wadsworth.
Berg, B. L. (1995). *Qualitative research methods for the social sciences* (2nd ed.). Allyn and Bacon.
Berger, P. L., & Luckmann, T. (1967). *The social construction of reality: A treatise on the sociology of knowledge* (3rd ed.). Anchor Books.
Bogdan, R. C. & Biklin, S, K. (1992). *Qualitative research for education: An introduction to theory and methods.* Allyn and Bacon.
Brearley, L. (2000). Exploring the creative voice in an academic context. *The Qualitative Report, 5*(3/4). Retrieved from http://www.nova.edu/ssss/QR/QR5-3/brearley.html.
Chan, Z. C. Y. (2003). Poetry writing: A therapeutic means for a social work doctoral student in the process of study. *Journal of Poetry Therapy, 16*(1), 5–17.
Collier, J., & Collier, M. (1986). *Visual anthropology: Photography as a research method.* University of New Mexico Press.
Curtis, J. (1989) *Mind's eye, mind's truth: FSA photography reconsidered.* Temple University Press.
Dunlop, T. (1998). From the trenches: Some personal thoughts on college renewal for the new millennium. *College Quarterly*, Winter, 35–46.
Ellis, C., & Bochner, A. P. (2000). Autoethnography, personal narrative, reflexivity: Researcher as subject. In N. K. Denzin & Y. S. Lincoln (Eds.), *Handbook of qualitative research.* Sage.
Eisner, E. W. (1981). On the differences between scientific and artistic approaches to qualitative research. *Educational Researcher, 10*(4), 5–9.
Finley, S., & Knowles, J. G. (1995). Researcher as artist/artist as researcher. *Qualitative Inquiry, 1*(1), 110–142.
Furman, R. (2004a). Using poetry and narrative as qualitative data: Exploring a father's cancer through poetry. *Family, Systems & Health, 22*(2), 162–170.
Furman, R. (2004b). Exploring friendship loss through poetry. *Journal of Loss and Trauma, 9*(1), 181–187.
Gee, J. (1991). A linguistic approach to narrative. *Journal of Narrative and Life History, 1*(1), 15–39.

Langer, C., & Furman, R. (2004). Exploring identity and assimilation. Research and interpretative poems. *Forum: Qualitative Social Research, 5*(2), http://www.qualitative-research.net/fqs-texte/2-04/2-04langerfurman-e.htm

Lewis, L. S., & Altbach, P. G. (2000). Faculty versus administration: A universal problem. *International Higher Education, 2*(1). 35–45.

Marshall, C., & Rossman, G. B. (1989). *Designing qualitative research*. Sage.

Percer, L. H. (1992). Going beyond the demonstrable range in educational scholarship: Exploring the intersections of poetry and research. The *Qualitative Report, 7*(2). Retrieved from http://www.nova.edu/ssss/QR/QR7-2/hayespercer.html.

Poindexter, C. C. (2002). Meaning from methods: Re-presenting narratives of an HIV-affected caregiver. *Qualitative Social Work, 1*(1), 59–78.

Richardson, L. (1992). The consequences of poetic representation. In C. Ellis & M. G. Flaherty (Eds.), *Investigating subjectivity: Research on lived experience* (pp.125–173). Sage.

Schatz, M. S., Furman, R., & Jenkins, L. (2003) A space to grow: Using the dialogue approach in multinational/multicultural social work. *International Work, 46*(4), 481–494.

Stein, H. F. (2003). The inner world of workplaces: Accessing this world through poetry, narrative, literature, music and visual art. *Consulting Psychology Journal Practice and Research, 55*(2), 84–93.

Stein, H. F. (2004). A window to the interior of experience. *Families, Systems, & Health, 22*(2), 178–179.

Willis, P. (2002). Poetry and poetics in phenomenological research. *Indo-Pacific Journal of Phenomenology, 3*(1), 1–19.

Part III:

Poetry and Education/Teaching

Chapter 17

Using Poetry and Written Exercises to Teach Empathy

Empathy is a core principle in social work and other helping professions (Johnson, 1992). It is an important factor in professional helping that cuts across theoretical orientations (Corsini & Wedding, 1995) and levels of practice—that is, individual, group, family and community work (Ivey, Pedersen, & Ivey, 2001; Hepworth, Rooney, & Larsen, 2002). It also is a key to competent multicultural helping (Lum, 2002; Wehrly, 1995). Being empathic is perhaps the central skill that allows practitioners to adhere to the adage "start where the client is," a key factor in establishing good helping relationships (Corey, 1995).

In spite of its importance, being empathic is often difficult for students and new practitioners. Some students struggle with the acceptance of clients who have multiple problems or who may be viewed as "resistant." Empathy is an easy concept in theory or when one agrees with the value and behavior of a client, but far more difficult in challenging practice situations.

Empathy can be broken down into concrete teachable components such as reflective listening, yet true and meaningful empathy may be far more complex and difficult to teach. As Rashkin and Rogers noted (1995):

> Empathy is an active, immediate, continuous process. The counselor makes a maximum effort to get within and to live the attitudes expressed instead of observing them, diagnosing them, or thinking of ways to make the process go faster. Such understanding must be acquired through intense, continuous and attentive attention to the feelings of others, to the exclusion of any other type of attention. (p.142)

The purpose of this article is to demonstrate how exercises associated with poetry and bibliotherapy can be useful in assisting faculty of the helping professions to teach empathy to their students. It will also be relevant to those supervising new helping professionals. The article will help meet this aim in several ways. First, a brief exploration of the concept of empathy will be discussed. Second, exercises that can be useful in teaching empathy will be presented. Third, examples from the writings of social work students will serve as case examples.

Empathy

Empathy has been defined as the understanding of a person from their frame of reference, perspective, or vantage point (Okun, 1992). Murphy and Dillon (1998) define empathy as the ability to immerse oneself in the experience of another without losing one's own sense of self. Brems (2001) posits that empathy cannot be achieved without understanding a client on affective, cognitive, and behavioral levels. Yalom (1995) suggests that underlining any consideration of technique or theory in therapeutic practice is the need for a helping relationship characterized by acceptance, genuineness, and empathy.

Carl Rogers (1980) was perhaps the first theorist to truly appreciate the importance of empathy to the development of human relationships. In his description of empathic listening, he highlights that true empathy is a way of *being* with a client. Indeed, empathy is perhaps the most central concept and skill to his client centered theory and practice. Egan (1994) recognizes the importance of empathy as a set of techniques, as an art, as well as a way of being. He argues that it is a primary mode of human contact that forms the basis of human relationships. In their classic chronicle of dilemmas in helping, *How can I help*, Dass and Gorman (1999) explore the importance of *the listening mind*, that part of each of us that can deeply attend to and respond to the needs of others: in short, empathy

Empathy is essential for various reasons. Empathy allows for ethical decisions making and altruism (Hurlbut, 2002). Without empathy, one is less likely to make pro-social choices based upon ethical reasoning. Researchers have explored the importance of empathy as a prerequisite for social justice. It is suggested that empathy is a requisite feature in the possession of a social consciousness (Blader & Tyler, 2002). Empathy has been shown to be lacking in children and adolescents with a history of substance abuse and criminality (Broom, 2002). Clearly, the development of empathy is essential for personal and social well-being.

Exercises to Increase Empathy

This section will explore various types of written exercises that I have used in teaching undergraduate and graduate social work students. It is my hope that readers of this article will borrow from and change these exercises to meet the needs of their students and clients.

Remembering Empathy Poem

Students are encouraged to remember a time in their lives when they felt deeply accepted and understood by someone. They are to remember the context in as much detail as possible, using as many senses as they can. Students are encouraged to explore what the other person did to make them feel so accepted, valued, and cared for. When students are able to clearly see, feel, and/or hear the situation, they are asked to spend ten to fifteen minutes writing a poem about their experiences. The goal is to have them describe the event utilizing as much sensory detail as possible. It is valuable to give students the opportunity to share what they wrote. The instructor can facilitate a discussion of the common themes that students wrote about. This exercise can be a valuable introduction to the topic of empathy or helping skills.

The Letter Poem

In this exercise, students in field practicum are asked to think about a client with whom they are having a difficult time. Students are asked to imagine themselves as this client. Some students might want to close their eyes and visualize this person. Some may take a more cerebral or "rational" approach. It is important to encourage students to utilize their dominant sense in order to help them in this process. They should be encouraged to imagine how this client feels about themselves, their life, and what it is like to be receiving assistance from the helper (the student participating in the exercise). This part of the exercise can work well by guiding the students through a visualization of their clients' lives. After several minutes, the student still imagining that they are the client will write a letter poem to the worker (themselves). In so doing, students are assisted in exploring how people feel about being in the role of client, and how they might perceive their helpers. The case example below will illustrate this point.

Sentence Completion Exercise

Sentence completion exercises help students feel comfortable by taking away the forebodingness of the blank page (Jacobs, Masson, & Harvill, 2002). The following sentence completion exercise is useful in helping students who need more structure for their written work.

My client feels _____ about their life.
My client sometimes is resistant to my help because_____
I respect my client because_____
My client possesses the following strengths: _____
Sometimes I underestimate my client by_____
My client has overcome the following difficulties_____

Resilience Poem

In this exercise, students are encouraged to focus on an empathic understanding of resilience and strength. Too often, helpers focus on what is wrong with clients and seek to understand only their problems and pains. An effective helper, however, is able to draw out clients' strengths, and help them reframe their experiences. Clients also tend to focus only on what is difficult and problematic in their lives. In this exercise, I have utilized a poem written by a women staying in a women's shelter that Sister Arlene Hynes (1987), one of the pioneers of poetry therapy, worked with. I read the poem three times to the class, and ask students to do one of two assignments. They are invited to either write a response letter to the client, focusing on their strengths, or write a poem reframing the original from one of trauma to triumph, victimization to resilience.

> Understand
> I am beginning to understand
> the horror of my situation
> the bleakness of my life
> the emptiness of my future
> cuts me like a knife
>
> I am begging to understand
> the madness of who you are
> the hollowness of the day
> the sadness of the fighting
> what else can I say?

> I am begging to understand
> the joke life played on me
> how futile are my dreams
> the absence of my anger
> the silence of my screams.

Poems from In-Class Interviews or Films

Some courses come before students have had significant experience with clients. In such situations, they can be encouraged to interview each other and write an empathic poem or paragraph about person they interviewed. Once a student completes their work, they are encouraged to share it with the person about which it has been written. The subject of the poem can give the writer feedback regarding the degree to which they were fully understood. The student can then be encouraged to revise the poem incorporating their new understanding.

Films can also be used as the subject for writing empathy poems. The instructor shows a film in class that is rich in emotional content and has students write a poem from the perspective of one or several of the important characters. This exercise allows instructors to assess the degree to which students are able to be empathic. In-class discussion of the poems can help students expand their skills by helping them see what other students have attended to.

One film that I have found particularly helpful in this exercise is the *Great Santini* (Carlino, 1979). This fine film depicts the story of the life of a military family in the South. Based on a novel by Pat Conroy, this movie explores the nature of relationships in a highly structured, patriarchal family. Family members respond to issues of alcoholism, domestic violence, and trauma with amazing clarity. The film also explores the dynamics of relationships between fathers and sons, mothers and daughters, and men and women. When the father dies in an airplane crash, the family is forced to face their own ambivalent feelings toward him in the resolution of their grief as well as in the development of new means of meeting their needs. This film is particularly valuable, as students often find themselves identifying with one family member over another and must struggle to understand and have compassion for other members, in particular the father.

Social Problem Poem

Another means of increasing empathy that does not involve writing about a client directly is the social problem poem. In this exercise, often useful in social policy or history courses, students are asked to research a social problem, such as poverty or discrimination. They conduct a literature review that helps them gather material to use in the creation of a poems, letters, or paragraphs. These writings can be written in the voice of specific people who were involved in the policy issue, or real or imagined people who suffer the consequences of the social problem. This assignment is valuable as an option for a final, integrative paper. In such an assignment, students use various types of writing (letters, poems, short essays, simulated newspaper clippings) to document the issue they are exploring. I am currently using poems in this manner to explore the social problems related to managed care.

Case Examples

The letters presented in this section were written by students in a Bachelors of Social Work group practice class. Students were asked to complete letters written from the voice of a client that they had a difficult time with, as described in the letter exercise previously discussed. Above each example, I will explore the significance of the exercise to each student and provide some context, when needed, to help increase the reader's understanding.

In the first example, the student takes on the voice of a client whose wife told him something secret and taboo about her past. Through adopting the voice of the client, the student began to appreciate just how difficult it had been for the client not only to discuss the situation, but to even come for help. Through completing the exercise, this student was able to come to terms with how hard it has been for the client to trust him.

> I really need you to understand how embarrassing this is for me. There is no one I can talk to who won't judge me. It's not as if I am even looking for help, because I know you can't imagine my situation. I am really just looking for understanding. I hope that this is completely confidential. Part of the difficulty is not being able to talk to anyone—I mean I have to call the crisis hotline in the middle of the night when my wife is called into work. I can't even bring myself to talk to her about it. I love her so much, but the taboo surrounding what she told me makes me shy away from a discussion. Like we don't talk about it happening and I have so many emotions. Sometimes I even feel jealous and sometimes pure disgust. But how can I be disgusted or angry at someone that I love so much? It's just that we dated

for so long and I didn't find out until a year into the marriage. Can anyone hear this conversation? I don't want to disclose much about myself but I'm a professional and what would people think if they found out.

In the following example, a student working with the elderly in a nursing home writes from a perspective of a woman struggling with the realities of her new dependence, her perceived abandonment at the hands of her family, and the difficulties of being cared for by strangers. In writing this piece, the student was able to clearly place themselves in the shoes of someone they previously only saw in behavioral terms as difficult to get along with, demanding, and hostile. By understanding the context of the client's behavior, the student was able to increase the degree to which they felt empathy toward her.

> My life has been a hard one. A long one. I have always had to fight for what I needed and even more for the things I wanted. I have always taken care of myself and my family and expected nothing. Then I began to age. Standing up for myself was not only harder for me to do figuratively, but physically also. Those who I have in my life gave up on me and placed me here with you, a stranger who comes in and treats me like a person without a face. I hate asking for help and I hate having to ask blurred faces of strangers even more. You are one of the many in this army of people taking care of me. I don't know you and you don't know me, but you think you do. You see me as a whiner, a mean old lady, a stubborn fool, a foul mouth beast. I don't mean to be. I am who I am. A person fighting for my independence and what is left of my pride.

The next letter was written in the voice of a veteran struggling with alcoholism. While processing this exercise in class, the student who wrote the letter, also a veteran, discussed how doing this exercise helped him become more empathic. First, it made him realize that he was not responsible for the client's behavior, that he could only do his best to help, and nothing more. Second, this insight helped him realize that he was doing too much of the work, and needed to help the client take more control of his own growth. Last, it helped him realize that even though he shared many of the same experiences as this man, he needed to work hard towards developing empathy with all his clients.

> I don't know where to begin. I know you have spent much energy and time in tying to help me and I always drop the ball. It's getting to the point where I don't want to see you because I feel so bad about not meeting your expectations. Then I drink to feel better, and I drink and drink and drink. Not that I need an excuse to drink, but then I feel bad again cause I know that the drinking gets in the way. And this, this therapy, is starting to take the fun out of my drunks, and this is pissing me off. I know that I am rambling, not making any sense, and this pisses me off too. It seems like about the only thing I am good at is being pissed off. And that's the point, I guess. I don't want to be pissed at you and I am sort of stuck there. Don't try to help me so damn much; that is what your good at, but that pisses me off too. I hope you understand.

In the following letter poem, the student sought to understand the perspective of a child with whom she works. Through writing this poem, she was able to explore how difficult it has been for the client to accept a change in her helper's role. She was able to come to understand how the client felt: unsupported, jealous, and abandoned. By engaging in this exercise, she was able to assess her own behavior through the eyes of another.

> I used to really like you. You were funny and silly at camp. You were my favorite provider. But then you started working at the school. I really liked it at first. But then you started bossing me around. I felt like I couldn't laugh with you anymore. All the kids wanted to sit by you and not me, that's why I stopped liking you. I would go home and get yelled out and bossed around, then I would go to school and you would not support me either. All I needed was a little patience. When I was being mean, I just needed to see that you would be there the next morning. Don't tell me when I am doing something wrong;, tell me when I am doing something right. Give me choices, not ultimatums.

In each of the examples above, students were able to increase their level of empathy for clients with whom they had been struggling. By so doing, they were able to not only understand the feelings of their clients, but also were able to critically evaluate their own helping behavior, as well as the social context in which they were providing services.

Conclusion

A key question is whether empathy is a skill that can be learned or a preexisting personal trait. It seems to be both. Research has demonstrated that empathy can be learned in clinical situations (Cautela, 1996) and through normal developmental experience as well (Mastrich, 2002). It has also been demonstrated that empathy can be improved in the training of helping professionals through intensive training methods (McLeod, Deane & Hogbin, 2002). It has been my experience that through the use of written exercises, students who already possess a high degree of empathy can improve this capacity, and those who struggle with expressing empathic reactions can improve their empathic responses. Future explorations should seek to test the degree to which this experience is true, and to what situations it is generalizable.

References

Brems, C. (2001). *Basic skills in psychotherapy and counseling*. Brooks/Cole.

Blader, S. L., & Tyler, T. R. (2002). Justice and empathy: What motivates people to help each other. In M. Ross & D. T. Miller (Eds.), *The justice motive in everyday life* (pp. 226–250). Cambridge University Press.

Broom, E. W. (2002). *An examination of factors related to the cognitive and affective empathy levels of adjudicated youth*. Dissertation Abstracts International, 63(2-A). US: University Microfilms International.

Carlino, L. J. (Director). (1979). *The Great Santini.*

Cautela, J. R. (1996). Training the client to be empathetic. In J. R. Cautela & W. Ishaq (Eds.), *Contemporary issues in behavior therapy: Improving the human condition* (pp. 337–353). Applied Clinical Psychology.

Corey, G. (1995). *Theory and practice of group counseling* (4th ed.). Brooks/Cole.

Corsini, R. J., & Wedding, D. (1995). *Current psychotherapies* (5th ed.). F. E. Peacock.

Dass, R., & Gorman, P. (1999). *How can I help?* Alfred A. Knopf.

Egan, G. (1994). *The skilled helper: A problem-management approach to helping*. Brooks/Cole.

Hepworth, D. H., Rooney, R. H., & Larsen, J. A. (2002). *Direct social work practice*. Pacific Grove, CA: Brooks/Cole.

Hynes, A. M.(1987). Biblio/poetry therapy in women's shelters. *American Journal of Social Psychiatry, 7*(2), 112–114.

Hurlbut, W. B. (2002). Empathy, evolution and altruism. In S.G. Post. & L. G. Underwood. (Eds.), *Altruism & altruistic love: Science, philosophy, & religion in dialogue* (pp. 309–327). Oxford University Press.

Ivey, A. E., Pedersen, P. B., & Ivey, M. B. (2001). *Intentional group counseling: A microskills approach*. Brooks/Cole.

Jacobs, E. E., Masson, R. L., & Harvill, R. L. (2002). *Group counseling: Strategies and skills*. Brooks/Cole.

Johnson, L. C. (1992). *Social work practice: A generalist approach* (4th ed.). Allyn and Bacon.

Lum, D. (2002). *Social work practice and people of color: A process-stage approach* (4th ed.). Brooks/Cole.

Mastrich, J. (2002). *Really winning: Using sports to develop character and integrity in our boys*. St Martin's Press.

McLeod, H. J., Deane, F. P., & Hogbin, B. (2002). Changing staff attitudes and empathy for working with people with psychosis. *Behavioural & Cognitive Psychotherapy, 30*(4), 459–470.

Murphy, B. C., & Dillon, C. (1998). *Interviewing in action: Process and practice*. Brooks/Cole.

Okun, B. F. (1992). *Effective helping: Interviewing and counseling techniques* (4th ed.). Brooks/Cole.

Raskin, N. J., & Rogers, C. R. (1995). Person-centered therapy. In R. J. Corsini & D. Wedding (Eds.), *Current psychotherapies* (5th ed.; pp. 128–161). Itasca, IL: F. E. Peacock.

Rogers, C. R. (1980). *A way of being*. Houghton Mifflin.

Wehrly, B. (1995). *Pathways to multicultural counseling competence*. Pacific Grove, CA.

Yalom, I. (1995). *The theory and practice of group psychotherapy* (4th ed.). Basic Books.

Chapter 18

Beyond the Literary Uses of Poetry: A Class for University Freshmen

The uses of poetry therapy—or poetry in service of growth, change and transformation—have been expanding. Poetry has become increasingly utilized as a tool of change in health care settings (Stuckey & Nobel, 2010), international development (Furman, 2006a), and even in business (Zinkhan, 1994). These less traditional uses of poetry have become increasingly important and represent an expansion of the domain of poetry therapy (poetry as change) that complements more common uses such as psychotherapy, personal expression, and community change (Furman, Riddoch, & Collins, 2004).

Poetry has also become increasingly recognized as a powerful tool of inquiry and social research, as exemplified by a recent issue of *Educational Insights* dedicated to the topic (Prendergast, 2009). Poetry has been used by scholars as a means of increasing researchers' understanding of their data and finding ways of presenting data in more meaningful ways (Furman, 2006b & c; Willis, 2002). Given that poetry holds great utility and promise as a tool for inquiry, it follows that the non-literary uses of poetry would have the potential to be useful in the educational process; indeed, poetry has made its way into various educational settings (Furman, 2005). For instance, Furman, Coyne, and Negi (2008) utilized the writing of poetry to help students process their feelings regarding social development paradoxes encountered in an international social work course in Nicaragua. Similarly, Langer and Furman (2004) used poetry as a means of exploring ethnic and racial identity to improve social work students' ability to engage in culturally sensitive practice. Recently, an entire issue of the journal *Learning Landscapes* explored the ways poetry has been used in various educational settings and with students of all ages, from those in early childhood education to graduate education (Butler-Kisber, 2010).

Given that poetry has been successfully used as a method of inquiry within the classroom, it seemed like an exciting possibility to develop a course that both studied the non-literary uses of poetry while utilizing poetry as a vehicle to achieve academic goals. The possibility of this parallel process, the uses of poetry as content and method, has intrigued me as a potentially powerful means to structure a college course.

The purpose of this paper is to explore the outcomes of my exploring these synergies: the course "Beyond the Literary Uses of Poetry." This freshman course at the University of Washington. Tacoma allowed students to learn about the non-literary uses of poetry using experiential, hands-on methods that help students develop new communication and analytical skills.

About the Course

The complete and technical name of the class was Introduction to Social Science 123: Beyond the Literary Uses of Poetry. The class was part of the undergraduate freshman "core" at the University of Washington, Tacoma (UWT). UWT is young campus, part of the University of Washington, one of the prominent public research universities in North America. UWT began in 1990 as an upper division and graduate university and accepted its first freshman only five years ago. The Freshman Core is a series of courses that highlight interdisciplinary learning and inquiry and seek to prepare students with the analytical skills they need to succeed in college and beyond.

The course description below explores some of these skills and theme.

> In this course, you will explore the non-literary uses of poetry. Unlike courses that explore the literary merits of poetry, in this course you will come to view poetry as a vehicle through which social and personal aims are achieved. You will learn to view poetry as a means of documenting and presenting human experience and social research, as a tool in therapy and change and community engagement, among other topics. You will learn to use poetry as a means of exploring key aspects of your own lives, and as a means of acquiring the important skills of self-reflection, data analysis, and public speaking.

Additionally, the goals of the course and the overall goals of the Freshman Core provided structure for the course. It is clear from a review of each of these goals that the writing, reading, and performance of poetry could easily be used to facilitate learning and meeting many of the social science objectives.

Goals of the course:
1. Students will develop an understanding of the non-literary use of poetry.
2. Students will gain an understanding of the multiplicity of human experience as depicted through poetry.
3. Students will acquire skills and become familiar with the research method of autoethnography and will develop research skills congruent with this method.
4. Through understanding how poetry is used as a tool for community development and social change, students will define their roles and responsibilities as members of a broader community.
5. Through various writing exercises, students will increase their ability to write to various discourse communities.
6. Students will develop the capacity for public speaking and performance.

Goals for Freshman Core Covered in the Course

Communication
- Express ideas clearly in writing and speaking in order to synthesize and evaluate information before presenting it.
- Enter/place themselves into an existing dialogue (intellectual, political, etc.).
- Identify, analyze, and summarize/represent the key elements of a text.

Global Perspective
- Think outside of cultural norms and values, including their own perspectives, to critically engage the larger world.
- Sharpen inquiry and critical thinking skills.
- Self-assess personal strengths (personal, academic, social) and how they can help overcome weaknesses.
- Approach complex issues by taking a large question and breaking it down into manageable pieces.
- Make meaningful connections among assignments and readings in order to develop a sense of the "big picture."
- Collect, evaluate, and analyze information and resources to solve problems or answer questions.

Weekly Topic, Speakers, and Experiences

Weekly topics reflected the various non-literary ways that poetry is used. Of course, no exploration of poetry would be complete without discussing some of the basic literary concepts of poetry. During the first week, we discussed definitions of poetry, and explored the distinction between poetry as a literary form and use of poetry for non-literary means. During the second week, we explored poetry as a tool of research and inquiry, focusing on innovations in post-modern research as a tool for understanding the world (Furman et al., 2007). Week two expanded on the theme of inquiry and investigation, moving into non-systematic uses of poetry as a vehicle to document social life. During week two, we had our first speaker/presenter, a well-known local poet whose performance pieces document important urban themes such as the paradoxes and contradictions of gentrification and development.

The speaker laid the groundwork for our third week's topic—poetry as performance. During this week, we explored skills that would prepare students for the end of the semester, when they would each perform a poem in front of the class. To prepare for their performances, we discussed various strategies, skills and tools for public speaking and performing poetry. Students learned the importance of audience, the expression of emotion, how to induce empathy, along with the use of volume, intonation, cadence, facial expressions, and body language. We listened to poets from various "schools," read their work (utilizing online recordings and videos from YouTube); this included the beats, academic poets, and slam poets. During week four we delved into poetry as a tool for self-exploration. It was during this week that I introduced the major assignment for the course, the poetic autoethnography assignment. This assignment connected what we learned about poetic inquiry during the first week with the current topic and presented students with a structured means of exploring an area they wished to investigate in their own lives. In this sense, the students were asked to become the archeologist of their own experiences (Stein, 2004). As the assignment was such an integral aspect of the course, I present it in its entirety below.

Poetic Autoethnography Assignment:
Introduction to Social Sciences: Beyond the Literary Uses of Poetry

As we have and will discuss, autoethnographies are explorations into important aspects of the self (in this case, yourself) that can also explore "truths" about groups of people, or about humankind as a whole. For the purpose of this assignment, we will be using my two articles on research poems and autoethnographies as models. That is, you will be utilizing aspects of the methodology that I have used to explore a topic about your life that you deem worthy of self-exploration/research.

Tasks

Step one: You will select an autoethnographic topic that you wish to explore. By January 20th, you will submit your topic to the instructor. If it makes sense to me, I will immediately approve it. If not, we will talk about it.

Step two: Over a three week period, you will write narratives about the topic that you selected. You will be given ten minutes per class to write these narratives, and should write several on your own. On Feb. 10, you will show your narratives to the instructor, in class. Overall, you need to have written a total of ten narratives, of approximately one to five paragraphs in length each. These narratives may be handwritten.

Step three: You will code your narratives, utilizing the method described in the articles and explored in great detail in class. You may work independently, in small groups, or in pairs outside of class to engage in the coding process.

Step four: Go back to your narratives and find the passages that best represent the themes you discovered. Using those representative lines, you will create five poems. You may choose to either use your original lines, or you may make minor revisions. Revisions should only be made if they help you more accurately present the themes you are exploring. You may place your poems into one of several poetic forms/structures we have explored- Pantoums, Tanka, or free verse (not technically a "form" or "structure," as we shall explore).

Products
- A one-paragraph discussion of your topic
- At least ten journal entries about the topic you will explore
- Your coding system and a one-page explanation of it

- A two-page exploration of the process of engaging in this work. This should explore what it was like to do this assignment, what you learned, and what difficulties you overcame. Also, discuss what this has taught you about your own strengths and limitations
- At least five research poems that explore several of the themes you identified.

Using poetry to explore the self, provided a useful introduction to poetry therapy, a topic that we discussed during weeks five and six. Two different practicing poetry therapists visited our class during the week and presented their work. Both also engaged students in writing exercises that they used with their clients. Students had the opportunity to read their poems and share what the experiences meant to them. During week eight, we learned the uses of poetry for community change. During this week, three homeless women, part of a women's collaborative, discussed the role poetry played in their overcoming substance abuse, mental illness, and homelessness. They discussed how they used their self-published book to education the public about homelessness, substance abuse, and women's issues. During week nine, we explored poetry as a tool of social protest. We read poetry protesting the Vietnam War, the current wars, environmental degradation, and the violation of immigrant's rights. Given that most of the students were between 18 and 20 years old, they particularly resonated with these themes. When I teach the course again, I will have protest poetry be the topic of the second week of the course.

Additional Teaching Methods and Considerations

Teaching methods were designed to demonstrate the non-literary uses of poetry and meet learning objectives. Nearly each day students engaged in what is termed "low risk" assignments to help them become more confident as writers. Low-risk assignments are those that are designed to get students to write with minimal pressure and with few expectations other than that they write; they typically are not graded. Such assignments help new college students become comfortable with viewing writing as a daily part of their lives and as a method of inquiry. For instance, after a guest speaker, students were asked to engage in a "free write" for five minutes about their reaction to the speaker.

Students were given the opportunity to read their work out loud, but there was no pressure to do so.

Students engaged in many experiential assignments during the semester. Each week, in-class writing assignments were designed to simultaneously amplify themes of the course and meet the learning objectives of the class. After a lecture on poetry therapy, students were asked to write a poem about what they had learned during the class session. This exercise helped students to synthesize what they learned and place it within the context of other course information and objectives. Assignments such as this also help students understand the value of making a written record of their learning. In this sense, they learned that writing was not only the end product of what they learned, but a critical means by which to process information and learn.

Conclusion

Poetry has many uses within higher educational settings. The reading, writing, and performing of poetry can be of value as a means of meeting educational goals and objectives. The parallel process of studying the non-literary uses of poetry while utilizing many of these tools in a freshman course seemed to represent a new use of poetry therapy. The interdisciplinary approach adopted by the course can help new students learn to think outside of disciplinary boxes that can hinder problem solving and learning.

References

Butler-Kisber, L. (Eds.) (2010). Poetry and education: Possibilities and practices. Special issue, *Learning Landscapes, 4*(1), 45–53.

Furman, R. (2005). Using poetry and written exercises to teach empathy. *Journal of Poetry Therapy, 18*(2), 103–110.

Furman, R. (2006a). A qualitative study of social development paradoxes in Guatemala using the research poem. *Journal of Comparative Social Welfare, 22*(1), 37–48.

Furman, R. (2006b). Poetic forms and structures in qualitative health research. *Qualitative Health Research, 16*(4), 560–566.

Furman, R., Coyne, A., & Negi, N. (2008). An international experience for social work students: Self-reflection through poetry and journal writing exercises. *Journal of Teaching in Social Work, 28*(1–2), 71–86.

Furman, R., Langer, C., Davis, C. S., Gallardo, H. P., & Kulkarni, S. (2007). Expressive research and reflective poetry as qualitative inquiry: A study of adolescent identity. *Qualitative Research, 5*(3), 301–315.

Furman, R., Riddoch, R., & Collins, K. (2004). Poetry, writing & community practice. *Human Service Education, 24*(1), 19–32.

Langer, C. L., & Furman, R. (2004). Exploring identity and assimilation. Research and interpretative poems. Forum: Qualitative Social Research, 5(2). http://www.qualitative-research.net/fqs-texte/2-04/2-04langerfurman-e.htm

Prendergast, M. (Ed.). (2009). Poetic inquiry. *Educational Insights, 13*(3).

Stein, H.F. (2004) A window to the interior of experience. *Families, Systems, and Health 22*(2): 178–179.

Stuckey, H. L., & Nobel, J. (2010). The connection between art, healing and public health: A review of current literature. *American Journal of Public Health*, 100(2), 254–263.

Willis, P. (2002). Poetry and poetics in phenomenological research. *Indo-Pacific Journal of Phenomenology, 3*, 1–19.

Zinkhan, G. (1994). Poetry in advertising. *Journal of Advertising, 23* (Winter), iii–vii.

Chapter 19

An International Experience for Social Work Students: Self-Reflection Through Poetry and Journal-Writing Exercises[1]

Becoming a social worker requires more than merely learning knowledge and theories (Garcia & Van Soest, 1997). Practice wisdom, the integration of knowledge and intuition, lies at the core of social work practice (Goldstein, 1990). Social workers themselves are the vehicle through which theories and knowledge are put into action in the service of individual and group, and to facilitate social change (Furman & Schatz, 2002; Schon, 1983; Sheafor, Horejsi, & Horejsi, 1997). The perceived importance of self-reflection and intuition is becoming increasingly evident in helping professions. Even in fields such as nursing and medicine, which on the surface may appear to rely upon "objective" data, self-reflection is a vital skill in developing an empathic understanding of persons in need (Stein, 2003).

Self-reflection is particularly valuable in the development of culturally sensitive and transnational social work practice skills (Fox, 1983; Lee & Greene, 1999; Schwartz, Fluckiger & Weisman, 1977). Since the self is the vehicle through which interventions are enacted, removing the student/practitioner from their own social context can be disorienting at best, and may lead to maladaptive and counterproductive worker behaviors. In practice situations with clients, such behaviors or affective displays can interfere with the helping relationship. Techniques and capacities must be developed to help workers face these challenges. Self-reflection is a key means by which these difficulties can be mitigated. Through self-reflection, social work students and workers may develop the capacity to understand their own feelings, beliefs and behaviors while they are occurring, and ultimately learn to expand their behavioral repertoire in the here-and-now.

---

[1] Co-authored with A. Coyne & N. J. Negi (2018).

The purpose of this article is to explore the uses of poetry and journal-writing exercises as a means of helping students develop their reflective capacities within an international setting. This aim will be met in several ways. First, self-reflection and its importance to social work practice and education is explored. Second, the importance of self-reflection to international and cross-cultural practice is discussed. Third, the use of written exercises and poetry as a means of facilitating self-reflection is highlighted. Fourth, poems written in response to structured exercises by students who took part in an international experience in social work in Leon, Nicaragua are presented as examples.

Self-Reflection in Practice and Education

The capacity to self-reflect may lead to important behavioral changes and may alter maladaptive behavioral patterns (Hixon & Swann, 1993). Self-reflection is the means by which we make sense of our social worlds and develop a personal understanding of it. In the process of self-reflection, an individual's cognitive mediating mechanisms allow them to connect to and interpret their social world. Through self-reflection, one may develop the capacity to understand their own biases in relation to their life and personal history, thereby developing the capacity to understand their social conditioning in a critical, potentially transformational way (Freire, 1973). Self-reflection helps develop critical consciousness; through reflecting on class status, privilege, internalized oppression, and other structural barriers that become internalized, an individual may transcend, or be liberated from, oppressive environments and social contexts. Self-reflection is the mechanism that leads to epiphany: moments of clarity and existential realizations that can lead to life-altering change.

As early as 1917, Mary Richmond (1917) warned against the role of bias in social work practice. She posited that social workers must become aware of their own distorted thinking in order to be effective in planning interventions for clients. By 1940, Gordon Hamilton declared that "knowledge of the self is essential for the conscious use of relationship" and "one must be aware of how the self operates in any helping relationship" (Hamilton, 1951, p. 41). Similarly, Charlotte Towle (1987) underscored the importance of self-knowledge by addressing prejudices, needs, and responses. Today it is often generally understood that social workers and social work students must strive toward developing therapeutic awareness—an awareness of their own emotions, beliefs, and reactions.

Without properly understanding the root causes of their reactions, workers inadvertently attribute the cause of their emotions to the behaviors of their clients, thereby interfering with the helping relationship. Traditionally conceptualized as countertransference (Moursund & Erskine, 2004; Teyber, 2000), this emotional reactivity may be mitigated by engaging in intensive self-reflection (Aron, 1991). Self-reflection therefore is not entirely a personal, isolated event. Self-reflection may be a social process that binds the individual to others in a self/social transformational manner. Self-reflection may lead to action, with action leading back to self-reflection in a continuous feedback loop facilitating continued growth and development.

Imre (1982) describes this as personal knowledge, a knowledge of the self as expressed in roles and relationships with clients. Personal knowledge of our own strengths and limitations, our own vulnerabilities, and our capacities to be of service to others is necessary for effective practice. Through becoming less emotionally reactive, practitioners are able to attend to clients' needs more effectively by being more present in the "here and now" (Dass & Gorman, 1999; Teyber, 2000).

In a similar concept, Goldstein (1990) explores the notion of practice wisdom, a synthesis of knowledge, skills, values, and experience actively processed through the reflective capacities of a trained and fully human worker. Schon (1983) describes the process by which this self-reflection occurs. To Schon, the reflective practitioner simultaneously pays attention *to* their client and their own internal reactions *about* the client. This reflection-in-action allows the worker to connect their thinking and their actions, which in turn influence subsequent thinking and behavioral responses. Ideally, the end result is a more complex, effective behavioral repertoire that becomes internalized as part of the worker's way of being with clients. For instance, Ringel (2003) links self-reflection with creativity, critical thinking, and student/worker sensitivity.

Self-Reflection in International and Cross-Cultural Work

Scholars and practitioners in other fields have stressed the importance of self-reflection for international and cross-cultural work. Komins & Nicholls (2003), through their experiences with developing an educational program in Turkey, found that critical self-reflection is crucial for understanding cultural and social realities other than one's own. They note that factual knowledge void of critical self-reflection is insufficient for effective cross-cultural education. Genor and Schulte (2002) stress the importance of self-reflection in cross-cultural educational experiences, citing the self-reflective process as a valuable tool for exploring beliefs regarding race and ethnicity. They utilize guided self-reflection as a mean of breaking down resistance to cross-cultural educational practices.

Journaling, Poetry and the Self-Reflective Process

The writing process has been known to facilitate the process of self-reflection. Richardson (2001) views writing as a method of discovery about the self and the world. To her and other post-modern scholars, the process of writing is itself a method of discovery, a method of inquiry. To write about the world is to write about the self, and to write about the self is to write about the world. In this sense, writing poetry, narrative, journal entries, and other exercises may be useful tools for self-discovery and self-reflection, as well as a means of inquiry into the world.

Of course, self-reflection can and does exist without the writing process. However, the writing process may force the subject to reflect on emotions and feelings that were previously unexplored. For example, in a commentary on Furman's (2004) autoethnography about his father's cancer, Shapiro (2004) observed that Furman, in writing self-reflective narratives in response to poems written ten years previously, became an archeologist of his own experience. The process of reflecting upon writings and experiences written ten years before and exploring these reflections through writing, allowed Furman to achieve a greater understanding of the complexity of his own emotions. Furman (2005) also used the same methodology in exploring the death of his dog, and his experiences as an adolescent (unpublished manuscript). Such self-reflections help explore the multiple realities hidden within complex human experiences.

Writing has been used as an important resource to increase students' self-reflection process in various fields (Furman, 2003/2004; Heath 1998; Orem 1997; Williamson 1997). Furman (2003/2004) previously explored the uses of structured poetry classroom exercises to increase the self-reflective capacities of students. He recommends poetry exercises that help students explore their own strengths and potentials as well as their mistakes. He notes that in addition to encouraging self-reflection, the use of poetry can help vary pedagogical approaches, thereby preventing student apathy and boredom. Langer and Furman (2004) advocate using written exercises to help students explore the cultural realities of native peoples. The authors developed exercises whereby students work in pairs to create poems from traditional qualitative research text. In this exercise, students are forced to grapple with the core messages of the text and develop an intimate sense of the research participants' experience. By closely attending to their subject's world, and by having to make editorial decisions about what data to include and exclude, students working in pairs can engage in dialogue about cultural contexts other than their own.

Writing poetry and other creative-writing experiences may also promote the development of strengths and resiliencies. Various commentators have observed that engaging in the creative process helps people maximize their potential (Makin, 1998; Talerico, 1986), and draws out strengths that may not have been previously apparent (Gil, 1990; Taft, 1939). Oiler (1983) observes that poetry allows us to hold our typical interpretations of experiences temporally in abeyance. By slowing down the interpretative process, the use of poetry gives the mind time to creatively reflect upon alternative meanings and interpretations, potentially liberating the mind from stereotypical ways of seeing the world. Through the use of image and metaphor, the process of writing can open the doors of the mind, and allow it to transcend limits.

An example of the usage of writing as a tool to facilitate self-reflection is included to illustrate this process. Whether the poems can be generalized is a matter of debate; this paper is conceptualized as exploratory in nature, the goal of which is to present exercises that social work and other faculty can use to facilitate development of their students' professional use of self. Faculty are encouraged to adopt the exercises and techniques for their own uses. While generalizability may not be applicable to the poetry and narratives presented here, Stein (2004) suggests that poetry is valuable to the degree to which it is "metaphorically generalizable." Poetry may be based upon specifics, but may become universal when its metaphors and images resonate with the reader as important or true. In this sense, the examples presented below may also be viewed as very tentative data about students' experiences in this particular international context.

Self-Reflection and an International Social Work Experience

Five students participated in a course sponsored by a school of social work in the Midwest. For eight years, social work students from several universities had the opportunity to travel to Leon, Nicaragua to study social work and social welfare from a Nicaraguan perspective. For ten days, students visit orphanages, hospitals, social service agencies, and other social institutions. They meet with social work students, educators, and social workers in Nicaragua and dialogue with them about the nature of social work practice in our respective counties. Faculty usually serve as translators and facilitators of dialogue during these exchanges. Each day, the students are asked to reflect upon their experiences through group dialogue with one or both of the faculty. At the end of group sessions, students are given reflective prompts designed to help them focus on key issues related to the experience and their professional use of self. Students are asked to write in their journals for a minimum of a half-an hour each day.

This past year two MSW students and three BSW students participated in this international experience. The poems and narrative reflections presented below are reflective responses of three students who choose to participate in this study. One student did not take the course for credit, and therefore was under no obligation to turn in their work, and one student refused to have her poems presented in this paper.

Examples of Writing Exercises and the Poems

For each of the exercises and prompts, students were told that they could choose to write in traditional prose form or arrange their words into poetic structure. Some of the advantages of poetic form and structure were briefly explored (i.e., the economy of words, metaphor, repetition, and the power of evocative language), yet students were given free rein to explore their feelings in any form that they wished. The authors chose to give minimal instructions about the structure of the assignments, as it was posited that students exploring a new international context would feel too overwhelmed if they needed to worry about learning new means of expression.

Exercise One: Processing the First Day
The first day in a new country can be an intense experience. This is especially true in a country as poor as Nicaragua; the second poorest

country in the Western Hemisphere. In order to help students give voice to their feelings and experience during their first day, they were given the choice of two exercises. The first exercise starts with an incomplete sentence that serves as a prompt: Yesterday I was, today I am. Sentence completion exercises are valuable aids in helping decrease students' fear and anxiety of writing and the self-reflective process; they reduce the fear of the blank page, which can be intimidating. The stem in the first exercise was designed to help students reflect upon themselves in two different contexts, and supports a constructivist view of self as evolving within context.

In the first example, the student candidly explores her sense of naivete and the difficulty of her first international encounter.

Yesterday I Was, Today I Am

Yesterday I was
a naïve, frightened American girl
missing the comforts of home
wishing the "meaning" of this trip
would know me upside the head

Today I am
a tired,
less naïve,
frightened American girl
who better understands
the term comfort
yet still searching
for a meaning

Another student wrote her response to this prompt as a more traditional journal entry. It is presented in its entirety. In the passage, she explores her feelings of hope and awe; her entry has the quality of a personal challenge to herself.

> Today is a bright, wonderful piece of greatness. Today was new, enjoyment and filled with social work ideas running through my head. I would like to return in one year to learn the language. Life is wonderful when you are living something new daily. Today was adventurous—the volcano, the strength of

this country. I tried the pottery wheel today—artists are peaceful, humble, honored, and needed in this world.

Today was the day I changed my mind on my life. I am going to live every day to the fullest—saying thank you, having an open mind, helping the world in which God sent me on this trip. When you live here all your ideas change about what is important. Not looks, not size, not money but LOVE of yourself, love of family/friends —what great power this country has.

Everybody says it's the AMERICAN way but why is it the best way? Today was the day I build myself up for the pain I shall see on Monday. Till then I am being thankful for today and only for the past but still looking for the future but not overlooking today... Till the sun comes up and my blue eyes open again.

For the second prompt, students were simply asked to reflect upon and write about their first day. The goal was to help them move into their own private, reflective worlds and back to the external world again. This was facilitated by asking them to focus on *things*, sensory data about what they saw, heard, smelled, and directly experienced. Focusing on sensory details also may help develop observational skills, essential for all facets of practice.

This student wrote a list that took on a poetic form of its own. Through juxtapositioning, this list of separate images is punctuated at the end of the poem by her very real feeling of fear.

Things That Stood Out

poverty
people ask for money
all of the selling on the street
selling everything
houses of blocks
everyone outside
animals all over.
I cannot imagine
what it would be like
not to have any money.
Scary

Exercise Two: Reflecting Upon the Orphanage

Visiting an orphanage that specializes in caring for special-needs children is an emotionally difficult experience for students. They at times feel overwhelmed with the severity of the children's' problems, the lack of resources, the severe overcrowding, and with their own sense of impotence. While with the children, students often vacillate from extreme attachment to total detachment. As a means of helping them reflect upon their experiences and explore their attachments, students were asked to write a letter or letter poem to a particular child. Letter poems and other forms of reflective addresses are useful in helping students explore the complexity of their relationships and have been used to facilitate growth in various practice courses (Furman, 2003/2004).

The four poems presented below were each written by different students. Some of the poems were started by the author while they were actually at the orphanage. Engaging in reflective work directly following encounters with the children may have helped students process their difficult feelings and may even provide a structured task that can be grounding.

Dear Emilio

I feel as if
I see your pain
through your yes
but don't understand it.
It makes me feel
inadequate
as a human.
I want to fully grasp
what your life has brought you,
but I don't think I ever will,
or even can.
You struggle to eat
yet so tiny of body
breaks my heart
I am comforted
by the care you receive.
What do you feel
the world has to offer?
Do you feel hope?

Does anyone instill hope within you?
Are you in pain?

Dear Angelo

When I first saw you in the little chair
in the little room
I was hooked.
What a cutie you are,
your eyes so beautiful and big.
You are perfect at eight months.
Why wouldn't your mom want you?
Maybe she does, but cannot have you.
I don't know your story.
What is your story?
I want to take you home,
to show you love,
what you deserve,
the best life.
Perfect baby, beautiful boy.

I can't take you home,
there are laws I cannot pass,
cannot get through.
But if I could, I would.
I will pray for you.
This letter will help me remember.
Your life at the orphanage
has very good workers—
that is good for you,
but you all,
deserve much more.
A home.

Gladys

looks around,
talks with her eyes,
feels with her smile,
chases you with her big brown eyes,
touches you with her smile,

listens with her eyes,
Gladys hold up her hands,
in a reaching cry,
pulls at your heart,
in a whispering cry.

Hector

So awesome
so full of life
in such a tiny
malformed,
deformed body
I stare at you
wanting to touch
wanting to talk
wanting to understand
your life
your body

Conclusion

The process of writing a poem or journaling thoughts seems to have facilitated the development or refinement of students' self-reflective capacities. Writing as a tool for self-reflection was especially useful within the international context, where cross-cultural variations are often difficult to grasp for beginning international practitioners and students. The exercise of requiring students' to engage in structured writing assignments allowed for structured time to self-reflect on often-overwhelming feelings that arise within international or foreign settings.

There are some limitations to the study. First, there was no pre-test of students' self-reflective capacities, it is not clear that these exercises did indeed improve student refection. It may be that the exercises presented did not develop self-reflection, but merely encouraged students to engage in the process. This may not be a significant limitation, as an important goal of social work practice and education is to highlight and accentuate existing strengths. Many students do have the capacity to look at themselves critically and merely need the forum to do so; other students struggle with developing this capacity. These exercises may be valuable with both groups of students and those who fall somewhere in the middle. Further, while the authors believe that the writing exercises did indeed facilitate student self-reflection, it is conceivable that the exercises merely documented such reflection.

Despite these limitations, this study offers a significant contribution to the field of international social work. International experiences can be valuable for the professional development of social work students. These experiences seem to lead to a type of cognitive dissonance that compels students to begin to question their own class- and culture-based assumptions. Poetry and journal exercises seem to aid in this process. Yet, these experiences are designed to help the development of skills of social work students in the United States, and may be of no benefit to the people that these students encounter. Mohan (2002) chastises, "Put bluntly, social work's internationalism smacks of hypocrisy and opportunism for which schools and graduates of developing nations continue to pay—quite unduly—a heavy price" (p. 124).

This is a legitimate concern. Hopefully, by engaging in the process of self-reflection, students will come to understand their own power and privilege, and will themselves guard against neo-imperialistic leanings in their international and cross-cultural encounters. As faculty, we have asked ourselves what structurally must occur for these experiences to be of benefit to those in the countries visited. Social work's adage—start where the client is—might be an important starting point for such an exploration. For instance, social work faculty at UNAN-Leon have been clear to point out the discrepancy between our social work methods and their practice and pedagogical needs. The authors of this paper have no clear answers as to how to resolve these issues but believe that the process of dialogue and collaboration will reveal potential solutions. At this point, we remain committed to the process. We believe that social work faculty must engage in their own reflective processes in order to continue their growth and development; we plan on engaging in this process more formally during subsequent international experiences.

References

Aron, L. (1991). The patient's experience of the analyst's subjectivity. *Psychoanalytic Dialogues, 1*(1), 29–51.

Dass, R., & Gorman, P. (1999). *How can I help?* Alfred A. Knopf.

Fox, J. R. (1983). Affective learning in racism courses with an experimental component. *Journal of Social Work Education, 19*(3), 69–76.

Freire, P. (1973). *Education for critical consciousness*. Seabury.
Furman, R. (2003/2004). Poetry as a tool for self-reflection in social work education. *Arête, 27*(2), 65-70.
Furman, R. (2004). Using poetry and narrative as qualitative data: Exploring a father's cancer through poetry. *Family, Systems & Health, 22*(2), 162–170.
Furman, R. (2005). Autoethnographic poems and narrative reflections: A qualitative study on the death of a companion animal. *Journal of Family Social Work.*
Furman, R. (unpublished manuscript). Poetic explorations of adolescent identity: Autoethnographic poems.
Furman, R., & Schatz, M. S. (2002). Teaching crisis intervention: Working with the whole student. *Journal of Police Crisis Negotiation, 2*(1), 31–42.
Garcia, B., & Van Soest, D. (1997). Changing perceptions of diversity and oppression: MSW students discuss the effects of a required course. *Journal of Social Work Education, 33*(1), 119–129.
Genor, M., & Schulte, A. (2002). Exploring race: Teacher educators bridge their personal and professional identities. *Multicultural Perspectives, 4*(3), 15–20.
Goldstein, H. (1990). The limits and art of understanding in social work practice. *Families in Society, 80*(4), 385–395.
Gil, D. (1990). *Unraveling social policy*. Schenkman.
Hamilton, G. (1951). *Theory and practice of social case work*. Columbia University Press.
Heath, H. (1998). Keeping a reflective practice diary: A practical guide. *Nurse Education Today, 18* (7) 592–598.
Hixon, J. G., & Swann, W. B. (1993). When does introspection bear fruit? Self-reflection, self-insight, and interpersonal choices. *Journal of Personality and Social Psychology, 64*(1), 35–43.
Imre, R. W. (1982). *Knowing and caring: Philosophical issues in social work*. University Press of America.
Komins, B. J., & Nicholls, D. G. (2003). Cultivating critical self-reflection in an international context: The development of an American studies curriculum in Turkey. *College Literature, 30*(3), 68–87.
Langer, C. & Furman, R. (2004). The Tanka as a qualitative research tool: A study of a Native American woman. *Journal of Poetry Therapy, 17*(3), 165–171.
Lee, M. Y., & Greene, G. J. (1999). A social constructivist framework for integrating cross cultural issues in teaching clinical social work. *Journal of Social Work Education, 35*(1), 21–37.
Makin, S. R. (1998). *Poetic wisdom: Revealing and helping*. Charles C. Thomas.
Mohan, B. (2002). New directions for doctoral education: Lessons from the Asian experience. *New Global Development, 18*(1/2),123–135.
Moursund, J. P., & Erskine, R. G. (2004). *Integrative psychotherapy*. Brooks/Cole-Thomson Learning.
Oiler, C. (1983). Nursing reality as reflected in nurses' poetry. *Perspectives in*

Psychiatric Care, 21(3), 81–89.

Orem, R. (1997). Journal writing as a form of professional development. In *Proceedings of the 16th Annual Midwest Research-to-Practice Conference in Adult, Continuing, and Community Education*, S. J. Levine, Ed.). East Lansing: Michigan State University.

Richardson, L. (2001). Getting personal: Writing stories. *Qualitative Studies in Education, 14*(1), 33–38.

Richmond, M. (1917). Social Diagnosis. The Free Press.

Ringel, S. (2003). The reflective self: A path to creativity and intuition in social work practice education. *Journal of Teaching in Social Work, 23*(3/4), 15–28.

Schon, D. A. (1983). *The reflective practitioner: How professionals think in action*. Basic Books.

Schwartz, F., Fluckiger, F. A., & Weisman, I. (1977). A cross cultural encounter: A non-traditional approach to social work education. San Francisco: R & E Research Associates.

Shapiro, J. (2004). Can poetry be Data? Potential relationships between poetry and research. *Families, Systems, & Health, 22*(2), 171–177.

Sheafor, B. W., Horejsi, C. R., & Horejsi, G. A. (1997). *Techniques and guidelines for social work practice* (4th ed.). Boston: Allyn and Bacon.

Stein, H. F. (2003). Ways of knowing in medicine: Seeing and beyond. *Families, Systems & Health, 21*(1), 29–35.

Stein, H. F. (2004). A window to the interior of experience. *Families, Systems, & Health, 22*(2), 178–179.

Taft, J. (1939). A conception of the growth process underlining social casework practice. *Social Casework*, (October), 72–80.

Talerico, C. J. (1986). The expressive arts and creativity as a form of therapeutic experience in the field of mental health. *Journal of Creative Behavior, 20*(4), 229–247.

Towle, C. (1987). *Common human needs* (revised ed.). NASW, Inc.

Teyber, E. (2000). *Interpersonal process in psychotherapy* (4th ed.). Brooks/Cole.

Williamson, A. (1997). Reflection in adult learning with particular reference to learning-in-action. *Australian Journal of Adult and Community Education, 37* (2), 93–99.

Chapter 20

The Poet/Practitioner: A Paradigm for the Profession[1]

> The social values of a professional group are its basic and fundamental beliefs, the unquestioned premises upon which its very existence rests. Foremost among these values is the essential worth of the service that the professional group extends to the community. The profession considers that the service is a social good and that community welfare would be immeasurably impaired by its absence (Greenwood, 1957, p. 52).

Throughout its history, social work has grappled with its professional role and identity (Arkava, 1967; Berlin, 1990; Dziegielewski, 2004; Kolevzon & Maykranz, 1982; Meyer, 1973). The search for professional identity may be essential to professional life and is engaged in by numerous professions. Defining a profession is a dynamic, evolving process deeply linked to shifts within the society the profession serves (Payne, 1997). Social change exerts pressures upon a profession to adapt to society's evolving needs (Kreuger, 1997). When a profession fails to adapt to its social context, professional drift occurs (Shulman, 1991). In such instances, members of a profession lose touch with the profession's mission, its values, and its modalities for meeting its aims. Postman (1992) has noted that social means of production have changed faster during this century than during any other millennium in history. Professions now exist in a state of flux and must engage in a constant process of creating and re-creating their role vis-à-vis society. This process has special currency for a profession such as social work, which is not merely a passive player in the process of social change but is itself a change agent acting upon the forces that simultaneously act upon it.

---

[1] Co-authored with C.L. Langer & D.K. Anderson (2006).

The purpose of this article is to explore a new paradigm for the professional social worker: the poet/practitioner. The training and practice of the poet are congruent with many aspects of social work practice. Examining the skills, attributes, and values of the poet, and their congruence to social work values, skills and knowledge, may lead to a paradigm with the capacity to focus social workers on the essential features of the profession. This paradigm, which highlights the humanistic, creative, and socially conscious role of the social work practitioner, may be particularly important today, given the medicalization of social problems and the conservatization of society.

This paper will achieve its aims in several ways. First, a discussion of historical paradigms that have guided the profession will be presented. Second, the nature of poetry and the poet will be addressed. Third, a historical account of poetry and the poetic in social work practice and education will provide an additional historical context for the discussion. Fourth, a new paradigm for the profession, the poet/practitioner, is proposed.

Historical Paradigms for Social Work Practice

Proponents have advanced various paradigms for the profession of social work (van Wormer, 1997). According to Goldstein (1990), social work has traveled down two distinct epistemological tracks, the positivist and the humanistic. These two worldviews are apparent in the different paradigms that social workers have adopted as guides to professional action. Various historical trends and innovations within the profession have led to shifts between offshoots of these two early positions. The scientist/practitioner became a popular paradigm, stemming from the influence of logical positivism and advances in the biological influences in human behavior. The roots of this paradigm can be traced to Flexner's (1915) infamous admonition of social work. He stressed that social work was not yet a profession, as it did not possess its own discrete, communicable body of knowledge. The reeling young profession, in its quest for status, respectability, and perhaps efficacy, began to veer from its previous path of compassionate social humanism exemplified by the early proponents of the rank-and-file movement (Axinn & Levin, 1975). Shortly after Flexner's admonition, Healy (1917) advocated for a scientific paradigm for the profession, while Southard (1919) explored the possibility of the medicalization of individual and social problems. Perhaps the most significant early movement towards the adaptation of the scientific paradigm was the publication of

Richmond's (1917) classic text *Social Diagnosis*, a thesis characterized by causal descriptions largely adhering to a medical model of assessment and treatment. This paradigm continued to thrive during the middle to late twentieth century. In large part due to the early successes of psychotropic medication in treating the mentally ill, large segments of the profession became increasingly aligned with the scientific model. These ideas continue to permeate social work research, education, and practice, despite strong criticisms regarding its congruence with the profession (Heineman, 1981).

Between the world wars, two competing schools of social work came into prominence: the functional and the diagnostic schools. These two perspectives differed markedly in how they viewed the purpose of social work and the nature of individual change (Yelaja, 1986). Partly continuing the tradition of Richmond, proponents of the diagnostic school viewed human problems as diseases caused by intrapsychic conflicts. The functionalist eschewed pathology-based paradigms and focused on the individual's capacity to transcend psychological and social obstacles.

Competing with the diagnostic school's scientific conceptualizations, the functional school adopted practices congruent with the humanistic approach (Robinson, 1949; Taft, 1939). Expanding the work of Otto Rank (1945), an artist who broke with Freudian orthodoxy, the functionalists eschewed positivistic notions and instead advocated for a more humanistic, holistic understanding of the human experience (Pray, 1949; Smalley, 1967; Taft, 1958 & 1962). Many maxims and principles of practice wisdom, such as "start where the client is" and the centrality of client self-determination, are functional principles that have been subsumed into generic social work practice.

Dissatisfied with what he saw as a move toward arrogance and omniscience in social work, Krill (1986) explored the notion of "the beat worker." Influenced by existential themes, Krill critiqued the scientist/social worker paradigm as a myth, based not on an understanding of the essentials of human behavior but on the desire for power, control, and prestige. Echoing functional themes, Krill implored practitioners to work in partnership with their clients toward reaching their self-defined goals and to eschew the arrogant role of expert.

While highlighting the importance of the social worker as scientist, Sheafor, Horejsi, and Horejsi (1997) also assert the need for social workers to use both head and heart when interacting with clients and providing services. By adding the component of heart to the classic paradigm of the scientist practitioner, the authors acknowledge the importance of the intuitive aspects of helping to social work practice. The strengths perspective has also advocated for a model of human behavior based upon resiliency, strength, and wholeness (Maluccio, 1981; Weick, Rapp, Sullivan, & Kisthardt, 1989). Proponents of this perspective affirm the importance of human intuition, and recognize the centrality of the creative, life-affirming will of each individual (Saleebey, 2000). The client is viewed as the expert and author of her own experience (Lewis, 1996). Still, the scientist/practitioner remains the dominant role in social work practice. Social workers now seem more concerned with notions such as evidence-based practice and billable hours than with self-actualization, community development, or empowerment.

The Poet and Poetry

What is the nature of the poet and her craft? Poet Timothy Liu helps focus this exploration by rhetorically inquiring: "What about poetry as a soulful experience? What about poetry that can teach us how to live?" (Hennessy, 2004, p. 4.). The task of the poet is far greater than the mere writing of words that rhyme or comply with a pattern or scheme. Jane Hirshfield (1997) described the role of the poem as the "clarification and magnification of being." The poet's task is to document and clarify her existence and the existence of others through the medium of language. Baraka (2003) explores the social aspect of the medium in his contention that poetry is both a reflection of and commentary on society. It is this dialectic that provides poetry and art currency, relevance, and power. The poem is both personal and social, in the same manner that the personal is political. Poetry challenges poets to understand themselves and their world. The poet is called upon to develop the requisite skills to make connections between the simultaneously separate and connected domains of her intrapsychic and social selves.

To define a poet as anyone who writes a poem is akin to defining anyone who helps people as a social worker. Like social workers, poets have learned time-honored skills that aid them in their practice. To use the term "professional" in the traditional sense is problematic; very few poets earn their living solely from their art. What distinguishes the poet is a dedication to the *craft* of poetry. The dedicated poet is as or more concerned with the aesthetics of a poem as with the content or the message of a poem. The poet does not rely on extraordinary events alone in her quest to make powerful poetry; through various linguistic tools she seeks to highlight the significance of everyday existence. Wordsworth (1979) asserts that the remarkable feature of the poet is her sensitivity. The poet hones her sensitivity to develop a keen understanding of the human condition. In addition to the interest in the social world, the poet is also concerned with the nature of the human soul.

The importance of sensitivity, a concern with the relationship between the individual and the social world, a need to comprehend the psyche and the soul, and a belief in the inherent beauty and goodness of people are some of the attributes that social workers and poets have in common. Perhaps it is for these reasons that the arts and humanities, poetry, and the poetic have held an important place in social work history.

Poetry and the Poetic in Social Work Education

The liberal arts and humanities have long played an important role in social work and social work education (Goldstein, 1984 Lowe, 1985; Pumphrey & Pumphrey, 1961. Reid and Peebles-Wilkins (1991) implore social work educators to renew the historic commitment of educating social workers in the liberal arts tradition. The Council on Social Work Education requires that social work education be based on a liberal arts foundation in the humanities (CSWE, 2002). The functional school, so central to the development of generic social work practices, was largely based upon the ideas of the artist Otto Rank (Rank, 1945). Social work was viewed more as an art than a science for much of its early development. While social work has lost some of its connections to the arts and humanities, they continue to strongly influence the profession. This may be largely due to the influence of culturally sensitive models of practice. Such models recognize that practice methods must be syntonic with ethnic groups whose worldviews differ markedly from that of the scientific paradigm (Langer & Furman, 2004a, 2004b). As such, poetic and narrative ways of knowing and helping may increase in their importance as ethnic minorities become larger segments of the population.

Devore and Schlesinger (1977) explore the value of utilizing literature to lend insight into the complexities of urban life. The use of literature in practice and education, also known as bibliotherapy, relies heavily upon poetry as a means of educating and healing (Rossiter & Brown, 1988). Poetry therapy has become an important discipline with many practitioners drawn from the social work profession. Poetry has been utilized in social work practice with children (Mazza, 1981, 1996 & 1999; Mazza, Magaz, & Scaturro, 1987), the elderly (Edwards, 1990; Goldstein, 1987), as well as with poor and oppressed populations (Edwards & Lyman, 1989). Poetry has also been used clinically in various practice contexts such as hospice (McLoughlin, 2000), medical facilities (Genova, 2003; Leedy, 1987), and schools (Wright & Chung, 2001). Poetry has even made its way into social work education. Mazza (1987) explored the use of poetry in various courses throughout the social work curriculum, noting that poetry can: 1) help sensitize students to emotional practice issues; 2) illuminate key dynamics of human behavior; and, 3) add value to teaching social work practice skills. Furman (2005) demonstrates how poetry can be a valuable aid in teaching empathy and can also aid in the process of self-reflection (Furman, 2003/2004).

Poetry has been used by social work practitioners from a variety of theoretical frameworks. Furman, Downey, Jackson and Bender (2002) explore how poetry is used when practicing from a strengths perspective. Poetry has also been used as a tool in existential (Furman, 2003; Lantz, 1997) and cognitive (Collins & Furman, in press) social work practice and has even found its way into social work research. Poindexter (2002) uses the research poem as a means of exploring the relationship between HIV-infected people and their caretakers. Langer and Furman (2004b) employ poetry as a means of exploring issues related to Native American identity, and Furman (2004) has utilized poetry for the studying the impact of cancer on families.

The Poet/Practitioner

In this section, a new paradigm for practice is considered: the poet/practitioner. It should be noted that the practice attributes highlighted are not new; they form the core of good social work practice. Also, a simple definition of the poetry/practitioner is not provided; it is defined through various value considerations and is not easily reduced. It is meant to serve social workers as a guide to focus their growth, development, and work. The goal here is to demonstrate the congruence between the poet and the social worker. This new paradigm can help refocus the profession on humanistic values and practice that have been important aspects of our history and may be threatened by the for-profit environment many social workers now operate within.

The Poet/Practitioner: Connecting the Head, the Heart, and the World

The outstanding poet is able to draw connections between thought and feeling. The poet who possesses a mastery of her craft avoids sentimentality. To avoid sentimentality, she relies upon concrete and specific images. She eschews abstract generalizations and focuses on sensory data. As the poet develops her skills, she reaches out to the natural world for images and metaphors that universalize her personal experiences. These images drawn from the external world serve to concretize poems in "real life." By so doing, the poet creates a work characterized by intense, emotional experiences without having to *tell* the reader what to feel. The poet allows the reader to experience whatever emotions are triggered by her subjective reactions to the images conveyed through the poem. By so doing, the poet fuses the affective world with the external world, thereby contextualizing human emotion in the social environment. The poet respects two seemingly contradictory aspects of human emotion. Feelings are simultaneously deeply personal and essentially universal experiences that occur within social contexts. The poet understands that the human condition must be understood through the lens of the individual and the social context in which they live. The poet understands that it is through our minds and our hearts that we meet with and join our social worlds.

As with the poet, the poet/practitioner must understand human emotion and cognition within a social context (Werner, 1986). The poet/practitioner processes a deep appreciation of the importance of ecological factors on clients' lives and on the centrality of working within this context to ensure change (Dietz, 2000). The poet/practitioner looks for connections between the selves of their clients, many of whom are isolated and alienated from others, to the external world. In spite of the desire to find a unifying theory of human behavior that explains all human phenomena in a neat, reductionistic manner, the poet/practitioner understands the complexity of being. In each encounter with a client; the poet/practitioner attends to the hearts and minds of individuals who live and function in social worlds. In spite of the desire of corporate managed-care organizations to treat the individual as a set of symptoms to be reduced to predictable treatment protocols, the poet/practitioner respects the inherent wholeness of each client. As with the poet, the poet/practitioner simultaneously respects what is different and the same about us. The poet/practitioner not only seeks to understand diversity, but is acutely attuned to the similarities of human beings and human behavior. Both poetry and practice demand the capacity to observe and utilize patterns. In practice, recognizing the patterns that occur in the life-course of individuals, families, or groups allows us to contextualize presenting problems, and seek solutions of appropriate depth and meaning. Treatment plans that result from this holistic view of the person include interventions from the biological, psychological, social, spiritual, and creative domains. The poet/practitioner doggedly resists pressures to medicalize clients. Instead, she responds to her clients' right to choose from among various strategies, allowing her clients to be self-determining and to maximize their values.

The Poet/Practitioner: Possessing the Spirit of the Playful Child
Writing poetry encourages an attitude of play. Through playing with words, the poet knows that she must experiment. Rigidity is the enemy of poetry. By engaging in the creative process, the poet strives toward flexibility. Each poem presents its own dilemmas. Through a sense of play that demands diligence and persistence, the poet works through moments of being stuck. Think of children building a bridge with blocks. They struggle mightily to arrange blocks in just the right manner. Left to their own devices, they may spend hours in their arrangements, allowing their creative sense and fantasy to sweep them away. Through their play, they learn to create, think in new ways, and perhaps most important, to innovate.

Poetry also encourages this playful innovation. The poet experiments with combinations of words, new images, strange and varied syntax to help a poem transcend *what it was*. To do so, the poet must let go of her sense of what is known. In the moment of creation, the poet attempts to let go of all she has learned, trusting that she has integrated previous lessons into her being. While she never turns her back on the conscious use of her skills, the poet understands that truth, beauty, and innovation often occur precisely when she suspends her rational, problem-solving functions and adopts an attitude of play.

As with the poet, the poet/practitioner has learned a great deal of knowledge and skills. Her professional training has taught her valuable lessons in regard to assessing and treating clients. Yet, individual clients are as different as individual poems. As each poem is a new combination of words and structures, each client presents a new constellation of experiences, feelings, beliefs, and social realities. Each client seeks to be understood for who they are. Approaching each new client with the sense of wonder and play that the poet brings to the page allows the poet/practitioner to partner with each client in the co-

construction of the helping experience. The poet/practitioner seeks to learn from each client; she adopts a sense of wonder and curiosity that helps her clients feel valued. To encounter the client and truly *know* them, she must let go of all her perceptions about who they might be. While listening, the poet/practitioner lets go of what she has learned in the same way that the poet or child experiences the world with a sense of wonderment.

The poet/practitioner does not neglect her training. Skills of observation are essential to this process. The poet/practitioner uses all of her skills to attend to clients' words, how they are being said, and attempts to see the world through her client's' eyes. The poet/practitioner is flexible, adaptable, culturally competent, and understands the importance of holistic assessment and intervention.

Perhaps most central to the concept of play is the notion of fun. Social work practice can and should be fun (Furman, 2001). Fun does not imply frivolity; clients present real problems that are serious and cause them much pain. Yet, the poet/practitioner works hard at enjoying her work in spite of having to contend with the pain and suffering of others. She chooses to infuse humor into her sessions, and can learn to appreciate what she actually does: gets paid to be of service to others. The poet/practitioner brings this attitude to her work with colleagues as well. In so doing, she is sought out for inspiration and encouragement. She feels increasingly connected to others, who in turn enrich her life.

The Poet/Practitioner: Respecting Subjective and Deep Knowledge
To be a poet means to live in the world of the subjective. In some ways, this constitutes a paradox, in that the poet seeks to observe and document observable features of the external world. Poets pay attention to details. In the process of writing a poem, the poet observes the small details that make up an individual, be that "individual" a leaf, a crack in the wall, or a person. On the other hand, the poet understands that what makes a poem unique is the poet's subjective experience of the external world. The poem is simultaneously a document of realities external to the poet and their own internal world. The poet values and appreciates the differences.

Poet/practitioners use a variety of techniques to begin to understand the hidden meaning of a client's words. Paraphrasing and reflecting both content and meaning are certainly not among the least of these skills. Encouraging clients to think in terms of metaphors, which shall be discussed in depth in another section of this paper, is sometimes useful because it allows some distance from the issue. Gaining distance is an important aspect that poetry brings to a difficult situation. So too, the poet/practitioner must engage in self-reflection, an important tool of social work practice (Schon, 1983; Ringel, 2003), in order to ensure that she is providing clients with accurate reflections of emotions, beliefs, and experiences.

The Poet/Practitioner: Seeking the Truth
Poet James L. Smith (2003) refers to the creation of the poem as "the distillation of the essence of being." The poet seeks truths about the self and others that not only hold truth for the individual, but offer a glimmer of truth for all humanity.

Seeking the truth is perhaps the ultimate goal for the poet/practitioner. Clients must sometimes gently, sometimes painfully, face difficult truths if they are to make lasting changes. Since truth is a relative term, understanding truth from the client's perspective is essential. The importance of an accurate assessment cannot be overstated. Fact and truth are not always interchangeable concepts. As a poet continually seeks the right words or phrases, the poet/practitioner must help clients sift through a multitude of potential meanings in order to find the one that resonates with a client as truth; the direction they believe is their live path.

In helping clients seek their truth, the poet/practitioner helps clients to explore their own constriction of meaning in their lives. Helping clients explore meaning potentials in their lives is an important and neglected aspect of social work practice (Krill, 1978); too often practice is overly focused on problem solving and symptom reduction. While problem solving and symptom reduction certainly have their place and can help clients in the short term, developing a sense of meaning and purpose may be the most essential task of living (van Deurzen-Smith, 1997; Willis, 1994; Yalom, 1980).

The Poet/Practitioner: Facilitating the Development of Meaning
In the act of creating poetry, the poet works toward gaining self-awareness. She explores the relationship between the self and the world. In so doing, she must be able to understand her own sense of values. The poet asks herself: What is it I care about? What is it that gives me meaning? The poet writes to make sense of the world and, in turn, creates a world of meaning and purpose. The poet imbues the world with new meanings that she creates, new meanings that explore what it means to be alive, and what it means to be human.

While the poet strives to create a personal meaning for herself, she also seeks to illuminate meanings to and for others. So too, the poet/practitioner seeks to maximize an individual's self-meaning in the world. The insights that can be discovered in the therapeutic process are similar to the insights one gains while writing poetry.

The poet/practitioner must be very self-aware and must consistently develop this self-awareness. The therapeutic relationship is dependent to some extent on a high level of self-awareness. The goal of the relationship is to enhance the client's sense of meaning and purpose in the world. Since poet/practitioners are frequently in the profession "to help people," they must guard against feeling as if they are the ones who liberate the client, taking credit for the work the client has done. This is not to say that the poet/practitioner does not also gain from the therapeutic relationship; personal and professional growth is certainly an important aspect of the helping process. However, it does mean that the practitioner is much more limited in ownership of outcome than is the poet in rejoicing at a finished work.

The Poet/Practitioner: Reflecting upon Practice
When asked to define the type of poet he is, Mark Doty (2003) referred to himself as a "meditative narrativist"—that is, one who reflects upon and gives voice to a story. The process of reflection is essential to both poet/practitioner and poet. The poet creates from a place of nothingness. The page is blank and full of both emptiness and possibility. Through various written and imaginative processes, the poet reflects upon their experience and seeks new ways of understanding. One method, called automatic writing, is particularly useful (McKinney, 1976). The poet writes for five minutes about a topic, person, or situation without censoring her thoughts. She writes as quickly as possible. After, the poet reads what they have written and seeks connections between tangential thoughts, feelings, and events.

The poet/practitioner engages in a similar process during interviews with clients. Clients often come to us with ambivalent or conflicted feelings and disjointed stories that they have difficulty sorting out. Through active listening, reflection, and interpretation, the poet/practitioner helps clients bring order to their experiences by valuing the stories clients share, searching for patterns, peering through the disjoined parts, and eventually helping clients make sense of their meaning.

So too, the poet/practitioner must develop the capacity of self-refection as a means of understanding her own emotional responses to clients. The capacity for reflection is essential for the professional poet/practitioner (Brennan, 1973), as the self is the vehicle for change. What we often refer to as practice wisdom is dependent upon a practitioner's capacity to deeply engage upon her experiences. DeRoos (1990) defines reflection in practice, or reflecting-in-action as "the conscious evaluation of action during the course of action" (p.283.) Chan (2003) recognized the importance of utilizing poetry as a means of self-reflection and as a tool to help her survive the strains of doctoral work. Furman (2003/2004) explores how social work students may utilize poetry as a means of expanding their ability to be self-reflective.

The Poet/Practitioner: Using Metaphor
Metaphor lies at the heart of poetry. Metaphor, the symbolic use of language where an object or event represents another object or event, allows the poet to evocatively explore the human experience. By exploring experiences metaphorically, the poet allows for the subjective feelings and perceptions of an individual to represent the universal. By utilizing metaphor, the reader is able to project her own experiences onto the written metaphor she is reading. In a very real sense, the poet encourages the reader to enter into her world and make it their own. The poet seeks to connect to their readers' humanness, to their authentic selves. In so doing, the poet encourages empathy and normalization by demonstrating that individual human pains, while personal in their experience, are indeed shared by many.

Not only are metaphors important to the process of connectedness, but to the process of growth and change. People hold core metaphors that represent their images of themselves, their lives, and their futures. Metaphor is central to many systems of helping, including various family therapies (Carter & McGoldrick, 1989; Nichols & Schwartz, 1995), narrative (Freedman & Combs, 1996), and constructivist practice (Franklin, 1995; Laird, 1995).

By speaking in metaphoric language, clients are able to safely discuss issues that are often too painful to address directly. For example, it may be easier for a couple to explore their "broken vessel" than for them to discuss their broken marriage. By allowing time for the couple to describe their "broken vessel," a poet/practitioner can gently move to help them make "repairs" to their "vessel."

Metaphors help the poet/practitioner understand the patterns of life as they are manifest within the individual. By understanding patterns that occur within the lives of clients, the poet/practitioner can help clients understand their own behavior more fully and place them within the context of the human condition. By helping clients see the metaphorical or even archetypal patterns of their own behavior, the poet/practitioner helps clients reduce guilt and blame. Once these immobilizing feelings are reduced, clients may work on changing routinized, problematic behavior less defensively.

The Poet/Practitioner: Advocating for Social Change

While some might think of the poet and poetry as concerned only with personal and private concerns, a great many poets have been catalysts for social change. Since the practice of poetry is predicated on developing a relationship between the external social world and internal personal perceptions, the conscious poet becomes aware of oppression and inequity. Whether sensitive by disposition or training, poets possess the observational tools to comprehend the causes of systemic barriers in their environments; many poets have become involved in working toward the amelioration of such barriers. For instance, poets have stood on the vanguard of various revolutionary movements throughout the world, most notably in Latin America (Cardenal, 1982). The minister of culture for the former Sandinista government of Nicaragua, the poet/priest Ernesto Cardinal, implemented a literacy campaign utilizing poetry as a means of educating the poorest Nicaraguans. In the United States, *Poets Against the War* (2003) organized poets against the most recent war in Iraq. Over five thousand poets have posted poems protesting US intervention in Iraq.

Poetry has also been used in ways that more closely approximate social work macro practice. For example, poetry groups have been conducted to validate the ethnic heritage of Puerto Ricans who have been discriminated against (Holman, 1996). These groups sought to help members become aware of the impact that oppression has had in their lives and transcend the effects. Poetry has also been used as a valuable tool in community organization and the development of intergenerational community spaces (Furman, Riddoch, & Collins, 2004). In a qualitative study of community organizers, Community Arts Network (2002) found that using stories, metaphors, and narratives were important tools in the practice of community organization and empowerment. They found that community organizers used narratives as a powerful way of connecting people to one another within their communities. Narratives are valuable means of helping people from diverse backgrounds make connections between their often very different experiences. In short:

the expressive, interpretive and creative aspects of the arts and humanities carry special utility when dividing lines have been etched deeply in communities. Often with greater power than other modes of human discourse, collective engagement with art can heal wounds, break logjams and build bridges (Community Arts Network, 2002).

Social work is rooted in social change and social justice (Estes, 1997; Healy, 2001). As exemplified in the work of early social work pioneers, who worked to ameliorate the deleterious effects of industrialization on the urban poor, a primary purpose of social work has been to alleviate or eliminate social problems through social action and advocacy. The poet/practitioner must work to develop and maintain her social justice orientation. This is particularly difficult given the oppressive, reactionary forces at work in society. The poet/practitioner seeks to stay connected to the social issues that are important to her and her clients through observation and personal awareness. The poet/practitioner always seeks to place individual problems into the context of the immediate social environment, as well as the larger global community.

Conclusion

It may seem to the reader that the paradigm being advocated in this article is a throwback to another time, a time when the medical model was seen as merely *one* practice framework (or perhaps before it even existed). The reader may notice that this paper does not measure the efficacy of practice principles advocated herein. In truth, the authors of this paper are convinced that too much focus has been paid to evidence-based practice and other outcomes-based models. Often, such models are overly reliant on social work knowledge, to the exclusion of social work values. This notion is especially important to consider, given that empirical studies have called into question the degree to which social work practitioners utilize theory as their primary practice guide (Cocozzelli & Constable, 1985). Social work values are essential guides to practice. They are central to our profession and our professional identity. We are as concerned with preferred instrumentalities, or preferred ways of treating people, as we are with outcomes (Levy, 1973). In his seminal article, Gordon (1965) asserts that when social workers base decisions upon knowledge when values are called for, their interventions will be misdirected. While the authors of this paper advocate for the paradigm of the poet/practitioner, this is but one paradigm that may guide practice. It is essential that social workers adopt metaphors, paradigms, and models that are as informed by social work values as they are social work knowledge. Without clear guidance from social work values, we are at risk of becoming a technocratic profession of social engineer, instead of the champions of the disadvantaged and oppressed.

References

Arkava, M. L. (1967). Social work practice knowledge: An examination of their relationship. *Journal of Education for Social Work, 3*(1), 3–5.

Axinn, J., & Levin, H. (1975). *Social welfare: A history of the American response to needs.* Dodd & Mead.

Baraka, A. (2003). *Social change & poetic tradition.* Proceedings from the Conference of Contemporary Poetry. Retrieved January 24, 2003: http://english.rutgers.edu/baraka.htm.

Berlin, S. B. (1990). Dichotomous and complex thinking. *Social Service Review, 64,* 46–59.

Brennan, W. (1973). The practitioner as theoretician. *Journal of Education for Social Work, 9*(1), 5–12.

Cardenal, E. (1982). *En Cuba.* Serie Popular Era.

Carter, B., & McGoldrick, M. (1989). *The changing family life cycle: A framework for family therapy.* Allyn & Bacon.

Chan, Z. C. Y. (2003). Poetry writing: A therapeutic means for a social work doctoral student in the process of study. *Journal of Poetry Therapy, 16*(1), 5–17.

Cocozzelli, C., & Constable, R. T. (1985). An empirical analysis of the relationship between theory and practice in clinical social work. *Journal of Social Service Research, 90*(1), 123–141.

Collins, K., & Furman, R. (in press). Poetry therapy and cognitive therapy. *The Arts in Psychotherapy.*

Community Arts Network (2002). *Connecting Californian: Finding the art in community change.* Author: Retrieved July 22, 2002. http://www.communityarts.net/ concal/rationale.php

CSWE–Council on Social Work Education. (2002). *Revisions to evaluation standards.* Author.

DeRoos, Y. S. (1990). The development of practice wisdom through human problem-solving processes. *Social Service Review, 64,* 276–287.

Devore, W., & Schlesinger, E. G. (1977). The integration of social science and literary materials: An approach to teaching urban family life. *Journal of Education for Social Work, 14*(3), 6–7.

Dietz, C. A. (2000). Reshaping clinical practice for the new millennium. *Journal of Social Work Education, 36*(3), 503–520.

Doty, M. (2003). Poetry reading. *Nebraska Writers Conference.* University of Nebraska at Lincoln, July 17.

Dziegielewski, S. F. (2004). *The changing face of health care social work.* Springer.

Edwards, M. E. (1990). Poetry: Vehicle for retrospection and delight. *Generations, 14,*(1), 61–62.

Edwards, M. E., & Lyman, A. J. (1989). Poetry: Life review for frail American Indian elderly. *Journal of Gerontological Social Work, 14,* 75–91.

Estes, R. J. (1997). Social work, social development and community welfare centers in international perspective. *International Social Work, 40*(1), 43–55.

Flexner, A. (1915). Is social work a profession? *Proceedings of the National Conference on Charities and Corrections* (pp. 575–590). Hildeman Printing.

Franklin, C. (1995). Expanding the vision of the social constructionist debates: Creating relevance for practitioners. *Families in Society, 76*(7), 395–406.

Freedman, J. & Combs, G. (1996). *Narrative therapy: The social construction of preferred realities.* Norton.

Furman, R. (2001). Fun and humor in human service practice and education. *Human Service Education, 21*(1), 3–10.

Furman, R. (2003). Poetry therapy and existential theory. *The Arts in Psychotherapy, 30(*4), 195–200.

Furman, R. (2003/2004). Poetry as a tool for self–reflection in social work education. *Arête, 27*(2), 65–70.

Furman, R. (2004). Using poetry and narrative as qualitative data: Exploring a father's cancer through poetry. *Family, Systems & Health, 22*(2), 162–170.

Furman, R. (2005). Using poetry and written exercises to teach empathy. *Journal of Poetry Therapy, 18*(2),103–110.

Furman, R., Downey, E. P., Jackson, R. L., & Bender, K. (2002). Poetry therapy as a tool for strengths-based practice. *Advances in Social Work, 3*(2), 146–157.

Furman, R., Riddoch, R., & Collins, K. (2004). Poetry, writing and community practice. *Human Service Education, 24*(1), 19–32.

Genova, N. J. (2003). Expanding our concept of the medical literature: The value of the humanities in medicine. *Journal of the American Academy of Physician Assistants, 16(*3), 61–64.

Goldstein, H. (1984). *Creative change: A cognitive-humanistic approach to social work practice.* Methuen.

Goldstein, H. (1990). The limits and art of understanding in social work practice. *Families in Society, 80*(4), 385–395.

Goldstein, M. (1987). Poetry: A tool to induce reminiscing and creativity with geriatrics. *Journal of Social Psychiatry, 7(*2), 117–121.

Gordon, W. E. (1965). Knowledge and value: Their distinction and relationship in clarifying social work practice. *Social Work, 10*(3), 32–39.
Greenwood, E. (1957). Attributes of a profession. *Social Work, 2*(1), 45–55.
Healy, L. M. (2001). *International social work: Professional action in an interdependent world.* New York: Oxford University Press.
Healy, W. (1917). The bearings of psychology on social case work. *Proceedings of National Conference of Social Work,* 104–112.
Heineman, M. B. (1981). The obsolete scientific imperative in social work research. *Social Service Review, 55,* 371–339.
Hennessy, C. (2004). Timothy Liu: An interview. *The Writer's Chronicle, 36*(5), 4–11.
Hirshfield, J. (1997). *Nine gates: Entering the mind of poetry.* HarperCollins.
Holman, W. D. (1996). The power of poetry: Validating ethnic identity through a bibliotherapeutic intervention with a Puerto Rican adolescent. *Child and Adolescent Social Work Journal, 13*(5), 371-383.
Kolevzon, M. S., & Maykranz, J. (1982). Theoretical orientation and clinical practice: Uniformity versus eclecticism. *Social Service Review,* March, 120–129.
Kreuger, L. W. (1997). The end of social work. *Journal of Social Work Education, 33,*(1), 19–27.
Krill, D. (1986). *The beat worker: Humanizing social work and psychotherapy practice.* University of America Press.
Krill, D. (1978). *Existential social work.* Free Press.
Laird, J. (1995). Family-centered practice in the post-modern era. *Families in Society, 76*(3), 150–162.
Langer, C., & Furman, R. (2004a). Exploring identity and assimilation. Research interpretive poems. *Forum: Qualitative Social Research, 5*(2). http://qualitative-research.net/fqs-texte/2-04/2-04langerfurman-e.htm
Langer, C. & Furman, R. (2004b). The tanka as a qualitative research tool: A study of a Native American woman. *Journal of Poetry Therapy, 17*(3), 165–171.
Lantz, J. (1997). Poetry in existential psychotherapy with couples and families. *Contemporary Family Therapy, 19*(3), 371–381.
Leedy, J. (1987). Poetry therapy for drug abusers. *The Journal of Social Psychiatry, 7(2) 106–108.*
Levy, C. S. (1973). The value base of social work. *Journal of Education for Social Work,* Winter, 34–42.
Lewis, J. S. (1996). Sense of coherence and the strengths perspective with older persons. *Journal of Gerontological Social Work, 26*(3–4), 99–112.
Lowe, G. (1985). The graduate-only debate in social work education 1931–1959, and its consequences for the profession. *Journal of Education for Social Work, 21*(3), 52–62.
Maluccio, A. N. (1981). *Promoting competence in clients.* The Free Press.
Mazza, N. (1981). The use of poetry in treating the troubled adolescent. *Adolescence, 16*(3), 400–408.

Mazza, N. (1987). Poetry and popular music in social work education: The liberal arts perspective. *The Arts in Psychotherapy, 13*(3), 293–299.

Mazza, N. (1996). Poetry therapy: A framework and synthesis of techniques for family social work. *Journal of Family Social Work, 1*(3), 3–18.

Mazza, N. (1999). *Poetry therapy: Interface of the arts and psychology*. CRC Press.

Mazza, N., Magaz, C., & Scaturro, J. (1987). Poetry therapy with abused children. *The Arts in Psychotherapy, 14*(1), 85–92.

McKinney, F. (1976). Free writing as therapy. *Psychotherapy: Theory Research and Practice*, 3(2), 183–187.

McLoughlin, D. (2000). Transition, transformation, and the art of losing: Some uses of poetry in hospice care for the terminally ill. *Psychodynamic Counseling*, 6(2), 215–234.

Meyer, C. (1973). Purpose and boundaries–Casework fifty years later. *Social Casework, 54*(4), 267–270.

Nichols, M., & Schwartz, R. (1995). *Family therapy* (3rd ed.). Allyn & Bacon.

Payne, M. (1997). *Modern social work theory* (2nd ed.). Lyceum.

Poets Against the War (2003). *Homepage*. Retrieved February 6, 2003. http://www.poetsagainstthewar.org

Poindexter, C. C. (2002). Meaning from methods: Re-presenting narratives of an HIV-affected caregiver. *Qualitative Social Work, 1*(1), 59–78.

Postman, N. (1992). *Technopoly: The surrender of culture to technology*. Random House.

Pray, K. L. M. (1949). *Social work in a revolutionary age and other papers*. The University of Pennsylvania.

Pumphrey, R. E., & Pumphrey, M. W. (1961). *The heritage of American social work*. Columbia University Press.

Rank, O. (1945). *Will therapy and truth and reality*. Knopf.

Reid, P. N., & Peebles-Wilkins, W. (1991). Social work and the liberal arts: Renewing the commitment. *Journal of Social Work Education, 27*(2), 208–219.

Richmond, M. (1917). *Social diagnosis*. Russell Sage Foundation.

Ringel, S. (2003). The reflective self: A path to creativity and intuitive knowledge in social work practice education. *Journal of Teaching in Social Work, 23*(3–4), 15–28.

Robinson, V. P. (1949). *The dynamics of supervision under functional controls*: The University of Pennsylvania Press.

Rossiter, C., & Brown, R. (1988). An evaluation of interactive bibliotherapy in a clinical setting. *Journal of Poetry Therapy, 1*(2), 65–73.

Saleebey, D. (2000). *The strengths perspective in social work*. Allyn and Bacon.

Schon, D. A. (1983). *The reflective practitioner: How professionals think in action*. Basic Books.

Sheafor, B. W., Horejsi, C. R., Horejsi, G. A. (1997). *Techniques and guidelines for social work practice* (4th ed.). Allyn & Bacon.

Shulman, L. (1991). *Interactional social work practice*. Itasca, IL: F. E. Peacock.

Smalley, R. E. (1967). *Theory for social work practice.* Columbia University.
Smith, J. L. (2003). Personal communication. Boulder, CO.
Southard, E. E. (1919). The individual versus the family as a unit of interest in social work. *Proceedings of National Conference of Social Work*, 582–587.
Taft, J. (1939). A conception of the growth process underlining social casework practice. *Social Casework*, October, 72–80.
Taft, J. (1958). *Otto Rank.* The Julian Press Inc.
Taft, J. (1962). The Forces that make for therapy. In V. P. Robinson (Ed.), *Jessie Taft: Therapist and social work educator* (p. 178–190) Philadelphia: University of Pennsylvania.
van Deurzen-Smith, E. (1997). *Everyday mysteries: Existential dimensions of psychology.* Routledge.
van Wormer, K. (1997). *Social welfare: A world view.* Nelson-Hall.
Weick, A., Rapp, C. A., Sullivan, W. P., & Kishardt, W. E. (1989). A strengths perspective for social work practice. *Social Work, 89*, 350–454.
Werner, H. D. (1986). Cognitive therapy. In F. T. Turner (Ed.), *Social work treatment* (pp. 91–129). The Free Press.
Willis, R. J. (1994). *Transcendence in relationship: Existentialism and psychotherapy.* Ablex.
Wordsworth, W. (1979). The prelude, 1799, 1805, 1850: Authoritative texts, context and reception, recent critical essays. In J. Wordsworth, M. H. Abrams, Stephen Gill (Eds.). Norton.
Wright, J., & Chung, M. C. (2001). Mastery or mystery? Therapeutic writing: A review of the literature. *British Journal of Guidance and Counseling, 29*(3), 277–291.
Yalom, I. D. (1980). *Existential psychotherapy.* Harper/Collins.
Yelaja, S. A. (1986). Functional theory for social work practice. In F. J. Turner (Ed.) *Social work treatment* (pp. 46–67) The Free Press.

Permissions

Chapter 1
Furman, R., Downey, E. P., Jackson, R. L., & Bender, K. (2002). Poetry therapy as a tool for strengths-based practice. *Advances in Social Work*, *3*(2), 146–157. Reprinted with permission.

Chapter 2
Collins, K. S., Furman, R., & Langer, C. L. (2006). Poetry therapy as a tool of cognitively based practice. *The Arts in Psychotherapy*, *33*(3), 180–187. Reprinted with permission.

Chapter 3
Furman, R. (2003). Poetry therapy and existential practice. *The Arts in Psychotherapy*, 39(4), 195–200. Reprinted with permission.

Chapter 4
Furman, R. (2007). The mundane, the existential, and the poetic. *Journal of Poetry Therapy*, *20*(3), 163–180. Reprinted with permission.

Chapter 5
Furman, R. (2012). A poetry group for cognitively impaired older adults: A brief report. *Journal of Poetry Therapy*, *25*(3), 173–178. Reprinted with permission.

Chapter 6
Furman, R., & Dill, L. (2012). Poetry therapy, men and masculinities. *The Arts in Psychotherapy*, *39*(2), 102-106. Reprinted with permission.

Chapter 7
Furman, R., Enterline, M., Thompson, R., & Shukraft, A. (2012). Poetry matters: A case for poetry in social work practice. *Journal of Social Intervention: Theory and Practice*, *21*(1), 5-17. Reprinted with permission.

Chapter 8
Furman, R. (2004). Exploring friendship loss through poetry. *Journal of Loss and Trauma*, *9*(2), 181–187. Reprinted with permission.

Chapter 9
Furman, R. (2006). Poetic forms and structures in qualitative health research. *Qualitative Health Research*, *16*(4), 560–566. Reprinted with permission.

Chapter 10
Furman, R. (2006). Autoethnographic poems and narrative reflections: A qualitative study on the death of a companion animal. *Journal of Family Social Work, 9*(4), 23–38.

Chapter 11
Furman, R. (2007). Poetry and narrative as qualitative data: Explorations into existential theory. *Indo-Pacific Journal of Phenomenology, 7*(1), 1–9. Reprinted with permission.

Chapter 12
Furman, R. (2004). Poetry as qualitative data for exploring social development and human experience in Latin America. *Journal of Latino/Latin American Studies, 1*(3), 81–104. Reprinted with permission.

Chapter 13
Furman, R. (2015). Autoethnographic Explorations of Researching Older Expatriate Men. *Creative Approaches to Research, 8*(3). Reprinted with permission.

Chapter 14
Furman, R. (2019). The tenderness and vulnerability of older expatriate men: A poetic inquiry of research and autoethnographic poems. *Journal of Poetry Therapy*, 1–6. Reprinted with permission.

Chapter 15
Furman, R., & Dill, L. (2015). Extreme data reduction: The case for the research Tanka. *Journal of Poetry Therapy, 28*(1), 43–52. Reprinted with permission.

Chapter 16
Szto, P., Furman, R., & Langer, C. (2005). Poetry and photography: An exploration into expressive/creative qualitative research. *Qualitative Social Work, 4*(2), 135–156. Reprinted with permission.

Chapter 17
Furman, R. (2005). Using poetry and written exercises to teach empathy. *Journal of Poetry Therapy, 18*(2), 103–110. Reprinted with permission.

Chapter 18
Furman, R. (2014). Beyond the literary uses of poetry: A class for university freshmen. *Journal of Poetry Therapy, 27*(4), 205–211. Reprinted with permission.

Chapter 19
Furman, R., Coyne, A., & Negi, N. J. (2008). An international experience for social work students: Self-reflection through poetry and journal writing exercises. *Journal of Teaching in Social Work, 28*(1–2), 71–85. Reprinted with permission.

Chapter 20
Furman, R., Langer, C. L., & Anderson, D. K. (2006). The poet/practitioner: A paradigm for the profession. *Journal of Sociology and Social Welfare, 33*, 29. Reprinted with permission.

Index

Adolescents 4, 47, 75, 92, 121, 232, 252
Aguinaldo, J. P. 154
Altruism 232
Alzheimer's Disease
  see dementia
Anderson, D. K. 263-277
Anxiety 6, 8, 20, 36-37, 40-41, 43, 54, 78, 138-140, 255
Aristotle 4, 35
Atget, J. E. A. 209
Auden, W. H. 38
Autoethnography i, 111, 119-122, 130-131, 137, 153, 171-181, 185-190, 207, 209, 243-245, 252
Automatic writing 39, 273

Bakhtin, M. M. 135
Baraka, A. 266
Beck, A. T. 19-20
Bender, K. 1-16
Berg, B. L. 217
Bibliotherapy 4, 231-232, 267
Brems, C. 232
Buber, M., 48
Bukowski, C. 4, 35, 78, 166

Camus, A. 141
Carver, R. 71
Case studies 137
Chan, Z. C. Y. 136, 274
Choice 13, 29, 37, 95, 140-141, 146, 181, 232, 238
Cognitive dissonance 260
Cognitive therapy 19-22, 24-31
Collaboration 5-6, 10, 24-25, 131, 151, 202, 217
Collaborative poems 9
Collins, K. S. 19-31

Colorado State University 100
Community development 243, 266
Conroy, P. 235
Constructivist psychology i, 7, 20, 22, 118-119, 154, 193, 255, 274
Council on Social Work Education 267
Coyne, A. 249-260
Creech, S. 131

Death iii, 36-37, 40, 49-50, 54-55, 101, 103-105, 118-131, 138-140, 143, 145, 156, 158, 161-162, 176, 180-181, 195, 252
Dementia 66-67, 69, 95, 153
Denzin, N. K. 110
Depression 8, 20-22, 25-26, 30, 43, 78, 135-136, 138, 214, 220
DeRoos, Y. S. 274
Dill, L. 74-85, 192-202
Diagnostic Manual of Mental Disorders i
Domestic violence 10-11, 235
Downey, E. P. 1-16
Dread 36-37, 54, 135, 138-140, 143, 145, 147

Egan, G. 232
Eisner, E. W. 120, 152, 194, 207
Ellis, A. 21
Empathy ii, 9, 47, 119, 167, 173, 231-239, 244, 268, 274
Empowerment 5-6, 12-13, 15, 31, 75, 89, 91, 152, 266, 275
Enterline, R. 88-96
Epistemology 22, 136, 150-151, 175, 193, 205-207, 216, 224-225, 264

see also logical positivism, post-modernism
Ethnography 15, 94, 150, 172, 175, 185-186, 192-193, 196, 211, 215, 218, 222
see also autoethnography
Evidence-Based Practice 266
Existential theory (psychology and philosophy) 35-44, 46-50, 134-148

Flexibility 13, 84, 91, 270
Flexner, A. 264
Fook, J. 5
Frankl, V. 49
Free verse 245
Freud, S. 22
Frost, R. 29

Gee, J. 174, 195, 208
Geer, F. C. 10
Gender 75
Gender identity 75
Ginsberg, A. 48-49, 110-111
Glicken, M. D. 77
Goldstein, H. 264
Gordon, W. E. 277
Great Santini, the 235
Greyrock Writing Institute 100
Grief 118-131
Group Therapy ii, 9, 12-14

Haiku 27, 112, 115, 187, 192-193, 196
Hathaway, B. 85
Healy, L. M. 264
Heidegger 138
Hero's journey 91
Hirschfield, J. 31, 38, 135, 171, 266
HIV 120, 136, 154, 174, 195, 208, 268
Hodas, G. 75
Homophobia 79
Hugo, V. 114
Humanities 22, 88-89, 109, 116, 153, 175-176, 185, 215-216, 221, 267, 276
Hynes A. 10-11, 234

Immigrants 246

Jackson, R. L. 1-16
Johnson, L. 7
Journal of Poetry Therapy iii, 23
Journal writing i, 23, 250-253
Jung, C. 91

Kelly, G. 19
Krill, D. 265

Langer, C. L. 19-31, 205-226, 263-277
Latin America i
Lazarus, A. A. 27
Lerner, A. 5, 8
Linear cause 135
Literary criticism 96
Liu, T. 266
Lived experience 46-47, 89, 92, 94, 112, 119-120, 134, 136-137, 150-151, 153-154, 167, 171, 173-176, 186, 190, 193, 208-209, 216, 219
Locklin, G. 80
Logic 135, 144
Logical positivism 22, 120, 134, 152, 154, 171

Madhuubuti, H. 81
Magnification 31, 38, 111, 173, 216, 266
Managed care 28, 89, 269
Martin, J. 114
Masculinity 74-85, 178, 180-181
Maslow, Abraham 6
Maslow's hierarchy of needs 6
Maughamm, S. 37
Mazza, N. i-iii, 15, 23, 35, 38-39, 268
Meaning 23, 35-41, 43, 47, 49, 61,

71, 76, 79, 89, 91, 93, 95, 104, 110-133, 115, 135-138, 140-142, 145-147, 172-173, 176-178, 192-195, 202, 208, 212, 215-216, 220-221, 224, 225, 241, 253, 255, 270-273
Metaphor i, 7-8, 10, 13, 23-25, 29, 35, 43, 49, 52, 69, 80, 88-93, 100, 111, 116, 121, 130, 135, 144, 153-155, 194, 208, 215-216, 219, 253-254, 269, 271, 274-275, 277
Mohan, B. 260
Mullan, H. 141, 147
Mundane 46-64

Narrative i-ii, 7, 22, 27, 47, 90-91, 111, 115-116, 119, 121, 123, 131, 134-148, 153, 174-176, 192-193, 195, 208-210, 213, 215, 245, 252-254, 267, 274-276
Narrative poem 80
Negi, N. J. 249-260
Nietzsche, F. 38

Oiler, C. 109, 253
Ontology 193
Oppression i, 11-12, 30, 36, 47, 76, 110, 150, 152, 199, 250, 268, 275-277

Pantoum 109, 114-115, 172-173, 175-181, 245
Pet loss 118-131
Phenomenological research 137
Photography i, 205-226
Poindexter, C. C. 120, 136, 154, 174, 195, 208, 268
Poetic transcription 109
Poets Against the War, 275
Positivism
  see logical positivism
Post-modernism 193
Posttraumatic Stress Disorder 10
Poverty 211, 254-256

Psychagogi 35

Qualitative research 93-95, 99-105, 109-116, 118-131, 134-148, 150-167, 171-181, 185-190, 192-202, 205-226

Rank, O. 88, 265, 267
Rationale Emotive Behavioral Therapy (REBT) 20
Reflective listening 231
Reiter, S. 23
Responsibility 36
Richardson, L. 113, 120, 136, 154, 175, 195, 208
Richmond, M. 265
Risk-taking 6, 47, 76, 187
Robinson, A. 122
Rogers, C. 232

Sabo, D. 83-84
Saleebey, D. 6
Sanders, D.
Sartre, J. P. 36, 46, 141
Schizophrenia 40-43
Self-actualization 266
Self-awareness 38, 74, 80, 273
Self-reflection ii, iii, 147, 155, 178, 249-260, 268, 272-274
Shapiro, J. 123, 252
Shukraf, A. 88-96
Smith, J. 135, 194, 272
Social justice 88, 209, 232, 276
Socratic dialogue 207
Southard, E. E. 264
Springsteen, B. 77
Star Wars 91
Stein, H. F. 130, 154, 208, 253
Strengths-based 1-16, 84
Substance abuse 5, 9, 20, 78, 138, 200-201, 235
Szoto, P. 205-226

Talerico, J. C. 6-7
Tanka 109, 112, 115-116, 174,

187, 192-193, 195-202, 232, 245-246
Thompson, R. 88-96
Trauma 10, 36, 47, 234-235
Triangulation 176, 197
Types of poetry 23

University of Washington, Takoma

242

Valery, P. 93
Van Deurzen-Smith 35-36, 138
Veterans 4, 9-10, 74, 92, 237
Vietnam War 10, 211, 246

Wadeson, H. 23

Author Biography

Rich Furman, MFA, MSW, PhD, is full professor of social work at the University of Washington, Tacoma. Rich has 25 years of experience as a clinical social worker, organizational leader, therapist, coach, and scholar. He has held leadership positions in higher education and non-profit organizations and was the founding director of one of the largest community-based, children's wraparound programs in the United States. He is the author of over 18 books and 120 peer-reviewed articles and recognized as one of the international leaders in expressive, arts-based qualitative methodologies. Rich provides strengths-based, insight-oriented coaching for scholars and leaders at all stages of their careers. Rich has conducted workshops on writing and publishing throughout Asia, Latin America, and Europe. In 2019 he crossed an item off his bucket list by completing a of Master of Fine Arts in Creative Nonfiction from Queens University of Charlotte's Latin America MFA program. Rich's books of poetry include *Trotting Race of Time* by University Professors Press.

www.ingramcontent.com/pod-product-compliance
Lightning Source LLC
Chambersburg PA
CBHW051630230426
43669CB00013B/2242